CONTEMPORARY
FRENCH PHILOSOPHY

A STUDY IN NORMS AND VALUES

Contemporary French Philosophy

A STUDY IN
NORMS AND VALUES

COLIN SMITH

LONDON
METHUEN & CO LTD
11 NEW FETTER LANE · EC4

First published in 1964
© 1964 Colin Smith
Printed in Great Britain by
Butler and Tanner Limited
Frome and London

CONTENTS

PREFACE

I have tried in this study, first, to extract from French philosophy and literature of the past thirty years or so a theme which I hope will give unity to the book more satisfactorily than would a strictly chronological method of treatment. This theme, which is dualistic, is outlined in the introduction. Secondly, I have attempted to fill in some of the more academic background to the kind of French philosophy which is widely known here as 'existentialist'. Sartre, Camus and other fashionable writers cannot be overlooked, however well known they may be by now. What needs to be realized, however, is that the philosophy which they propound arises out of the whole history and background of continental philosophy in this century, and is not a philosophico-literary invention of theirs; yet I have no wish to belittle them in pointing this out.

I have taken important and typical works of a number of philosophers for fairly detailed analysis, rather than tried to condense into inadequate summaries more of what they have to say. Certain currents of thought are thinly represented, e.g. religious philosophy, either because they fall outside the picture which I wish to present, and which I regard as central to recent French thought, or because in a few cases I feel ill-fitted to do justice to them.

I wish to thank Professor H. B. Acton and Mr Maurice Cranston for their interest and encouragement in this work, and for valuable suggestions in matters of detail. I am also indebted to the Leverhulme Trust for having enabled me to devote two terms of study leave to its preparation at an earlier stage.

C. S.

University College, London
April 1963

INTRODUCTION

I should like to qualify the philosophy dealt with in the following pages as 'open', borrowing an adjective from Bergson (*The Two Sources of Morality and Religion*) and Gaston Bachelard (*La Philosophie du non*), as it seems to convey the idea of experience and activity as some sort of forward-looking evaluation, rather than as conformity to essences, norms or pre-established standards and concepts. Openness is the distinctive aspect of experience which is stressed by much of twentieth-century philosophy. Yet conformity and some sort of fidelity to what is in existence, or to what can be posited as a norm, is manifestly not only part of human living as normally thought of, but even of 'authentic' or creative living, for without it creation would have no identifiable starting point.

This duality[1] is what I am concerned with. We are by now familiar with the primacy of 'choice', the creation of values, the rejection of notions of substance, as themes of recent continental philosophy. Indeed, the philosophy of our time seems generally to favour the return to a critical, 'open' approach, after a period of much system-building and postulation of dominating cosmic principles after the manner of Hegel. Generally speaking, when we look back over the modern period, we are struck by the progressive abandonment of concepts of substance and continuity, in favour of views of human experience, natural processes, etc., as fundamentally discontinuous and contingent. Gaston Poulet, in his *Etudes sur le temps humain*, quotes Aquinas as saying that it is only when all the operations of the soul are resolved in the pure contemplation of intelligible truth that the soul enters into that uniformity which makes it resemble the angels. Now this idea of a uniformity, without further qualification, to which we feel that we ought to have some sort of access, came to be abandoned with

---

[1] Which existentialists call that of essence and existence.

the secularization of thought. Descartes was struck by the discontinuity of time, and the need to postulate continuous creation, even as a process of conservation. Hume remained unwilling to defy logic by dissolving certain, to him irreducible, kinds of discontinuity; and Goethe declared 'Time is my field'. The acceptance of time, of real change, and the renunciation of the quest for eternity, strikes us as essentially modern.

By the eighteenth century a general assault was being launched on such notions as that of the soul, of causality and of morality as rooted in something more basic than circumstance and need. It is tempting to see this analytical and destructive approach as finally triumphant in the present century, when time ousts eternity, verbs show themselves as more satisfactorily expressive of reality than nouns, and existence precedes essence. It is, however, clear that there is a limit to the extent to which reality can be seen as fragmentary without its becoming meaningless, and it is, I think, the implicit purpose of many contemporary French writers to show that this limit must not be transgressed, precisely because, as they hold, consciousness is nothing but the conferment of meaning. So schools such as Gestalt psychology and phenomenology (which conceives activity as by its nature sense-giving) supervene by way of reaction against the dissolution of experience into atomic fragments, *actes gratuits*, and all the extravagances arising from a notion of contingency which allows nothing to derive from, or belong to, anything else. The dilemma of necessity and contingency is not so much debated between recent French philosophers as inherent in the outlook of most of them. This 'hybrid' outlook is characteristically that of many of the philosophers treated in the following pages, but I also devote some space to representatives of what may be called purely essentialist thought, notably André Lalande, whose 'involutionary' principle posited the kind of quasi-substance which is seen as 'running through' reality, and who offers a contrast serving, I hope, to throw into relief the relatively unpredictable factors which, in the view of others, govern our behaviour and evaluations.

I consider the bipolarity of conservative and creative experience under three headings. First, in relation to experience of being as each of us knows it in himself, and this is inextricably involved with the experience of time, and a possible desire to escape from it.[1] Secondly, in relation to reason and concepts. Thirdly, in relation to morality and value-judgements generally.

In the first of these categories we meet a thoroughgoing ontology of 'derealization' (or refusal to identify being, or fix it by analogy) in the work of Sartre. His conception of the duality of the self as acquired (*being in itself*), yet constantly self-transcending (*being for itself*), is probably by now more familiar to English readers of French philosophy and literature than any other notion in contemporary European thought, and I here devote a section to that part of its content which is relevant to my purpose. It is enough to say at this stage that restless as is the 'human reality' which it presents, it expresses the phenomenological view that creation, evaluation and action are intimately bound up with, though 'transcendent' to, the dead weight of our acquired being, and that freedom is dependent upon this paradox and this ambiguity.

As an introduction to the dualism which is my subject, and to Sartre with whom I first deal as the most internationally celebrated exponent of it, I begin the first section by considering a traditional preoccupation of philosophy: the failure of reality to conform to what it 'ought' to be, its failure to conform to a supposedly perfect and pre-existent model of itself, or the problem of what W. Koehler[2] calls requiredness. The disproportion between what is and what, we feel, should be, is referred to by Jean Grenier as an *écart*, or gap, and by Camus as a 'divorce' between ourselves – with our intimations of an ideal realm – and the world, a divorce which constitutes the absurdity of the human situation, according to him. This discontinuity is a familiar stumbling-block to any integrated account of experience, and Camus's empiricist course is to do away with one of the horns of his dilemma. Having recognized the divorce, he says, there remains no eternal principle

[1] Since, for phenomenologists, consciousness is consciousness of something, it is also bound up with meaning-giving; hence the title of Section I, 'The Search for Significance'.

[2] *The Place of Value in a World of Facts*, New York, 1938.

to invoke for the guidance of our lives, and we must therefore live quantitatively, quality having become meaningless. The fact is that quantity is here tacitly promoted to the status of a quality, being all that is now required of us, and being, it too, bereft of any compelling authority. But Camus either does not see this, or is content to regard quantity as the most empirically verifiable quality.

Sartre, although his novel *La Nausée* seems to suggest that he shares Camus's view of the 'divorce', and consequent absurdity, does not in fact, when he comes down to phenomenological method, in *Being and Nothingness*, see the *écart* or gulf in the same way. We are not cut off from significance, heroically holding an island of value against a chaotic and nonsensical universe. We are not, as Camus seems to imply that we are, utterly fragmented and discontinuous in ourselves, and faced with a world similarly without unity and significance. Yet neither, says Sartre, have we an essence. Nor is our situation to be read off as the point of intersection of necessary psychological laws. How then is it to be conceived?

It may be worth while to restate Sartre's position in non-Sartrean terms by saying that we *have* an essence, but that it is always provisional as long as we are physically alive. We do in fact accumulate our identity by the process of living, and it is surely a necessary part of that identity that it should have a history. This historical self is the limitation which provides us with a situation in which to act. We are condemned to be free in virtue of that situation which we never choose (though in some measure we *have chosen* it) but from which our choices operate. We have at any given time a self which is inevitably in process of modification by virtue of what we see required ahead of us. So what ought to be is not to be conceived as belonging to a static and eternal realm located outside the world, but as revealed in ever-changing forms ahead of us, always 'soliciting' and never possessed.

This carrot and donkey version of the self and its quest is naturally forward-looking; and, though conceived as pre-eminently a process of conferring meaning on reality, that meaning is always about to be realized or completed, never definitively present. Hence Sartre's description of the *for-itself* as an apotheosis never brought to completion. The general impression left is one of instability, of a human reality upon which we never really take a hold.

In contrast to this total rejection of any contemplative or reposeful view of experience, I then deal with an ontological work of Louis Lavelle, a philosopher of an older generation, but writing in the late nineteen-twenties and after. Lavelle, in the work here examined, is concerned with 'act', or 'the perpetual miracle of initiative', which brings about 'my insertion into the world'. The world is thus in a sense there for Lavelle, and we participate in it, so that the element of novelty and undoubted creativity is attenuated unless we regard the Whole as exceeding the Given, which Lavelle does. Time presents itself as piecemeal, is given successively, and is the instrument of participation. The importance of the stress laid on the idea of participation lies in the possibility which it offers of seeing experience as realized, and not merely as value to-be-realized, as it appears predominantly in Sartre. The whole interest of these allegories of experience is to be found in the relative emphasis laid on living and re-living, on creation and contemplation. We shall see that by conferring value on each aspect of time, and not merely on the present and future, Lavelle is able to add to the favoured view of experience as adventure that of experience as an acquisition. This means, as will become clear from a consideration of the philosophy of Merleau-Ponty, finding a place in the realm of value for both time and eternity.

By contrast, one of the most uncompromising opponents of the notion of experience as a kind of congealed entity weighing down on living consciousness is Ferdinand Alquié. *La Nostalgie de l'être* is presented as something discreditable to be got rid of, and the duty of philosophy, according to M. Alquié, is to unmask and denounce attempts to objectify being, as is done, for instance, when it is identified with the totality of things. About 'being' nothing can be said, and the true, perennial ontology is in time. A parallel thesis is put forward in the same author's *Le Désir d'éternité,* and here I begin to consider conservation and creation in relation to *reason.* Again the desire for the unchanging is a vain one, the pursuit of a chimera. It takes two forms, the emotional and the intellectual refusal of time. The first is seen in a conscious, or even more in an unconscious attachment to our past, which we come to see as our realized self, and almost inevitably as an incubus upon our present and future, in the sense that habit, or habitual thinking, or unconscious obsession are obstacles to spontaneity. Alquié's position in these works, expressed in an undramatic way and in a traditional philosophical language, appears to be the extreme anti-essentialist one, that we should not look for some essence of individual or collective being upon which to fall back in contemplative lassitude. Time marches on, and we must march with it. It will be seen that we are slipping from metaphysics into psychology, and indeed confusion of, or rather indifference to, the distinction between the two is frequent in the philosophies under consideration. There is, of course, all the difference in the world between speculation about the thinking subject, which is metaphysical, and the advocacy of an attitude to our past actions, which may be called – in accordance with French tradition – moral. The latter deals unmistakably with experience, the former with what is inaccessible and transcendent to experience. But what these philosophies are concerned with is attitudes to aspects of the self, and 'category mistakes' which may influence these attitudes. The attitude tacitly recommended is negative, and amounts to 'not regarding the active self as an object'. The *cogito* is that which is always metaphysically 'behind' us, and from which we work. Yet so also behind us – but this time temporally – is our being *in itself.* The thinking subject, constituting reason, and also in a sense one's historical self-up-to-this-moment, are not to be seen as legitimately amenable to conceptualization, since the resultant concepts tend to clog and immobilize the experience which they are designed to serve but cannot embody.

Alquié's treatment of the theme of the eternity of reason fills the second part of *Le Désir d'éternité.* The diminished element of continuity in determinism, as compared with causality, shows, in effect, that identity does not reside in reality at all. Is eternity then a false notion, irrelevant to anything connected with our activity? No; but what we are warned against is the spurious introduction of eternity *into* that activity. We must recognize that the 'eternal subject' transcends time, and, by unifying its instants, apprehends it. This spirit is impersonal; it is an activity not an entity, in fact it is the sense-giving activity which synthesizes the instants of time by refusing their disjointed multiplicity. Thus the intellectual and emotional refusals of time are respectively activity and passivity (or passion), the fruitful and the parasitical. Reason is not to be confused with its own creations and made into a kind of ideal object, which, in the form of Ideas, hovers over appearances. It serves to mediate between time and eternity in the interest of action.

Though this 'derealization' may be a plausible analysis of 'constituting reason', however, there is some quality of objectivity and permanence in 'constituted reason', as manifest in scientific and social systems of law. I include some consideration of Lalande's view of the rational activity of mind as assimilatory, that is, as tending to incorporate new fact or experience into an acquired and indestructible 'body' of knowledge. In contrast to this are 'open' philosophies, such as those of Bachelard and Morot-Sir. In these latter we see the evolution of scientific truth, by successive 'conversions', as analogous to the development of the personal history as presented by Merleau-Ponty. Just as the dynamic personal history shows both resistance and yielding to a series of existential choices, so science has an appearance of being established, until such time as its internal tensions produce new hypotheses and a consequent reassessment of the significance of reality.

Most of these philosophers are reasonably tolerant of a carrying over from past into present and future in some form or other. M. Vladimir Jankélévitch takes up the experience of regret and remorse (which Alquié sees as futile retrospective attachments and passions) and concludes that remorse at least, is, in relation to the act which we would see undone, a necessary phase in purging ourselves of the act's paralysing effects. To try to sidestep the painful experience of contrition is, in effect, to try to skip over a stretch of time – the time of remorse – which we feel ill-fitted to tolerate. But, says Jankélévitch, the world is such that we cannot do this. We must live through our repentance if we want to have done with it and its cause. Just as our deed will not leave us alone, equally it will not allow us to thrust it unceremoniously aside. Our time is something which we must accept, and this means that our present is to some extent committed by our past. We cannot rationalize ourselves out of the consequences of our actions by stoicism, by seeing ourselves as a mere undifferentiated instance of a universal necessity, or by ironical detachment – or so Jankélévitch would have us believe. He does full justice to these idols of the intelligence, however, and devotes a volume to irony which is not the least interesting of his many books. Irony involves standing aside, as a spectator, from our self and our predicament, and seeing ourself as another, or as an instance. This universalization is an intellectual process related to those other acts of universalization which establish norms and laws, and which introduce some degree of homogeneity into the chaos of individual cases. The ironist is, therefore, seeking a kind of eternity by refusing to live his time in blind and self-centred, though ultimately therapeutic, unhappiness.

But this emotional attitude to the relations between past and present, which takes the form of a desire to preserve the past, or conversely unmake it, or somehow to conjure away the present consequences of its definitive pastness, is only part of the problem raised by time in human experience. The greater question is that of its composition and its direct relation to that experience. Its composition is, ostensibly, and for common sense, a quantitative one. It is reducible to instants, each one of which would seem to contain within itself a unit of experience; and such a conception is, of course, atomistic. If the instants of time are discontinuous, it would seem that the experiences which it sustains are equally so, and the questions then are: how are the instants of time welded into experiences, and how are experiences interrelated to form the individual's experience as a whole? In other words, what are the boundaries of individual experiences, and are these latter mutually exclusive? Or again, what is the nature of the act which posits experiences as each in a way autonomous or meaningful, and thence interrelated in such a way as to give one's life as a whole meaning and individuality? Jankélévitch examines these questions in his *Philosophie première* in terms of creation and continuation. The creation which might naturally be imagined as an instantaneous *fiat* is not contained in any mathematical unit of time. It has not strictly assignable temporal or spatial boundaries, though it is necessarily elaborated and launched in time and space. It is related to the personal past and belongs to the existent world, though its originality is complete. It may then become in a sense repeatable and part of our continuity. This continuity itself, through its inner tensions, engenders fresh creative acts on both a small and a large scale; and this exemplifies the interdependence of creation and continuation.

With Merleau-Ponty we reach a philosopher for whom the synthesis of the creative and conservative aspects of experience is complete. His *Phenomenology of Perception* is one of the outstanding works of post-war French philosophy. The thesis is, in effect, that life is not a series of complete transformations, or a set of water-tight compartments of experience, as it would be if we were Camus's actor, who lives quantitatively, and despairs of personal continuity. Camus wanted to discredit the notion of human substance, as Sartre indicated when he described *L'Etranger* as a Humean novel. Merleau-Ponty argues that a decision to adopt a certain commitment, or loyalty, is a summing-up of a personal past, even though it may appear to run counter to that past, or even refute it. A decision of this kind is not an intellectual assessment of what we logically must become, but an expression, however unexpected, of what we are. Our progress through time seems to create and establish a distinctive individual being in ourselves, which we and others come to recognize, and to which we become attached, in conformity with our desire for eternity or an essence. We build up a certain resistance to chameleon-like variability. But in response to time and experience a tension may periodically accumulate, and eventually we are forced to reassess ourselves-in-the-world, and we undergo something analogous to a conversion. The word 'conversion' is often used by French philosophers in this connection. Our established self is seen to be

B

inadequate, and we revise it in some degree. The cup is full and one particular drop causes it to overflow. William James, in *Varieties of Religious Experience*, presents conversion to and from religious belief as an event of this kind. What comes finally as a revelation and break with the self, and brings a major personal readjustment, is being prepared inwardly over a long period of increasing tension. This personal readjustment is not made in response to (though it may be on the pretext of) e.g. reading the Bible or Charles Bradlaugh. That is to say, it is not comparable to stopping at traffic lights because they happen to be at red when we drive up. It is not primarily a response to a signal, but an expression of a self which is repudiating its now irrelevant essence. 'It is I who give a direction, significance and future to my life, but that does not mean that these are conceived; they spring from my present and past, and in particular from my present and past co-existence.' Merleau-Ponty examines the growth of class conscious-ness and its expression in revolutionary situations, and holds that genuine adherence to a political position is 'lived-through', and not the assent given by a pure, limitlessly free and eternal con-sciousness or *cogito* to a set of arguments suddenly put forward. Our decisions are expressions of the self even when they re-orientate it.

In the third part we reach the domain of ethics. Here Bergson's *Two Sources of Morality and Religion*, with its 'open' and 'closed' moralities, anticipates the anti-legalist and personalist ethics of more recent philosophy. But Bergson's forward-looking open morality is offset by his suggestion that an evolutionary tendency is operative in this field as an extra-temporal force dominating change. Lalande too, though his thesis postulates an *in*volutionary, instead of an *e*volutionary tendency, is thinking on the same quasi-naturalistic lines. Raymond Polin raises the question of genuinely creative evaluation, with its attendant difficulties. He distinguishes *values*, which are really acts of evaluation, from *norms*, which are the degraded products of such acts. These correspond, in the axiological field, to Sartre's *for itself* and *in itself* in the field of human reality. The discussion of this ethical dualism is carried further by Jankélévitch's *Traité des vertus*, which distinguishes between the virtues of initiation and those of continuation. Thus we are led on to the crux of the existentialist conception of morality, or 'authenticity', which may be described as first-hand virtue, or virtue which springs straight from the heart, from the *premier mouvement*, as distinct from second-hand virtue which follows precepts, that is, which practises conformity to Polin's norms. I here draw on English philosophical writing for discussions parallel to these, notably from Professor Nowell-Smith's *Ethics* and Bernard Mayo's *Ethics and the Moral Life*.

The difficulty of 'existential' choice is that its authenticity depends on its being spontaneous and heartfelt, and that this guarantee is really morally indeterminate, being a state of mind or feeling and not even remotely related to any behavioural content. The same could be said of any 'guarantee' one wished to name, of course, but English writers (e.g. Nowell-Smith) have tended to take a basis of altruism as a self-evident moral necessity, whereas the French have tended to deprive the authentic act of any generally socially orientated direction. This is not true of Jankélévitch, but it is of Sartre, who seems more concerned with the problem of the person (a sort of secular salvation) than of man as a political animal, despite his general air of being preoccupied with politics. Simone de Beauvoir makes persistent attempts to show that existentialist ethics will turn out to promote something resembling the greatest happiness of the greatest number, but this does not seem at all self-evident. Hence certain signs of a renascence of universality, represented here by Jean Pucelle.

The kind of philosophy I am concerned with is personalist, concentrating upon the individual in-the-world coming to terms with that world, and above all avoiding stagnation as a refuge from its ever renewed exigencies. What I here try to show, from the writings of the French themselves, is the mutual complementarity of existence and essence in feeling, knowing and acting; that is, in living with oneself, with the world and with other people, a process effected by perpetually throwing up meanings which are never anything but provisional.

PART ONE

THE SEARCH FOR SIGNIFICANCE

I

Absurdity. The gulf between man and his world. Camus

Jean Grenier, in a small book entitled *Choice*,[1] wrote: '*We are not in the world*, this thought is the genesis of philosophizing . . . It is not that the world seems bad, but that it seems *different*. Pessimism is not necessarily the starting-point of philosophical speculation, but rather a more general feeling, a feeling of strangeness.' In his *Myth of Sisyphus* Camus describes man as 'divorced' from his world. Yet on the other hand 'being-in-the-world' and *Mitsein* are key concepts of phenomenology. How are these apparently mutually exclusive positions reconciled, if at all? Is there any meeting-point between human sense and the world's nonsense?

The most extreme expression of the 'feeling of separation' [2] and strangeness spoken of by Grenier is to be seen in those two works of twenty and more years ago, Sartre's *La Nausée* and Camus's *Le Mythe de Sisyphe*. Here the world of things is presented as something intractable, incompatible with our rational and moral demands; it is the view of disappointed idealists. Because predictability is only intermittent and partial in the real world, and logical necessity entirely absent from it, we find French writers, just before and after the war, adopting a tragic, not to say melodramatic, attitude to life, which was seen as an 'interminable defeat'. Camus's *Myth of Sisyphus* purports to be a systematic exposition and justification of this attitude.

Camus's argument in this work runs roughly as follows. The absurd means, variously and interchangeably, in the first place the irrational, that which has no rational link with other things; secondly, the contingent, that which is without rational origin;

[1] *Le Choix*, Paris, 1941. [2] 'un sentiment d'écart', op. cit. p. 3.

23

and thirdly, evil. The mind seeks to establish relations between phenomena, and ultimately to bring everything under one comprehensive system. This search for rational unity is doomed to failure. The necessarily frustrated impulse to seek meaning in irreducible diversity constitutes the absurdity of man's position.[1] A consciousness of time, change, ultimate purposelessness and death which annuls everything is what distinguishes *l'homme absurde* from *l'homme quotidien*. Must this recognition of 'the walls of absurdity' lead to suicide? Not to physical suicide, because whatever ought to be the case, it in fact does not. The body's judgement is as valid as the mind's, and the body recoils from annihilation. In man's attachment to life there is something stronger than all the world's ills.[2] The real subject of the book is: Does the absurdity of life make intellectual 'suicide' a logical conclusion or not, and in any case what is this?

If we first examine the notion of absurdity a little more closely we see that although the role of reason and scientific progress is acknowledged, these can make sense of reality only to a limited extent. The predictability of things is only schematic, and it seems that the 'primitive hostility'[3] and 'that thickness and strangeness of the world'[4] are ultimately insurmountable. There is an almost universal tendency to wish to escape from this uncertainty and contingency, and this is what Camus means when he refers to *nostalgie* or *nostalgie d'unité*.[5] One is reminded of Ferdinand Alquié's *Le Désir d'éternité* and *La Nostalgie de l'être*. The ultimate unintelligibility of the world is to be accepted as an absolute limitation. Heidegger is quoted as saying that the finite and limited nature of human existence is more primordial than man himself: the fact that the mind cannot impose its patterns on everything, cannot understand everything, is not a relative handicap which may be abolished with the advance of knowledge, it is absolute. It is

[1] The word *absurde* is normally translatable as 'conscious of absurdity'. *Un esprit absurde, un homme absurde* apply to a man who has awakened to the gulf. The opposite is *l'homme quotidien* meaning man unaware of the emptiness of life, the ordinary man in his daily routine, the *concitoyens* of *La Peste*. Cf Heidegger's *Alltäglichkeit*.

[2] *Le Mythe de Sisyphe*, Gallimard, 1942, p. 20.   [3] ibid. p. 28.

[4] ibid. p. 29.   [5] ibid. pp. 32, 33.

l'irrémédiable. The basis of this view is that the notion of purpose is relative, so that no absolute purpose is conceivable, while on the other hand the universe is not strikingly self-sufficient in the sense in which, for example, a work of art is self-sufficient.

When we become aware of time and contingency we are tormented by a contrary insatiable desire for unity, purpose, meaning and eternity. This is our nostalgia. But man lives among disunity, plurality and time, which divide and bring with them merely the irremediable. Camus attacks the commonest forms of escape from the absurd, all of which he identifies as versions of Kierkegaard's 'leap' into a transcendent refuge, which carries man from the impasse facing the rational mind.[1] They are so many forms of intellectual suicide. By abandoning 'reason', escape is possible into some form of eternity. But to admit in any way that absurdity or contingency can be circumvented by recourse to a higher principle such as God, or pre-established harmony, is to *consent* to absurdity, to cease to be a rebel. The absurd has a meaning only in so far as one does not consent to it,[2] as Camus says, i.e. dissolve it by some form of assent. Camus quotes Jaspers on this question and accuses him of betrayal. Does not failure, asks Jaspers, demonstrate beyond every possible explanation and interpretation not nothingness but the being of transcendence? Cannot we, that is, escape from impotence and limitation by positing a supernatural, super-rational order in which all things are reconciled?[3] Camus will have none of this, and extols in contrast the man who is conscious of the incompatibility between his own desire for rationality in conflict with the hostility and irreducibility of the material universe. The absurd is essentially a divorce. The bipolarity presented to experience *is* the absurd and this must be preserved, not conjured away. Fusion and reconciliation of man with his world, by religious belief or search for metaphysical unity, is the great betrayal.

[1] Cf Nietzsche, *Thus spake Zarathustra*, 'Of Other-worldlings': A weariness that, with a single leap – a death-leap – desireth to reach the Ultimate, a poor ignorant weariness that willeth not any more to will: *this* created all gods and otherworlds.

[2] op. cit. p. 50.   [3] op. cit. p. 48.

What is involved in living within the walls of the absurd? Life becomes a condemnation, but one which liberates because we are not tied to an eternal vision, we take each experience as it comes, all being of equal value. We live quantitatively, not qualitatively. There is no quality, no value, no criterion by which things are justified. We have the 'divine disponibilité du condamné à mort', because we have nothing to live *for*. We become *engagé* because there is no point in not being. Life is lived quantitatively to the full, that is, it must be exhausted in manifold realization. The symbols chosen for this quantitative living are: Don Juan, the lover of many women; the actor, who plays many parts (thereby participating physically in many lives); and the artist, who bodies forth the shapes of his imagination.[1]

Thus, from starting with a denial of value and ultimate purpose Camus arrives, paradoxically and melodramatically, at a philosophy of action or rather of activity. It is never made quite clear by discursive means why despair, from which suicide appears an escape at least worth considering, should become a spur to activity and intense living. It is only through Camus's novels, particularly *La Peste*, that we realize, despite all the talk of meaningless, unfruitful and repetitive exertion, that Camus is in fact espousing as intrinsically worth while the cause of man's deliverance from evil. There is not much more here than an emotional response to the stubborn contingency of the given. Let us see if Sartre offers a more closely articulated commentary on its significance and implications.

---

[1] Tout être sain tend à se multiplier (*M. de S.* p. 98). L'acteur règne dans le périssable (ibid. p. 108). Si jamais la morale de la quantité pouvait trouver son aliment, c'est bien sur cette scène singulière (ibid. p. 109). Similarly, 'Créer c'est vivre deux fois' (ibid. p. 130). Creation is 'le grand mime . . . sans lendemain'.

2

Transcendence. The pursuit of meaning as a necessary but 'useless passion'. Sartre

Camus conceives the absurd in predominantly spatial terms, that is to say, the evil outside man can invade and corrupt him, and is to be thought of as an alien force intruding upon human nature. Sartre's contingency is, in one important respect, even more irremediable, in that it is almost always lost to any human power of modification. He calls it being *in-itself*,[1] which is primarily the condition of anything inanimate; anything which, in Sartre's language, coincides completely with itself,[2] is a *plenum*, all of one piece,[3] with no disposition to become other than it is, no potentiality.[4] But the term is not reserved exclusively for things, it designates also a constituent of 'human reality'. In order to make clear precisely what is the human *in-itself*, we must turn our attention to its complementary element, being *for-itself*. This is exclusively human, and is an aspect of consciousness which is defined as *une décompression d'être*. (The in-itself has been shown to be a *plenum* devoid of any principle of change.) The self cannot be grasped as a true existent, the subject cannot *be* himself, for coincidence with the self reduces it to a bare in-itself and dehumanizes it. The self is a kind of separation of the subject from himself, a kind of non-coincidence with himself, a constant escaping from his own identity, a constant pursuit of an unstable

[1] These terms gain nothing in clarity by being translated. But since I shall give most of my quotations from *L'Etre et le néant* in Hazel E. Barnes's translation, I pass on these somewhat stodgy, but as far as I can see, unavoidable expressions. *B.N.* refers to translation, *E.N.* to original text.

[2] *B.N.* p. 74 (*E.N.* p. 116). 'Of this table I can say only that it is purely and simply *this* table.'

[3] 'The density of being of the in-itself is infinite. It is a fullness.' (*C'est le plein.*) ibid.

[4] 'In the in-itself there is not a particle of being which is not wholly within itself without distance . . . not the slightest suspicion of duality . . . not the slightest emptiness in being, not the tiniest crack through which nothingness might slip in.' ibid. See also all Part II of this work.

inner equilibrium. The for-itself, we may say, is the dynamic aspect of the self, poised in the present and solicited by a future which constantly reshapes the self. The reshaped self is thrown back into the past and becomes henceforth unavailable, a dead weight, the in-itself of the self.

This in-itself, however, is not entirely discarded and without interest. The contingency of what is unavoidably *there* is for Sartre not something which requires at all costs to be circumvented, because of course it cannot be. The in-itself is merely another version of this contingency, this time that part of the self which the passage of time has put out of our reach, but which remains a formative force exerted upon the for-itself. The for-itself is free to advance into novelty, but it is not free to choose its starting point. This is, and always was, given. Sartre calls it the *facticity* of the for-itself, which means its contingency. It is what survives of the in-itself into the for-itself, which in turn is responsible for what it does, but not for where it operates.[1] So Sartre's for-itself is not entirely absurd and unfruitful. We constantly escape from it, but it is the condition of that escape.

When we come to consider modal contingency, which may be said to indicate the contingency of the parts and their interrelations as distinct from that of the whole,[2] we find that, in one way or another, recent philosophers regard it as a *condition* of freedom and not as a form of freedom. It is necessary to point this out, since there has been a tendency to see the principle of indeterminacy as evidence of some sort of will, as opposed to blindly determined forces, and this is treated as a vindication of freedom, and as conferring a new lease of life on human freewill.

---

[1] 'Being-in-itself can found its nothingness but not its being. In its decompression it nihilates itself in a for-itself which becomes *qua* for-itself its own foundation; but the contingency which the for-itself has derived from the in-itself remains out of reach. It is what *remains* of the in-itself in the for-itself as facticity and what causes the for-itself to have only a factual necessity; that is, it is the foundation of its *consciousness-of-being* or *existence*, but on no account can it found its presence.' B.N. p. 84 (E.N. p. 127).

[2] Which is *radical* contingency. The distinction is drawn by Grenier, *Le Choix*.

Boutroux's thesis on the contingency of natural laws[1] seems to have had such an implication, and the conception of the *acte gratuit* is probably the final curiosity to which this muddle can lead. It involves a confusion between two distinct pairs of opposites: coercion and freedom from constraint, regularity of occurence and randomness. Purposefulness in action is here perversely thought of as subordination to a determining force, namely motive, which leaves only random action, or the 'freedom of indifference', as a form of freewill. The philosophers with whom I am concerned have something more interesting than this to say of contingency.[2]

There is a complex interplay of necessity and contingency in Sartre's idea of human reality. Necessity is sandwiched between two contingencies. There is the radical contingency of my whole being, but, given that, I must of necessity be somewhere, at some time, and with certain attributes.[3] The particular content of somewhere and sometimes, however, and the particular attributes are again contingent. Reality is represented as thrust upon us along with certain resources for dealing with it, and then it is up to us to make of it what we can and will. We can neither choose another situation (in the widest sense of what we have and are and where we are) nor contract out of being-in-the-world. These elements of givenness are the means whereby we can *be* something in the existential sense. Our existence, moreover, augments the facticity of the for-itself, which is sustained by an ever-recurrent contingency from which the dynamic self can move on.[4]

Contingency, then, is the condition of freedom. 'We are a freedom which chooses, but we do not choose to be free' (*B.N.* pp. 484–5; *E.N.* p. 565). The fact of being unable not to be

---

[1] *De la Contingence des lois de la nature*, 1875.

[2] For Sartre's refutation of freedom of indifference, see *Being and Nothingness*, pp. 433 ff. (*E.N.* pp. 509 ff.).

[3] 'For human reality, to be is to be there.' *B.N.* p. 308 (*E.N.* p. 371).

[4] 'The for-itself is supported by a perpetual contingency.' *B.N.* p. 308 (*E.N.* p. 371). When Sartre talks of 'gratuity' he means gratuity of *basic positivity*, not of the ensuing act. E.g. the for-itself 'has the feeling of its complete gratuity; it apprehends itself as being there *for nothing*, as being *de trop*'. *B.N.* p. 84 (*E.N.* p. 126).

free is the facticity of liberty, and the fact of being unable not to exist is its contingency.[1] Contingency and facticity are one.[2] Sartre says this: We shall use the term *situation* for the contingency of freedom in the *plenum* of being of the world, inasmuch as this *datum*, which is there only *in order not to constrain* freedom, is revealed to this freedom only as *already illuminated* by the end which freedom chooses. Thus the *datum* never appears to the for-itself as a brute existent in-itself; it is discovered always *as a cause* since it is revealed only in the light of an end which illuminates it. Situation and motivation are really one (*B.N.* p. 487; *E.N.* p. 568).

We have here an extremely condensed exposition of the theory of what M. V. Jankélévitch calls the *organ-obstacle*, and in varying forms it is the core of virtually all French thought on the nature of being or existence and the realization of value. What Sartre means is this. Our *situation* is given fortuitously and might be regarded as a limitation, and indeed is a limitation. It is wedged into the *plenum* of reality and therefore cannot be done away with. But it is also an opportunity. It is *given*, but as a means, not an obstacle hampering free action – a means of realizing the new situation, which by its own limitation it suggests and the possibility of which it reveals. So the given is a motive, the obstacle is an instrument.

Liberty divorced from facticity is discussed by Orestes and his teacher at the beginning of Sartre's *Les Mouches*. The teacher extols detachment, intellectual or economic, and shows his pupil

---

[1] A comparable discussion of the necessity and contingency of *obligation* occurs in Bergson's *Les Deux Sources* (pp. 20–4). Any given habit, which we may call moral, is contingent, but the habit of contracting habits is a part of human nature analogous to instinct, and which Bergson calls 'le tout de l'obligation'. No individual habit is instinctive, but the totality of obligation is a kind of latent, schematic instinct into which variable elements are introduced, resembling in this the universal human tendency to speak, but to speak *different* languages. We feel obliged only if we are free, and each specific obligation implies freedom; but it is necessary that there should be obligations in general, and indeed obligation is the form which necessity takes in relation to the higher manifestations of life. Bergson's version of being 'condemned to be free' is the basis of the 'open morality'.

[2] *E.N.* p. 567.

how enviable it is to be rich, handsome, wise beyond one's years with second-hand wisdom, freed from every bondage and every belief, free for every commitment yet knowing that one must never become committed, in short, a superior person fit to be a university teacher. To which Orestes replies that the freedom which he enjoys is that of the thread of gossamer floating in the air. He is infinite possibility because life has not yet given him the facticity which is the material on which the for-itself works.[1] Sartre is often concerned, as here, with the guilt which is inseparable from authentic existence, as opposed to the suspended animation which is an attempt to evade choice. To drift, to accept one's status, i.e. to try to preserve a pure in-itself, is to betray the dynamic spirituality which is man's birthright. The intrinsic moral quality of the act, or of life, is secondary to its simply being an act, which carries its own salvation with it.[2] Orestes' own problem at the beginning of *Les Mouches* is to acquire a situation which the rest of the characters, including the population of Argos, already possess. His need is frequently expressed in spatial terms (the need to belong to Argos),[3] or in terms of action,[4] but fundamentally he is concerned with a certain quality of 'duration', of 'lived' time, as we see in Act II, tableau II, scene 8. Liberty has struck him 'like a thunderbolt'. But Electra does not feel free, for how can this crime, for which she feels guilty, be undone and her remorse dispelled? It is precisely the irremediability of the act which makes it valuable to Orestes. It is *his* act, his liberty,[5] being in-itself which is a point of departure, not something to be wished away and fretted over.

Clearly acts which, once accomplished, become part of the facticity of the in-itself and organ-obstacles of the for-itself are seen, temporally, as a constituent of duration. Since the point of view adopted is 'phenomenological' and not objective and mathematical, the act performed is (for me) always past: 'My past . . . is

---

[1] Quelle superbe absence que mon âme!... Ah! s'il était un acte, vois-tu, un acte qui me donnât droit de cité parmi eux!
[2] Cf *Saint Genet*, passim.   [3] Je veux être un homme de quelque part.
[4] Il faut que je me leste d'un forfait bien lourd.
[5] Plus il sera lourd à porter, plus je me réjouirai, car ma liberté, c'est lui.

the past *of this* present.'[1] It is not relative, but a personal possession[2] which is a means of the 'ever-growing totality of the in-
itself which we are'.[3] But when Sartre says 'which we are' he is
using the verb 'to be' with his customary ambiguity to include the
sense also of 'to become'.[4] It seems that Bergson's concept of
duration in effect conveys all that Sartre's odd linguistic thriftiness
achieves in this way. This semantic assimilation is natural when
we consider the current French tendency to equate act with being,
or reality with process. For although Bergson sees the living organism as always complete,[5] while Sartre sees it as never complete, the contrast is more apparent than real. The completeness
which strikes Bergson is an organic process of integration which
absorbs experience into itself, as opposed to inanimate being
which has no immanent principle of unity. The idea of completeness is suggested by a largely retrospective view of duration and
preoccupation with the role of memory, but this completeness is
not to be conceived as a finally static condition, as *L'Evolution
créatrice*, if nothing else, makes clear. In Sartre, whose philosophy
is predominantly forward-looking, the difficulty of conceiving a
developing totality is felt acutely. Since this development is anything but construction according to a preconceived schema
(Bergson and Sartre agree on this), there has to be talk of 'an
original project, a unification destined to reveal itself to us as a
non-substantial absolute'.[6] It is noticeable that M. Raymond
Polin, himself actively philosophizing in this field, has, as I see it,
been led astray by the ambiguity of the current French dynamic
conception of being, and criticized Sartre, who admittedly starts
from ontology, for 'identifying liberty with being for-itself,[7] and
slipping into a reduction of existentialist morality to lucid self-

---

[1] *E.N.* p. 154 (*B.N.* p. 110).   [2] *E.N.* p. 155 (*B.N.* p. 112).
[3] *E.N.* p. 159 (*B.N.* p.115).   [4] Cf *E.N.* p. 162 (*B.N.* p. 118).
[5] Cf V. Jankélévitch, *Bergson*, 1931, p. 8. 'Il n'y a pas d'ébauches d'organes,
de rudiments de fonctions.' One can regard as to some extent comparable
Merleau-Ponty's idea of an evolving experience, always in process of becoming; never definitive, yet constantly throwing up 'objects' (which may be
'unities of value') on its way.
[6] *E.N.* p. 648 (*B.N.* p. 561).
[7] Which, in a sense, is *not* being.

knowledge'.[1] I doubt if Sartre would agree that there can be any possibility of 'lucidly knowing' the *pour-soi*.

The traditional search to discover supposedly existing values belongs to a general conception of spiritual activity different from that of Sartre and the majority of French philosophers born in this century. What these latter are on the whole interested in is human activity in its relation to time, and in its ambiguous status as in part determining future experience and in part being the condition of free choice. It might appear that what is included in the paradoxical idea of organ-obstacle is simply means. The object, however, is to analyse these concepts not logically but into what might be described as their emotive components. The word 'means' does not suggest the idea, which the existentialists want to convey, of struggling with something barely adequate in order to make something of it.

Existentialists react against determinism, but this reaction tends to be accompanied by a simultaneous reaction against the freedom of indifference which, as we have seen, often appears as the alternative to determinism, only to be recognized as equally unflattering to the will, which wants to see itself as untrammelled while being necessarily motivated. Renouvier, as M. Jankélévitch points out,[2] points to indifference as the common postulate of both determinism and indeterminism, and it is to show the will as neither non-existent nor capricious that the notion of the organ-obstacle comes into being. It is an idea closely related to that of facticity in that the constituents of a situation are represented as the means of changing it or escaping from it. The idea is expressed simply by saying that we cannot will in a vacuum or that the desire for something else is not only necessarily felt in relation to what exists, but that it is realized by means of what exists. Much is owed, and acknowledged as owed, to the ideologists,[3] though

---

[1] R. Polin, 'La philosophie des valeurs en France' in *L'Activité philosophique contemporaine en France et aux Etats-Unis*, 1950, Vol. II, pp. 228–9.

[2] *Bergson*, p. 101. 'Tout motif est déjà du voulu... Ma volonté n'est pas en moi comme une étrangère ou une visiteuse.'

[3] *E.N.* p. 389 (*B.N.* pp. 324–5). Notably Destutt de Tracy and Maine de

c

Bachelard's term *coéfficient d'adversité* is much in favour to express the idea of universal resistance offered not only by what is opposed to our purposes, but also by what furthers them. 'Every means is favourable and adverse', says Sartre,[1] and the importance of this idea, along with that of facticity from which it is often scarcely distinguishable, in exorcising the evil spirit of 'freedom of in-difference' is seen in *Being and Nothingness*.[2] Liberty encounters limitations in the *given* which it transforms or abolishes (*qu'elle dépasse ou néantit*). The 'coefficient of adversity' shows that liberty, far from being destroyed by contingency (*la liberté n'est pas dirimée par le donné*), is in fact conditioned by it. We can be free only in relation to a state of affairs and in spite of it. This is just what M. Jankélévitch expresses by saying that the *quia* is often a *quamvis*.[3]

Within the closely related group of ideas which are conceived as aspects of action, facticity leads on, via the organ-obstacle, to the role of negation. Being and nothingness are for Sartre comple-mentary, and he quotes Hegel's assertion that there is nothing on earth or in heaven which does not contain being and nothingness.[4] What Sartre means, when he talks of the nothingness which haunts being,[5] or of realities which are 'inhabited' by negation as a condition of their existence, or of *négatités* which are syntheses of the negative and positive,[6] is simply that being something is ex-clusive of being something else. This is, of course, trivial as seen in the context of a static view of being, but when action is pre-sented as, however humbly, value-creating, then what is not there acquires importance.[7] The 'hole in being' (*ce trou d'être*) is no doubt part of the celebrated 'waste-pipe' imagery, but it also represents, more abstractly, the deficiency, the 'lack' which is felt

---

Biran, 'idéologues' of the early nineteenth century, who moved from a sensationalist position to a voluntaristic philosophy.

[1] loc. cit.   [2] *E.N.* p. 564 (*B.N.* p. 484).

[3] Cf 'L'expérience n'est possible que dans ce qui précisément l'incarne et, l'incarnant, l'entrave.' *Phil. prem.* p. 6. Also, for the positive aspect of this, cf *Bergson*, p. 241: 'l'élan suppose un point d'appui'.

[4] *B.N.* p. 13 (*E.N.* p. 49).   [5] *B.N.* p. 11 (*E.N.* p. 47).

[6] *B.N.* p. 21 (*E.N.* p. 57).

[7] 'Nothingness is always an *elsewhere*.' *B.N.* p. 78 (*E.N.* p. 121).

in a given situation, and whereby the 'value' of which the for-itself is the agent is brought into being.[1] A. N. Whitehead says much the same thing in *Science and the Modern World*: 'The real relevance of untrue propositions for each actual occasion is disclosed by art, romance and by criticism in reference to ideals. . . . An event is decisive in proportion to the importance (for it) of its untrue propositions.' Hence the Janus character of this negativity: the absence and otherness of the ideal suggested by reality, and the negation of reality by action in pursuit of its vision, expresses the partiality and exclusiveness of what we find given to us and what we do in relation to it. As M. Raymond Polin writes:[2] 'The invention of values consists precisely in a breaking up of relationships, in a refusal of identification and immanence.'

At this stage it is convenient to leave the question of positive value for a while, and return to consideration of the in-itself. It has been stated already that this term is applied primarily to anything inanimate, with no potentiality or disposition to change. It is that which has an essence.[3] The in-itself, like the absurd, can invade the human field, and when it does it manifests itself as 'bad faith'. It is significant that an evaluative word is here used because, in some versions of 'bad faith' at least, the existentialist is intent upon effecting a transvaluation of important traditional values, and giving a pejorative connotation to what may well be considered, and certainly has been considered, laudable: for example, the propensity to acquire a stable and predictable personal character. What we may describe as a rational approach to human psychology appears to Sartre as 'une conduite d'excuse'. This 'apologetic' procedure consists in seeing within us opposing forces comparable to things, in trying to link up discrete objects and events in space and time,[4] in providing us with a *human nature*

---

[1] 'Descartes . . . has given a name to this possibility which human reality has to secrete a nothingness which isolates it – it is freedom.' *B.N.* pp. 24–5 (*E.N.* p. 61).

[2] *La Création des valeurs*, Paris, 1944, p. 98.   [3] Vide supra, p. 27.

[4] '. . . to fill the void which encircles us, to re-establish the links between past and present, between present and future.' *B.N.* p. 40 (*E.N.* p. 78). Cf *B.N.* p. 557, *E.N.* p. 643, on 'the illusion of substance' (*l'illusion substantialiste*).

productive of our acts, when it should be recognizing a *human reality* which is ceaselessly transcendent, that is to say, which is constantly escaping from – therefore transforming, therefore renouncing – its own essence. We are, in short, reduced by this procedure to being never anything but what we are, to a reintegration into being, as opposed to becoming. This degenerate form of being is described as 'existing in the mode of the in-itself'.[1] The attack on 'determinism' is frequently made in *Being and Nothingness*,[2] and it is interesting to consider what it implies concerning the nature of existentialism. What Sartre calls psychological determinism and the attempt to 'reify' (*chosifier*) complex human impulses, motives and mental processes is in fact part of man's age-long effort, not to increase his servitude, but on the contrary to deliver himself from constraints which limit his freedom of choice. Increased knowledge of ourselves and our environment, with its consequent reduction of the domain of hazard, has always appeared as a gain, and it seems premature to allow ourselves the luxury of forgoing it. Yet this is what existentialists often appear to want to do, and one wonders which of two contrary but not mutually exclusive motives predominates in determining their outlook. They may consider that progress has carried us far enough from the adventurous insecurity of our pristine state, and desire a dash of uncertainty to relieve the boredom of modern comfort. This attitude, however, has already, in an age of acute physical insecurity, an old-fashioned, Nietzschean air about it, and it is more probable that *Angst* involves a homeopathic recourse to insecurity as the best hardening treatment in a world where philosophy offers no consolations. It is significant that the philosophers and writers whom we generally class as existentialist are acutely conscious of the tragic significance of the human lot rather than power-seeking in the worldly sense. Nietzsche's will to power stood for a tragic energism of like kind. To be free, therefore, does not mean to be successful, but to exercise 'autonomy of choice'. We may, as Sartre says, choose failure, or the impossible.[3]

[1] *B.N.* p. 56 (*E.N.* p. 95).   [2] *B.N.* pp. 439 ff. (*E.N.* p. 515).
[3] *B.N.* p. 483 (*E.N.* p. 563).

The distinction between in-itself and for-itself is obviously parallel to that between material and spiritual in more orthodox language; except that spirit, or soul, is traditionally regarded as substance, whereas Sartre establishes discontinuity, which he usually calls transcendence, as all-important in this sphere. But the similarity between the concept of 'the body' and in-itself is striking, for Sartre uses the symbol of viscosity,[1] evocative of bodily humours, to convey the idea of 'the flesh', which absorbs and degrades the spiritual principle.[2] But the scope of this dichotomy does not stop here. It is characteristic of Sartre to convey 'human reality' in terms of time, and it seems that towards the end of *Being and Nothingness* the need to avoid what M. Ferdinand Alquié calls 'the affective refusal of time'[3] is expressed in Sartrian imagery. Our dynamic, free self is 'insidiously and invisibly held back by the suction of the past', and obliged to watch 'its slow dissolution in the past from which it flees . . . the horror of the viscous is the intense fear that time may become viscous',[4] and that we may become bogged down in our own past.

In-itself conceived as the immobilization of the dynamic self is treated frequently and at length by Sartre, in *Being and Nothingness* and in *Saint Genet*. One's essence is all that which the human reality apprehends of itself as *having been*,[5] and we can allow ourselves to become glued in our essence not only by deliberate choice, by Alquié's affective refusal of time, and by refusal of that which by its nature bears us on, but also in disguised and apparently innocent ways. Sincerity, the willing recognition by oneself of what one is, may be laudable or a form of 'bad faith'.[6] It is laudable if acknowledging one's faults leads one to disavow the being that they constitute. For then sincerity is an instrument of the for-itself. But it may be merely evidence of Sartrian 'bad faith' if it simply permits one to stand aside from oneself and treat oneself

---

[1] 'Slime (*le visqueux*) is the revenge of the in-itself.' B.N. p. 609 (*E.N.* p. 701).

[2] Sexuality and viscosity are regarded as 'a being in which the for-itself is swallowed up by the in-itself'. B.N. p. 614 (*E.N.* p. 796).

[3] *Le Désir d'Éternité*.   [4] *E.N.* p. 702 (my translation) (*B.N.* pp. 610–11).

[5] *B.N.* pp. 34–5 (*E.N.* p. 73).   [6] See *B.N.* pp. 62 ff. (*E.N.* pp. 102 ff.).

as an object of fascinated scrutiny. 'Drawing up a perpetual inventory of what one is, is to deny oneself constantly and to seek refuge in a sphere in which one is nothing but a pure, free act of contemplation' (*un pur et libre regard*).[1] Insincerity, on the other hand, may amount to a praiseworthy refusal to see the for-itself as incurably paralysed. A man who admits that he has been consistently guilty of homosexual behaviour but refuses to identify himself as *a* homosexual with the words 'Je suis un pédéraste', and who finds excuses for himself as some kind of special case, may well be refusing to accept an essence, a destiny, a category which closes the way to self-transcendence and change. His evasiveness enables him to retain his freedom.

One is almost tempted to say that through his treatment of the in-itself and for-itself Sartre has made any discussion of freedom superfluous. Living presents a succession of choices, and since choice must, in virtue of the meaning of the word, be free, the word liberty would seem otiose. At one time Sartre declares that existence precedes essence,[2] at another that liberty precedes essence,[3] and generally speaking it is clear that freedom is the sole attribute, or rather the being, of the for-itself or existential self. The human reality which unfolds in time is a being-for-choice and is only retrospectively objective.[4] The essence of man is in suspense in his liberty, writes Sartre,[5] he does not *first* exist in order *subsequently* to be free; there is no difference between man's being and his being-free. This paradox of being necessarily free, or being condemned to be free, simply restates the situation of the for-itself which vainly seeks to stabilize itself in static being, or in-itself. The discussion of freedom in *Being and Nothingness*

---

[1] *E.N.* p. 106 (my translation) (*B.N.* p. 65).
[2] *E.N.* p. 515 (*B.N.* p. 439).   [3] *E.N.* p. 61 (*B.N.* p. 25).
[4] See V. Jankélévitch, *Bergson*, pp. 90–1. 'Je suis incapable, livré à mes hésitations, d'anticiper sur leur issue: mais je prévois que je reconnaîtrai cette issue comme la seule possible quand je m'y engagerai. *Je ne sais pas* mais je devine que je vais avoir su. Je me trouve, en somme, dans la situation ambiguë d'une personne qui se sent connaître ce qu'elle se sent ignorer.' 'Le sentiment de la liberté n'est pas autre chose que ce savoir, plus cette ignorance.'
[5] *B.N.* p. 25 (*E.N.* p. 61). Cf also ibid. p. 440 (p. 516).

merely reiterates what has been said earlier in existentialist jargon, and for better or worse, this is after all Sartre's contribution to philosophy. The pages devoted to the roles of the in-itself and for-itself describe in phenomenological terms the feeling of freedom experienced by the person in action, or on the point of it: of freedom, as Jankélévitch aptly puts it, 'impenetrable only to the onlooker'.[1] Sartre's words: 'It is because human reality is inadequate (*n'est pas assez*) that it is free'[2] are unintelligible unless read in the light of the previous phenomenological analysis of the for-itself and of time.

It is clear that if, for human reality, to be is to choose oneself[3] then man is wholly responsible. Therefore, since action is paramount, although Sartre explicitly reserves discussion of morals for a future work,[4] some ethical recommendations can be seen to emerge. This raises the question of 'authenticity', which is a current contemporary French word for 'virtue', but this will be examined later. It is sufficient to say at the moment that although all actions are freely chosen, some are more so than others. What would normally be regarded as outside the control of the individual will is considered by Sartre to be an unconscious choice. A chronic feeling of inferiority is a consciousness of oneself in the world, an unconscious choice of oneself-for-others which Sartre prefers to call a *conscience non-positionnelle* or *conscience non-thétique (de) soi*, the bracketing of the preposition giving the reflexive pronoun an adjectival force, so that the self becomes an attribute or qualification of consciousness rather than an 'object' of it. But there is a thetic or positing consciousness which comes into existence through our recognition that we are separate from objective reality, a recognition which Sartre calls the 'internal negation'.[5] He does not make clear how this positing consciousness is generated, and one must suppose that he sees its source in frustrated desire or a sense of encountering an external resistance, but in any case some sort of 'leap' seems to be implied. Now this thetic consciousness is value-creating, because it sees the lack of

---

[1] *Bergson*, p. 38.   [2] *E.N.* p. 516 (my translation) (*B.N.* p. 440).
[3] ibid.   [4] *E.N.* p. 722 (*B.N.* p. 628).
[5] *B.N.* p. 463 (*E.N.* p. 541).

what it demands: 'We choose the world not in its contexture as in-itself but in its meaning—in choosing ourselves.'[1] We can, so to speak, endorse thetically our original non-positing choice, but then we risk being guilty of bad faith and inauthenticity.[2] In short we are offending Sartre's moral code, where virtue consists in taking the line of most resistance.

There appears to be an original choice which is non-positing and therefore 'innocent', but this may have to be cancelled out by thetic choice if this latter is to be authentic. This situation seems to be more effectively, if less elaborately, described by saying that we make something, or fail to make something, of our gifts in the time and place in which we find ourselves, that is, we start with data upon which we subsequently work. But Sartre wants to make the sphere of deliberate action so all-embracing that, as with freedom, the concept of will becomes superfluous, and that of involuntary action meaningless. A good deal of confusion arises from Sartre's attempt to bulldoze his way through ordinary linguistic usage in the search for phenomenological vividness. To say that an act is free would seem necessarily to imply that it is voluntary. Yet by representing all consciousness as involving choice, therefore free act, while at the same time distinguishing non-positing and positing consciousness (i.e. involuntary and voluntary acts), he surely contradicts himself.

Thus since freedom is identical with my existence, it is the foundation of ends which I shall attempt to attain either by the will or by passionate efforts. Therefore it cannot be limited to voluntary acts. *B.N.* p. 444 (*E.N.* p. 520).

In relation to freedom there is no privileged psychic pheno-

[1] *B.N.* p. 463 (*E.N.* p. 541).

[2] We may, however, *authentically* decide to endorse our non-thetic choice. The following remark on Camus's *Outsider* is interesting in this connection. 'He is responsible for the murder despite his innocence. The moment of conscience has arrived and he senses that he is guilty. Then Meursault fires four more shots . . . he consciously and deliberately repeats what he has just done unconsciously and unwillingly. The re-enactment is an implicit assumption of responsibility and an act of consent.' Louis L. Rossi, 'Albert Camus, the Plague of Absurdity', *The Kenyon Review*, Vol. XX, summer 1958, No. 3, pp. 399–422.

menon. All my 'modes of being' manifest freedom equally since they are all ways of being my own nothingness. *B.N.* p. 445 (*E.N.* p. 521).

The will is not a privileged manifestation of freedom. *B.N.* p. 452 (*E.N.* p. 529).

Sartre has often been criticized on account of his attitude to others, and his apparent fear of others. His whole philosophy is coloured by this. Wishing to remain independent of 'autrui', which is almost an abstraction, he tries to bring every datum of psychological life within the sphere of the individual's responsibility. We can thus always deprive others of power over us, even if it be only that of predicting our behaviour, a power which our circumstances, environment and make-up confer upon an onlooker. Sartre's fear of 'le regard' is intense, and he tries to rob the hostile gaze of an object by empowering the autonomous self to do away with any essence upon which 'autrui' may avidly or complacently seize. It is freedom 'whereby the for-itself escapes from its being and its essence, and whereby it is always something other than what can be *said* of it'. The for-itself is 'already beyond the name given to it, or the property recognized in it'.[1]

Freedom for Sartre, one ventures to say, becomes a somewhat depreciated concept, despite its constant use and the importance which he obviously attaches to it. Freedom has, paradoxically, been argued into a subordinate position, through the very prominence given to it. Without determinism or servitude the word freedom ceases to mean very much, and by endowing the for-itself with its character of evaluative mobility Sartre appears to have demoted the idea of freedom to a humbler and more relative field of application. If *we are* a freedom, freedom as an attribute can hardly be discussed.[2]

What is more important is the peculiar character of virtual nonentity which Sartre confers upon the for-itself which is none the

[1] *E.N.* p. 515 (*B.N.* p. 439).
[2] M. Alquié's comment seems relevant. 'It is clear that freedom, being ontological, cannot, strictly speaking, be known.' *La Nostalgie de l'être*, p. 115. Cf also S. de Beauvoir, *Pour une morale de l'ambiguïté*, 1947, pp. 35–6, where this objection is dealt with.

less a necessity. 'I am condemned to exist for ever beyond my essence.'[1] It is non-natural in the sense that it cannot be reduced to being in-itself, and thus made tangible. Sartre is really issuing a warning, a very long warning in *Being and Nothingness*, against the assimilation of valuation to judgement of what is, not so much through any abstract, speculative interest in the distinction between the 'is' and the 'ought', as because the evaluating self runs the risk of becoming somehow objectified and thus ceasing to be evaluative. The special nature of phenomenological investigation consists in its attempt to describe dynamic experience in time, and not to offer a schematization of that experience in some sort of arrested state.

Sartre's approach, perhaps for that reason, seems to be implicitly evaluative, since the for-itself not only necessarily characterizes life that is truly human, but is praiseworthy. The more we are, phenomenologically speaking, for ourselves, the better. Are we then back in a naturalistic ethic? If so, it is of a rather unusual kind, since the recommendation appears to be not to reduce obligation to reality but to assimilate reality to valuation. In other words, what we perceive and do is what we require, and to search for a reality independent of requiredness is a vain pursuit. The extent to which assessment of values invades Sartre's ontology is shown by the importance of the concept of 'authenticity' in his, and related, philosophies. 'Authentic' may be both a value word and a descriptive one. In existentialist contexts it exploits this ambivalence. It has in such contexts the generality of 'good' without seeming openly to commit its user to morality.

From the foregoing it becomes clear, I think, that although both Camus and Sartre subscribe to the notion of absurdity, Sartre reduces the 'separation' in a way in which Camus does not. Camus's commitment is a kind of unexpected humanitarianism at variance with the vision of a valueless world presented in *The Myth of Sisyphus*. Reality is 'out there', and the divorce is maintained between the human being and a hostile and intractable environment. Now Sartre's phenomenological approach saves

[1] *B.N.* p. 439 (*E.N.* p. 515).

him from the dismay felt by Camus on discovering that, having failed to ground value in reality, his morality has to be sustained by the strength of his own feelings. Sartre assimilates experience to evaluation, and in the assimilation the 'separation' is abolished, or rather transformed. From there being an unbridgeable gap between man and his world, man is henceforth *in the world*, and the 'separation' is always ahead of him, a gap perpetually requiring to be bridged, and being bridged only to be reopened. The inhuman and the human, the *in-itself* and the *for-itself*, are interdependent and mutually complementary. The self has its ballast of acquired reality, but this is being constantly transcended or out-run.

A considerable change is seen in Sartre's general position in the first volume of his *Critique de la raison dialectique*, which appeared in 1960. In this work Sartre's thought moves towards dialectical materialism, and this reorientation involves some change in the idea of action as presented in *L'Etre et le néant*. One might expect that an absolute volte-face would be required concerning being *for-itself*, since there is after all a Marxist direction to history, leading on to a 'totalization' which is 'perpetually in the making as History and historical Truth'.[1] But the determinism of Marx and the predestination of Calvin leave room for effort and adaptation to concrete circumstance. Indeed the new 'human reality' of Sartre is one which finds its expression through the transformation of the material reality into means. 'Thought must discover its own necessity in its material object, while discovering *in itself, in so far as it is itself a material being*, the necessity of its object.'[2] This recalls Merleau-Ponty's conception of the embodied self – one's own dynamic body – as the source of all other objects. Whether or not there is in fact any influence of Merleau-Ponty here, or whether this view is inevitable in any Marxist philosophy, the fact remains that Sartre passes from a Kierkegaardian rejection of any rational or other 'mediation' (a rejection expounded in *L'Etre et le néant*) to the search for an acceptable mediation as the central problem of man. The reluctant existentialist Sartre[3] is

[1] *Critique de la raison dialectique*, Paris, Gallimard, 1960, p. 10. Cf p. 29.
[2] op. cit. pp. 131–2.
[3] Vide Preface, page 7. 'Je n'aime pas parler de l'existentialisme.' But

walking on a tight-rope over the abyss of essentialism, which in this case takes the form of realizing a pre-existent historical truth and the consummation of time. How is the feat negotiated? No doubt we shall have to wait for the second volume of this wordy work for a final answer, even if we get it then. A few indications are, however, here available.

There is still no human essence; nevertheless 'communication is always possible'.[1] This might appear a considerable concession for Sartre, who has always seemed inclined to deny, in effect, any fruitful and collaborative *Mitsein*. The Other, with his hostile and dispossessing 'gaze', has always stood in the way of creative being 'for itself'. Alterity, at least in the shape of Other People, has always seemed, in personal relations, to constitute a threat. It still seems to do so, but now the Other is less deliberately menacing; he is doing his own best for himself, in putting into operation his own *praxis*, and perhaps even acting in the interest of others for a time; yet the illusory *Mitsein* is a Hobbesian 'pledged society' of enemies. Moreover, through a perversity inherent in the mediation of things, an outcome is produced which Sartre calls the '*pratico-inerte*', which serves nobody's interest. It is an outcome in which the realized and 'crystallized' intention is no longer anything but an obstacle.

Transcendence is now defined as 'existence-outside-the-self in relation to the Other-than-the-self and the Other-than-man', and 'as the mediation between the given which is undergone and the practical significance'. The stress is now on the material world as the instrument of the intentional, albeit material, body, and on the process of meaning-giving. Our being, in so far as it issues into significant action, is outside ourselves, or more accurately it is a process of realizing objects and objectives outside ourselves. Here Heidegger's support is invoked as the champion of Marxism in so far as Marxism makes my being dependent on external action, in

---

existentialism will remain valid until it has exerted its influence upon Marxism. Cf Maurice Cranston, *Sartre*, Oliver & Boyd, 1962, p. 89. 'He wants Marxism to purge itself of its nineteenth-century materialistic concept of determinism and accept from existentialism a rational concept of human freedom.'

[1] op. cit. p. 105.

so far as 'Being is Another in me' and as 'man is himself only through Being, which is not identical with him'.[1]

Thus only through the mediation of material reality is significance brought to light, and human reality made to exist: man is 'mediated' by things to the extent that things are mediated by man.[2] But this mediation, in the form of *praxis*, is self-stultifying in that its materialization produces the obstructive *pratico-inerte*. Sartre gives the example of Chinese peasants who, in the course of many centuries, have cleared their land of trees in the interest of cultivation, with the result that now there are no trees to hold the top soil, which is consequently carried into the rivers and is the cause of widespread flooding. So trees, which were an obstacle to an intention, are now cleared away, and their absence has in its turn become an obstacle to the very cultivation which their presence impeded. The outcome of a common purpose shows itself as the triumph of an unintentionally hostile Other. A human *praxis* has become 'crystallized and inverted'.[3] The fate of collective enterprises is to become *antipraxis*, 'that is, praxis with *no author*, outrunning the given in the direction of rigid ends; the hidden significance is counter-finality'.[4] So it would seem that *praxis* and *Mitsein* must founder in 'alienated objectification'.

Sartre is clearly trying to keep *praxis* at the level of large-scale transactions between man and inanimate nature, which give rise, incidentally but also almost necessarily, to results which cancel out the creative effort initially expended, and display *antipraxis*,[5] in which 'a social heritage is transformed into a disaster'. At this level the disaster is not open to 'interpretation' – periodic flooding is unmistakably a physical scourge. It is not always possible, however, to see *antipraxis* as so unambiguously realized. Though fire and flood hardly allow themselves to be thought of otherwise than as calamities, it is only in a human context that any interpretation or valuation at all can be put on them, and we soon find Sartre having to concede that it is the human meaning which we

[1] op. cit. p. 248. Quoted from Waehlens, *Phénoménologie et vérité*.
[2] op. cit. p. 165.   [3] op. cit. p. 235.
[4] By which we are to understand the defeat of the object sought in the first place.   [5] ibid.

express and evaluate in the worked material. Indeed, he is forced back to what one might be justified in calling the orthodox phenomenological position, in which the pre-reflective 'given' is never accessible.

> If materiality is found everywhere, and is indissolubly linked to the meanings imprinted upon it by the *praxis* . . . and if the thing can bring forth its own idea, where then is *matter*, that is to say, Being totally devoid of meaning? The reply is simple: it is presented nowhere in human experience.[1]

So the attempt to overcome the resistance of brute, material reality becomes a metaphor rather than a description of the human situation, and we experience something analogous to this resistance '*in society*, where inertia, automatism and impenetrability act as brakes upon our actions'.[2] Hence the 'idée-objet', which is 'crystallized' or 'passivized' *praxis*, and which has its brief life as a creative force and becomes parasitical as soon as it has fulfilled its provisional function.

Sartre, in this work, is trying to reduce the dualistic philosophy of *in-itself* and *for-itself*, expounded in *L'Etre et le néant*, to a monism of matter. We shall see that the same attempt is in effect made by Merleau-Ponty, for whom the body as primary object throws up a succession of secondary objects in its relations with reality. Probably some influence has been exerted by Merleau-Ponty here, despite the estrangement between the two philosophers which occurred some years ago. Sartre says: 'Man is precisely that material reality through which matter receives its human functions.'[3] He also asserts that the universe of science is a rigorous chain of *meanings* (*significations*). These arise from practice and are reapplied to it for further elucidation, but each one is presented as provisional, however long it is in fact expedient to retain it. The only monism relevant to human reality, he says, is the monism of matter. It is the only one which banishes the 'purely theological' temptation to contemplate nature 'with no additions from outside'. We have come a long way from the world of 'la nausée'. From being the embodiment of absurdity and

---

[1] op. cit. p. 247.   [2] ibid.   [3] op. cit. p. 249.

the unmediatable, the material world is now the sole mediation for a mankind delivered of God, metaphysical unity, pre-established harmony, etc. Sartre would have us believe that he has effected a philosophical economy in discovering 'la médiation de la chose', but the sense-giving operation remains mysterious, and Sartre, as always, leaves too many loose ends.

3

Participation. A vindication of being-in-itself as meaningful. Louis Lavelle

I have taken Sartre as the obvious example of a philosopher for whom human reality is transcendent, that is, self-renewing and only retrospectively given. There are other writers of similar outlook, of course, but it may be better to defer consideration of these until the discussion of authenticity is broached. What one may call the Sartrian view, however, is not universal and indeed its exposition is not the most difficult to follow or reproduce, as one might imagine it to be from reading *Being and Nothingness*. The approach which contrasts with the creative view of existence is the one which considers experience as participation. Since to participate is to enter into a relationship with what is in some sense already there, this view has been described, in its axiological aspects, as the *objective* theory of values.[1] I think, however, that this description is likely to lead to confusion, since it would be impossible to be less objectivist concerning the source of the act and of action than, for example, Lavelle and M. Alquié. The word 'transcendent' indeed also fails to designate anything distinctive in either of the two schools compared with the other, so it will be necessary to choose other terms, and I think that perhaps 'the act as creation' and 'the act as participation' will establish the necessary distinction, or come near to doing so.

[1] R. Polin, *L'Activité philosophique contemporaine en France et aux Etats-Unis*, Vol. II, p. 218.

Participation is the term predominantly associated with Louis Lavelle, one of the foremost of recent French philosophers, who, although highly representative of this kind of philosophy, does not entirely avoid the pitfalls of his own difficult position. Very roughly this, as set out in his major work *La Dialectique de l'éternel présent*, is that our actions are contained in the totality of things so that they are instrumental rather than creative. That ever-vigilant killer of objectivist giants, M. Alquié, complains that this amounts to saying that 'there is no Being other than that of the Whole'.[1] Certainly the criticism needs to be made, for whatever Lavelle's own conception was, the reader is almost inevitably driven to see here a kind of Hegelian assimilation of being to some sort of totality. Alquié is justified in being a purist about this. We shall see, I think, on closer scrutiny, that Lavelle's philosophy is less impure than Alquié suggests.

Now what has Lavelle to say? He begins by stating what appear to him to be the two emotional attitudes underlying philosophical speculation. In the first place surprise at the 'perpetual miracle of initiative',[2] or 'my own insertion into the world'.[3] The mystery of this self-insertion resides less in the act performed than in the inner *fiat* whereby this act is brought about, in *ma présence active à moi-même*, in the feeling of responsibility towards myself and the world. This permanent initiative which is the point of insertion of myself into the world is the stuff of being; Lavelle holds that being and act are ultimately identical. The second striking factor of experience is 'that ever actual presence from which I never succeed in escaping'. This, to put it another way, is the *cogito* which enables me to pick out from the totality of being a being which is my own.[4] These elements coalesce into self-consciousness apprehended as freedom of initiative.

As far as being as a whole is concerned, it is all-inclusive and absolute.[5] There is nothing outside it, no underlying, generating

---

[1] *La Nostalgie de l'être*, p. 11. Cf Suzanne Bachelard, *La Conscience de rationalité*, P.U.F., 1958, p. 2: 'la conscience vigilante est, à sa manière, conscience première'.

[2] *De l'être*, p. 9.

[3] *De l'acte*, p. 10.   [4] *De l'être*, p. 9.   [5] ibid. p. 14.

principle which is its source, such as value or possibility, for these, in their way, are. If they were not, what compelling force could be attributed to them? How indeed could they be conceived? It is already clear that Lavelle is no believer in the 'creation of values', or even in a for-itself which is ever in process of escape from being. For Lavelle being is pure act, and pure act leads to participation.[1]

Pure act is the impersonal spiritual source[2] of individual initiative. If we wish to call this being, we may, but we are not entitled to allow being thus conceived to become solidified. We shall be naturally inclined to do so, because when we objectify we immobilize. Being would perhaps be helpfully described as a kind of potential energy, which, I should think Lavelle would say, is bound to be utilized in one way or another. Being is given to me, he says, as a power which I am left to use, and which is realized only by an internal operation which always depends on me for its performance.[3] But this potential energy does not belong to a source which is localized in me; being is universal, that is, there is nothing which can be affirmed yet which escapes it; it includes not only everything affirmed, but everything affirmable. Wherever it is present, it is present in its entirety.[4] It is univocal. Anticipating the difficulties and obscurities which this idea involves, Lavelle tries hard to extricate himself. If the totality of being is given, he asks, how can it be possible to add anything to it, for then all thought and action must be sterile. But, he replies, the Whole is *not* given. The given is only a part of it, and it includes also the possible and time. It is through the persistence of a prejudice which, he says, he is constantly condemning, that we conceive being in terms of the object as it presents itself to us in a momentary experience.[5] He goes on to elaborate his view by declaring that being is present everywhere and nowhere: nowhere because it is not identified with its modes; everywhere because every aspect of being implies every other, which appears to be something like a restatement of Whitehead's 'fallacy of simple location'.

The idea that being undergoes no sort of augmentation through the acts which might appear to add to it is stressed again and

---

[1] ibid. p. 16.   [2] Cf F. Alquié, *Le Désir d'éternité*, p. 111.
[3] *De l'acte*, p. 64.   [4] *De l'être*, p. 289.   [5] ibid. p. 290.

D

again.[1] It is noticeable that, without naming Sartre, Lavelle pointedly criticizes the conception of a wholly creative existence which leaves in the wake of its acts a trail of debris comprising mere rejected by-products of authentic living. The essence of being, he says, is to be only *in-itself*, to be the only term outside which there is nothing.[2] Elsewhere he complains more specifically of how misguided is the insistence upon the idea of being as a perpetual self-surmounting. This he rightly diagnoses as a certain immoderate self-assertion, and at the same time as the desire to escape from the self and be lost in a permanently indeterminate mode of existence. For, according to such a conception, only movement is significant, the forms assumed and things done being, as things, despised.[3] To English readers any significant distinction between one kind of anti-substantialism and the other will appear hard to grasp. We shall find, I think, that while seeing being as an activity, as does Sartre, Lavelle attaches greater importance to its products. These are not simply so much spent energy, they can be, and must be, re-utilized for further spiritual adventure and enrichment. Whereas for Sartre the creation of value is a prospective activity, the 'lack' always being ahead, for Lavelle the realization of value may equally be retrospective, the past having, no less than the future, a selection of possibilities, in this case actualized, to offer. It is true that he says 'the created is for the act only an instrument . . . it is always the created which passes, whereas the act itself is eternally reborn'.[4] The point is that the created thing can be many times instrumental, it is not burnt up like fuel or thrown overboard and irrecoverable. The implication of this is that Lavelle's dynamism does not preclude a contemplative any more than a materially productive life, for in both is participation achieved. Indeed production is in a sense

---

[1] *De l'acte*, pp. 15–16, 43, 106, 127, 172, 345. 'Participation ceaselessly diversifies and multiplies particular forms of being, by personal development and mutual enrichment, without adding anything to being itself.' '(Participation) operates in (Totality) by an act which is always identical and always new' whereby 'our own being is constituted by a double movement of borrowing and restitution, being indefinitely nourished by Totality without ever adding anything to it'.

[2] ibid. p. 127.   [3] ibid. p. 106.   [4] ibid. p. 16.

unimportant, it is the corollary of the act rather than its *raison d'être*. The act is its own end, for it serves to bear witness rather than to achieve.[1]

SUBJECTIVITY AND OBJECTIVITY

I have mentioned what Lavelle regards as the basic philosophical preoccupation: 'my active presence to myself', the inner *fiat* which initiates my participation in being, my 'insertion' into the world. Now in attempting to come to grips with this, Lavelle adopts a view common to a number of Christian philosophers, for which they invoke the authority of Descartes. The *cogito* is seen as bounded on two sides, so to speak, by the external world and by a transcendent inner one. Both make us aware of our limitations. Discussion of the outer reality may be postponed for the moment. The inner reality is felt as the basis of our individual being, and its 'otherness' is borne in upon us by the intimation of imperfection which we experience in relation to an 'anterior'[2] inner perfection. Thus the self is 'swamped'[3] no less from the inner side than from the outer, because it is the self which relates them to each other. In relation to exteriority the self is comparatively passive, whereas to the inner side it is autonomous and capable of penetration. This is similar to the discussion of the 'radical point of departure' by the late Pierre Thévenaz,[4] who conceives the identification of the essential self not so much as a turning inwards from external reality, as the penetration, from a familiar, peripheral self, into a central core which is the ability to doubt.

It is the inner reality, according to Lavelle, which in response to its feeling of inadequacy is impelled to initiate the act of participation. But participation is not to be understood as an intervention in an objective reality which is there already.[5] The act, in its accomplishment, bodies forth its own objective reality, and it is important to understand that subjective and objective are

[1] *De l'acte*, p. 15.

[2] 'Une intériorité parfaite qui est première par rapport à ma propre intériorité.' *De l'être*, p. 18.

[3] 'débordé'.   [4] *L'Homme et sa raison*, 1957.

[5] 'Philosophy begins where being ceases to be confused with the object, but is identified with the interior act . . .' *De l'être*, p. 17.

aspects of the act, and not independent entities. There is interdependence between the concepts of subject and object. We have
seen that the self experiences a certain lack in relation to an inner
perfection, an idea which appears to be a slight variant of the
ontological proof offered by Descartes. Now there is a corresponding 'aspiration' manifest in the external direction, which
shows how the object is related to the act. Here is what Lavelle
says about this:

> Objects or phenomena are the distinctive marks of [the act's]
> limitation, which it never ceases to encounter; but they do not
> express merely this limitation, or at least they express it by
> bringing to it, in the form of data which it must receive or
> suffer, *everything that it lacks*, which persuades it that without
> them it would *possess* nothing; whence it readily concludes that
> it would *be* nothing. The limitation of the self, however, is in a
> certain sense internal. But again the self is not pure interiority;
> in it interiority is always linked to exteriority; it has a body and
> a world exists for it.[1]

Now the implication of this idea of the act which fashions
objects on the boundaries, so to speak, of its efficacy, objects
which show that its power, or its participation, has succeeded in
extending thus far and no farther, objects which are, quite simply,
the intention and meaning of the self's activity, is brought out
towards the end of *De l'acte*. Passivity in us, says Lavelle, is not
the effect of an alien activity, but merely the sign of the limits to
which our activity has exerted itself.[2] The act and the objective
datum as Lavelle conceives them might well, I suggest, be described, adapting a distinction of André Lalande's, as constituent
and constituted reality. Reality is sometimes the act, sometimes
its empirical product. The interdependence and complementarity
of the subjective and the objective is discussed in Chapter 17 of
De l'acte. Lavelle here contests the one-sided view, as he sees it, of
empiricism which endows the 'given' with a reality which it
denies to the act, whereas, he maintains, the object is non-
existent without the act which brings it into being. 'In the world

[1] *De l'être*, pp. 17–18. My italics.   [2] *De l'acte*, p. 390.

of participation it is the coincidence of the two which constitutes true being.'[1] Because we are capable of activity and passivity, being may appear identifiable either with pure act or with the sum of the given. In fact consciousness, which is potentiality,[2] is the instrument of mediation between the act and data. Hence consciousness is always either turning inwards to the 'sovereign efficacy' from which it draws its own activity, or outwards, applying that activity to construct[3] out of reality new given situations corresponding to its successive operations. The perfection of participation is expressed by a due balancing of act and datum.[4]

It might appear from this that Lavelle's position is entirely idealistic, in that he denies the self-subsistence, if not the reality, of what is not 'act' or mind. But this is not so. What he says is this. It is often considered that the creative act produces a work outside itself, which could subsist, like the product of the artisan, without its maker. But there is no creative power other than the power to create the self, a power which draws all creatures into participation in its own creative essence; *pure act can create only beings and not things*. As for things, they are always the effect of the act of participation; not that it can bring them out of nothing, but that, as things, they express the act's limitation and passivity; they are less a sign of its perfection than of its impotence.[5] Now I think this is a significant statement. It means, surely, that there *is* a domain of objectivity, a pre-reflective reality; things, in the most general sense, are not unreal, but they are literally insignificant until brought into existence from the human point of view by the sense-giving processes of active mind, which out of *things* creates *beings*. The distinction is not basically the familiar one between inanimate objects and living beings, but between the reality which presents itself to what Sartre would call 'pre-reflective' consciousness, and the same reality when it has been endowed with form, or interpreted, by the mediation of the participating act.[6] The force

[1] ibid. p. 289.
[2] i.e. power to call up its reality seen either retrospectively or prospectively.
[3] 'en faisant surgir'.   [4] *De l'acte*, p. 290.   [5] ibid. p. 375.
[6] He does indeed use the term 'beings' in such a way that it seems to refer to *human* beings, and there is some confusion, but since the term is relevant

of the inwardly directed self can also be seen in the light of this. The particular 'beings' which are brought into existence out of raw objectivity are determined by the inadequacy or the requirements of the self in relation to its inner core. It is already clear that our internal-external dichotomy breaks down here, since the requirements of the self, the 'lacks', are always felt by a self which has been built out of its externalized, actualized or 'participated' acts. It is always impure in contrast with the basic *cogito* which measures its doubt against the perfection of certitude. It has never been pure, any more than Sartre's for-itself has ever started from scratch without an in-itself. In short the act selects its own data, and the process of selection – which is indistinguishable from creation – marks the finitude of participation.

We have seen that 'beings' (as opposed to things) are forms. There is, writes Lavelle,[1] a reciprocity between things and ideas (presumably the sort of awareness which makes nothing of the datum), but the only true reciprocity is intentional and operates between beings. Here 'beings' means 'other minds', which are of course in their activity form-giving. Reciprocity is possible between minds through the forms which are actually given. The ultimate impersonality of pure act ensures that the forms of human participation will not necessarily be incomprehensible between one person and another. The pure act upon which we all draw is a universality of being. I can, Lavelle explains, be reasonably sure that my ideas will be understood by others because they are drawn from the source of pure act in which all are capable of participating.

Returning to consideration of the relation of the act to the external world, we meet the familiar theme of the organ-obstacle. Creation is a divine act of self-realization, the world being the instrument of this creation rather than its object,[2] and this relationship has its counterpart in that of man to his works. Pure act is indeterminate in theory, but determinate in the inevitable fact which we recognize as the act of participation. A useful distinction

only to what Sartre calls *human reality*, the confusion has no serious consequences.

[1] *De l'acte*, pp. 411–12.   [2] *De l'être*, p. 22.

is established by Lavelle between act and action, when he describes the act as 'personal and secret' but necessarily transformed into action when it is brought up against a boundary mark which it tries to overshoot, and which in its turn gives the act its form.[1] Elsewhere[2] the operation of participation is equated with the suffering of limitation. The notion of the organ-obstacle is highly important on account of its role in that introspective pursuit of the ultimate genesis of action, which Lavelle calls 'the reflective act'.[3] Here the symmetry of outer and inner worlds is taken a step further when the pre-reflective consciousness is shown as the organ-obstacle of participation. Spontaneity is pre-reflective,[4] and reflection tries to catch it at its source. The contrasts of instinct and will in the domain of the practical, of sensation and thought in that of the theoretical, exemplify the distinction between these two forms of activity.[5] Before reflection, man is under nature's domination, responsive only to the will to live and multiply, which is the raw material of his participation. He may remain thus enslaved and never rise to genuine participation, remaining *quotidien* and on the animal side of lucidity. The essence of participation is to give him mastery of his own destiny, to enable him to assume responsibility for what he wills by producing his own reasons for acting. It is clear already that participation is the operation by which authentic living is achieved, by which the force which animates man is called into question, suspended, taken in hand or given a different direction.[6] But this effort at self-origination runs up against the organ-obstacle of spontaneity. Reflection aspires to become a first beginning, but it never transcends spontaneity. However, we are enabled by the reflective effort to see nature and instinct simultaneously as symbols of the fall and vehicles of participation.

Lavelle praises Le Senne's exposition of the role of the obstacle, of which I shall have occasion to write later, but considers that it is over-emphasized. A small obstacle, he thinks, is a better 'organ'

---

[1] ibid. pp. 292–4.   [2] *De l'acte*, p. 14.   [3] ibid. Chapter II.
[4] Spontaneity of life is intermediate between the inertia of matter and the activity of pure spirit.
[5] *De l'acte*, p. 29.   [6] ibid. p. 30.

for action. Such a datum is presumably not excessively absorbing for the reflective act, but absorbing enough for us to be unable to perceive it without becoming conscious of an activity which engenders it.[1] It is clear that Lavelle is more idealistic than Le Senne, for, he says, as far as the object which appears to be initially given is concerned, it is no more than the occasion of the act of reflection. So it is in fact never really given at all, but posited. Reflection starts from the given and reverts to the act which produces or explains it. To this extent it is immediately transcendent in relation to any experience contained in the pure datum. Thus in positing the given it posits itself and carries within itself the possibility of continuing to do so eternally.[2]

The important element in this idea is that the act of participation is really, so to speak, self-probing and self-actualizing, and productive of all that is in any way significant in the reality which it 'encounters'. If this is so, our attempt to control reality must be an attempt to accede to and dominate pure act itself, and this attempt implies an activity of valuation and realization of value, since we can 'take control' only in the interest of some specific ulterior aim.

THE IMPORTANCE OF THE GIVEN

Matter gives to mind both the instrument and the resistance which mind needs.[3] By now this is a familiar enough idea. The service which matter, or the object, or the given, does is to rescue pure act from the limbo of its purity, to convert our virtuality into actuality.[4] Matter is rather a crude word with which to designate the external world, since it is not really a question of stressing a spirit-matter duality. Lavelle is happier when he is talking about the *given*, and, like others, he allows himself moments of gratification at the semantic appropriateness of the term he has chosen to use. We must, he says, retain the noble word 'the given', which always implies some sort of gift. The given is often thought of as a starting point, but it is also in a sense a destination, for it is correlative to an act performed and also a sort of terminus and end.

[1] *De l'acte*, p. 32.   [2] ibid. p. 34.   [3] ibid. p. 323.
[4] ibid. p. 319.

Every operation of consciousness is directed to a certain datum, which it is for me to receive. In this datum the idea comes to fruition, the hope we feel for it feeds the desire which, without it, would remain for ever merely intentional.[1] Lavelle even goes so far as to concede a certain plausibility to the view, which of course he rejects, that the real is to be found in the object.[2] On the other hand, he says,[3] the primacy of the act is not in doubt, because although the mind can bring itself, with difficulty, it is true, but without contradiction, to imagine an act with no datum – because the datum always appears to be a limiting factor (*une borne*) – it is impossible to imagine a datum which is given to no one, that is, which is not actualized by the act which is limited by it. Whether we accept this as self-evident or not will depend, of course, on whether or not we have accepted the account which Lavelle gives of the nature of mental activity and participation. There is something rather Berkeleyan about this, and I think most empiricists would contend that all that the tree in the quad lacks when no one is there is an observer. He would certainly not be prepared to agree that the extinction of all life on earth, for example, would *ipso facto* abolish the earth and the solar system. Lavelle would probably reply that, on the contrary, it would, because, phenomenologically speaking, the earth and solar system are intentional entities,[4] 'beings' not things, or, in so far as they are things, of no philosophical significance and, indeed, nameless.

PARTICIPATION AND REQUIREDNESS

The above consideration as to whether the act or the given can be independently self-subsistent forces one prematurely to the conclusion, which it would be expedient to defer, that the act can never be regarded as axiologically neutral. Participation is nothing but a consenting to be, which, however, compels us to take our part in the work of creation. It brings home to me the fact that though I have not given myself being, at least I can give myself the being that I shall be.[5] I can, in simpler words, realize my true self or not. The problem of participation is not, he goes on, a second-order

---

[1] ibid. p. 303.   [2] ibid. p. 308.   [3] ibid. pp. 304–5.
[4] Merleau-Ponty would call them 'cultural objects'.   [5] *De l'acte*, p. 355.

problem, which involves asking how a self posited in the first place participates in a pure act which is theoretically independent of it. It is a first-order problem inseparable from the ever-present experience of an act which is beyond us and which is limited by our action and, moreover, of our assent to or refusal of it whereby we are precisely what we are. The relation between pure act and self is reproduced in that between soul and body. Their union is given to us and the problem is to know how to separate them, not how to unite them. This seems in all ways unexceptionable, and simply says that the ghost is not in the machine, but is the manner in which the machine works.

Participation, then, is ultimately not the medium of 'être' but of 'devoir-être'. The latter is difficult to translate; it often means 'obligation', but this meaning is too narrow here. Pure act, by providing the ground for participation, brings value into the world.[1] Lavelle explicitly distinguishes 'devoir-être' from total being or pure act. It expresses, he says, the inner call towards being which forces us out of nothingness to become, by choice and effort, what we are not, or at least what we are not yet. This, however, is not a Sartrian creativeness, but 'the assumption of the act by which Being creates itself', and which is promoted by our collaboration. Lavelle is always anxious to stress that action is derivative and related to something greater than itself, and the motive for this insistence is clearly theological. It is significant that he does not regard all possible action as equally legitimate, for he sees liberty as able to be misused, turning against God the power derived from him, and transforming the overweening self into a demon. There is only one form of sin: preferring oneself to God. Sartre, of course, regards self-deification, or a finally stabilized *in-itself-for-itself*, as the goal pursued, admittedly vainly, but legitimately, not to say almost necessarily, by the for-itself. In this Lavelle contrasts sharply with Sartre, but is close to him when he says that the mystery of liberty lies in my inability to *withhold* participation, for even in refusing it, I exercise it. The man who seeks escape from the world in suicide contributes by his act to the world's history.

[1] *De l'acte*, p. 357.

THE REFLECTIVE CIRCLE – 'CAUSA SUI'

As we have seen in discussing subjectivity and objectivity, the act is both received and performed, so that precisely when we believe that we are conferring being upon it, it is giving being to us.[1] Or the given is something we help to make. Now this process of receiving and at the same time performing the act is reflective by nature. The distinctively human activities of exercising foresight, or recollecting, or performing any mental operation which involves discrimination, necessitate, according to Lavelle, a turning back upon spontaneity in order to direct it and order it. They are forms of the act which seek the power, in engendering themselves, to engender all that is.[2] Now if the act merely coincided with the spontaneous impulse to being, we should live on what Sartre and Camus call the level of the *quotidien*. What distinguishes the reflective act is that it tries to reach and control its source, and to produce meaningful being, or rather being without qualification (Sartre's *human reality*) since being is by its nature sensegiving and sense-impregnated. But in so far as act is not spontaneous, it is necessarily not automatic, and something is *required* over and above what is given as mere raw, unformed thinghood. We have already met this in Sartre's 'lack', and shall meet it again in Le Senne's and M. Jankélévitch's 'fêlure'. Lavelle calls it the interval and states that it is universally experienced as a lack, which desire, will, fantasy or hope all try to make good. It is an 'ontological deficiency'.[3] The world is wholly formed in the interval separating the reflective act from the creative.[4] In a sense the reflection which discovers the world brings it into being. It provides that world with an inner space by which the two (act and world) are separated, only to be reunited, while in that space appear all the multiplicity of forms which bear witness to the efficacy of the reflective act. It cannot be maintained that the

---

[1] *De l'acte*, p. 13.

[2] ibid. p. 34.

[3] ibid. p. 200. It is not to be confused with Jankélévitch's 'interval', discussed later.

[4] ibid. p. 35. Cf p. 23: 'The world . . . fills the interval separating pure act from the act of participation.'

'outward journey' is stultified by the return since between them lies the world.

Later[1] Lavelle refers to his own work *La Perception visuelle et la profondeur* as illustrating the theory of the interval. We have in fact a form, not merely an illustration, of the interval in visual perception. The visual interval shows us objects in so far as they fail to coincide with us, at the same time opening the way to desire which leads us to close the gap and possess them. The depth of the visual image expresses the distance dividing possibility from actuality, and free movement converts one into the other.[2] He further illustrates the nature of the interval by citing the constituent and constituted reason of M. André Lalande.[3] Constituent reason is the faculty actively establishing rational relations, and constituted reason the physical laws, legal codes, precepts, etc., which are the completed and systematized output of the active reason. These latter serve also, by their imperfection, to encourage constituent reason forward to new syntheses. In this way both rational explanation and 'open' morality are the fruits of the reflective act. We have thus a reflective circle joining reflection and creation, which is simply the act 'causa sui'. The circular process in relation to morality is exemplified in repentance. The misdeed belongs to the past. Repentance cannot undo it, but it takes it up and in a sense repairs it. Our actions, says Lavelle, must become detached from us so that we may once more take possession of them, by giving them their spiritual value and meaning. The dogma of the fall and return to grace is a moral expression of the circular nature of a universe in which participation reigns. But, he adds, we must not take the mere coming of the individual being as constituting the fall, but the use he makes of the power at his disposal. If he falls, then it is in order that the return to God may be open to him through his own consent.[4] Now, of course, this is strikingly contrary to what Sartre would say. Repentance for him would be a fruitless adherence to the in-itself of the accomplished

[1] *De l'acte*, p. 32.

[2] Cf Merleau-Ponty's idea of depth as a 'motive' in *Phenomenology of Perception*.

[3] *De l'acte*, p. 34.   [4] ibid. pp. 40–1.

fact. Furthermore he would, I think, regard the 'fall' not as the misfortune of some, but as the necessary lot of all; he would regard it as God's fault, if anybody's, but also as authentic man's opportunity to 'participate' (though he does not use this term), an opportunity to be seized, as Orestes seizes it in *Les Mouches* where a guilt-ridden people exemplifies 'bad faith'. A similar contrast between the two philosophers is seen in their attitude to the 'interval'. Lavelle says that it is an interval only *for us*; for it expresses the plenitude of concrete being, always present, always offered.[1] I find this insistence on the presence of what has to be brought into being quite self-contradictory, and Sartre's view of value as created less fraught with difficulties.

THE DIALECTICAL ACT

I have dealt at some length with the reflective act which seeks the source of the modifications we bring to reality in the innermost core of the person. I now turn to the dialectical act, which is perhaps a little more 'phenomenal' in its emphasis. Its dual aspects are analysis and synthesis. Analysis is firstly the operation whereby we discern those elements in reality which we need in the direction of our personal life: but the discernment already creates them in a sense, for their existence is owed to the choice of them which we make.[2] It may be objected that in order to be chosen they must first be given, but we are now familiar with Lavelle's view that we make our given by making sense of it. The 'given' which is the merest raw material from which our world is composed is not considered to be, as such, accessible. We have given it to ourselves as significant before we have had time to apprehend it pre-reflectively. What we can influence is the participating act which is strictly our own, not the reality which can only theoretically be seized pre-reflectively. So analysis involves, in the second place, distinguishing the acts which collectively go to make our participation. It corresponds, inwardly, to the 'outwardly' analytic examination of the objects of consciousness which we perform. All the operations of consciousness are analytic, he says;[3] we are reminded that intelligence is the act by which we discern the

[1] *De l'acte*, p. 201.　　[2] ibid. p. 43.　　[3] ibid. p. 45.

elements of reality; willing is choosing; loving is preferring. Hence the act of participation is originally analytic, but on actualization it is immediately synthetic in that it forms ourselves and the world out of those discrete elements. But the synthesis is unstable; no sooner is it formed than it is once more subjected to analysis, under the motive force of the reflective act, and so the dialectical process perpetuates itself. The world, says Lavelle, is the system which we ceaselessly elaborate in order to conceive it, and subsequently break in order to live in it,[1] the world is always given and always a career open before us.[2]

THE QUODDITY OF THE ACT

We may say that the act of participation is bipolar and that these poles are respectively pure act and the world. Pure act, as its name suggests, cannot be assimilated to any form of action or force which may be manifestations of it, such as creative power, life force or cosmic energy. These are already realizations, limitations and data.[3] It is difficult to avoid assimilating Lavelle's 'participation' to creation of value when he says that there is nothing real elsewhere than in the act. When it appears that reality has been achieved, it has already slipped away or sunk to the level of material for a fresh act.[4] The 'real' is clearly the 'here and now' and this always eludes us as an object of possession. We may recall it (the process and value of recollection as seen by Lavelle have still to be discussed) but the passing and ever-recurrent act is always a move ahead of us, and leaves us with only an object to contemplate. Stendhal is talking of this feeling of ontological frustration when he discusses in his autobiographical works and diaries the difficulty of living through and at the same time dominating the experience of the moment. We cannot hold our action beneath our gaze as it is performed; only its fruits can be contemplated retrospectively, and these are not the act itself. The act is never a datum: it is, as we have seen, an aspect of being, and the word being is primarily a verb.[5] The fundamental act is the act of being, from which the notion of a state of being is

---

[1] *De l'acte*, p. 46.   [2] ibid. p. 53.   [3] *De l'être*, p. 23.
[4] *De l'acte*, p. 17.   [5] ibid. p. 63.

nothing but a derivative.[1] Being is not an attribute, because as act it is the source of all attributes, and cannot become one of them. It does not make sense to qualify it with any such epithet as 'existential'. Lavelle, intent on preserving the act from any 'essential' contamination, is fond of comparing it with light.[2] The act, he says, which draws all objects from nothingness and applies itself to them so that we may produce or know them without itself becoming an object among others, is comparable to light which envelops and illumines everything we see. Lavelle finds no word to characterize this act which is the cause of itself and of all things.[3] We shall find, I think, that Jankélévitch's *quoddity* is to all intents and purposes its equivalent.

Lavelle has interesting things to say about the 'transcendence' of all spiritual activity in relation to the states which manifest or express it, in Chapter 9 of *De l'acte*. The difference, he says, between the critical philosophy and true 'spiritualism' is the difference between the act conceived by induction, and seized immediately in its very accomplishment.[4] That this spiritualism is for Lavelle, as it is traditionally in French philosophy, closely allied to voluntarism, is shown towards the end of this important volume. It can be maintained, Lavelle argues, that understanding comes (logically?) first in the 'order of knowledge'; but its distinctive function is to recognize the existence and the primacy of the will by which it itself is put to work to throw light on all the will's procedures. There is, however, no *act* other than the one of which we are aware while we are actually performing it, and this act is always an act of will,[5] which cannot be known because it can never become an object for the intelligence, which it throws forward rather, one feels, as a torch throws forward a beam of light. But here again the dialectical character of the act becomes prominent, for just as intelligence has its origin in an act of will, so the act of will seeks as its end intelligibility. The action of will is transformed into contemplation when it has spent itself; after enabling us to pierce reality, it confers upon us the possession of it. Whence the inevitable impression that will is a quest while

---

[1] *De l'acte*, pp. 63, 65.   [2] ibid. pp. 22, 37, 61, 485.   [3] ibid. p. 113.
[4] ibid. p. 146.   [5] ibid. pp. 473–4.

intelligence bestows a possession.[1] We shall see that Alquié takes a different view of intelligence, regarding it as constituent and not primarily constituted. Lavelle regards intelligence as powerless to perpetuate its own efficacy without the initiative of will. Scepticism arises, he says, from our looking to intelligence to do what it cannot do, create.

TIME AND PARTICIPATION

Recent French philosophy has been much concerned with the question of time, and Lavelle is quite typical in this respect. Time plays an essential role in participation, and this role is discussed in *Du temps et de l'éternité*. Time marks the gap (*écart*) between totality of being and individual being,[2] the interval standing between the part and the whole, or between absolute act and act of participation.[3] This notion seems to come perilously near to imagining time spatially, as in some sense completed, and passing before us like the individual pictures in a cinematograph. The impression that this is so arises because Lavelle tells us that the 'act of consciousness and liberty' which is ceaselessly renewed cannot be actualized before the succession of events in time have provided it with an opening into which it can slip.[4] Such metaphors make it difficult to see time otherwise than as furnished for our use, to be filled with acts which are in some way preordained and even pre-existent. It is not, however, Lavelle's intention to give this impression, for he says elsewhere that this tendency to regard time as given must be resisted; space is given but time is not. Time is created and inseparable from the act of participation; it amounts to the same thing whether we apprehend ourselves as the ever-incomplete act whereby we make ourselves at all times, or whether we discover time.[5] (The use of the word 'discover' again suggests a hankering after a pre-existent totality.)

Time, however, is not a datum. It springs from a 'non-coincidence of the self with the present of the object'.[6] It is, in other words, bound up with awareness of the 'lack', or the interval,

---

[1] *De l'acte*, p. 478.   [2] *Du temps et de l'éternité*, p. 18.
[3] ibid. p. 20.   [4] ibid. p. 31. Cf *De l'acte*, pp. 250–1.
[5] *Du temps*, p. 54.   [6] ibid. p. 22.

and it is the instrument of the production of value, for Lavelle adds: 'Where perception occurs, there is no longer any time.'[1] This is a curious remark, but an interesting one, since it reveals the fundamentally dynamic and phenomenological (i.e. sense-giving) character of experience as conceived by continental philosophers. Perception is represented as a kind of repose or eternity, since while perceiving we are not 'called' or made aware of any interval to be filled, and therefore we do not create a time in which to 'coincide' with the object, for it is already there. In creating time we 'refuse' the present, which is given, and discover therefore our freedom in the interval.[2] Freedom is again, not simply freedom from external restraint, but a value-producing capacity and indeed activity. For that reason Lavelle says: 'All freedom is liberation.'[3] This liberation uses time as the organ-obstacle of participation. Pure freedom would achieve its end immediately, without requiring time. Absolute necessity would cancel out any preference and confound logical and historical order. Time is therefore a compromise between freedom and necessity; it makes individuation through liberty possible, but this is limited by a reality which comprises a situation and other freedoms.[4] It is also a product of reflection, of the refusal of the present object, a refusal which confronts the given world with a demand, and calls some new object into being which satisfies the lack.[5] Time is the apprehension of a past and a future of some *one* thing, 'the relation of each thing to itself' and not a succession of disconnected perceptions. Again we should note the evaluative implication of this.

Lavelle describes the experience of time as that of our insufficiency and poverty. The more we are conscious of the lack which is inherent in the reality we project, the more we are conscious of time which is the vehicle of the interval. Consciousness of time, in its purest form, is boredom, which is awareness of an interval

---

[1] Cf Merleau-Ponty: 'The non-temporal is the acquired.'

[2] This refusal of the present is the opposite of Alquié's 'refusal of time', as we shall see.

[3] *Du temps*, p. 92. Cf D. Christoff, *Recherche de la liberté*, P.U.F., 1958, passim.

[4] *Du temps*, pp. 97–8.   [5] ibid. pp. 168–9.

which nothing spans or fills.[1] But when time is filled with our activity we seem to live in an eternal present. It is this eternal present which Lavelle terms 'présence', distinguishing it from the 'present' moment. The present, which is acutely felt in a state of boredom, is what requires a future, what demands the mobility of time, to make good the insufficiency of this moment by hurrying on the next.[2] But presence is *absence of requiredness*, and is experienced not, admittedly, when we feel no lack, for that would be equivalent to Sartre's apotheosis through the coincidence, *per impossibile*, of *in-itself-for-itself* – but when we are fully active in filling the interval, so that the aim is as good as achieved.

We are, however, going a little too quickly, since before considering the trilogy of becoming, duration and eternity, the nature of time in its phases of past, present and future must be examined more closely. Lavelle's treatment of past and future, and the problem of prediction, resembles Bergson's. Only the past can be known, not the future. By 'known' here we are to understand something like 'possessed', contemplated in all its detail. But we may reply that we obviously do not know even the past in this way, since memory is selective and gives emphasis to certain features of past experience; indeed, Lavelle himself recognizes this, as we shall soon see. Nevertheless he is no doubt right to stress the strong sense of the concrete which fills us when we recall an event, compared with the, at best, schematized reality which we see lying ahead of us. The future is 'the essentially unknowable', and the error of fatalism lies in its treating the future as if it were the past, that is, as knowable. Whereas the intelligence gives meaning to the past, it is will which does so for the future. In order to preserve its originality the future must remain the object of a mobile, indeterminate thought never destined to be completed, as such, in the form of knowledge. When it is thus

---

[1] *Du temps*, p. 236.

[2] It is not so much the *present* as the *instant* which has to be contrasted with *presence*. 'While presence seems to abolish time, the instant seems deeply involved in time.' ibid. p. 239. Cf 'The instant is the place of participation'. ibid. p. 247.

completed, and no further modification can be brought to it, it has ceased to be the future.[1]

As the instant is the 'place' of participation, the past is the 'place' of knowledge. Knowledge is always posterior to being. The relation which is essential to knowledge is the causal one, and in persuading ourselves that the future is accessible to the knowing mind, we consider it in so far as it is determined by the past.[2] Furthermore the essence of the causal relation is the identity, though it may be concealed, of the terms, but the future cannot be prevented from showing originality, so 'inter-phenomenal' causality is reduced to regularity of succession, which represents a last resort in the matter of borrowing, from the past, the complete guarantee of knowledge.[3] A scientific law enables me to control the future by action only to the extent that it enables me to control the past by thought.[4] Despite this implication of a totally creative future, Lavelle once more confuses the issue by describing our situation in relation to the future as being 'on the brink, not of nothingness, but of unparticipated being'. We stand in a sense between two 'néants', that of the future and that of the past, but future nothingness is a mystery which defies knowledge, whereas past nothingness is annulled being, 'loaded with all our knowledge, even though that knowledge be buried with it'.[5] The knowledge that is buried with it makes the past in fact as incomplete in memory as is the future anticipated as an object of pseudo-knowledge. Indeed for Lavelle the past is not valueless, any more than the future. Both are subject to a process of selection, and Lavelle's originality lies perhaps in the fact that during a period of highly voluntaristic and future-centred French philosophy, he has been able to see value embodied in the past, that is, he has been able to see the past as a field in which discrimination has its place. There is a passage[6] in *Du temps et de l'éternité* which is of interest in this connection. The past is, in its status as a possession, our present. The memory of an event brings regret at its pastness and irrevocability, but in fact our present is enriched by this consciousness of detachment from the remembered

---

[1] ibid. pp. 270–2.   [2] ibid. p. 307.   [3] ibid. pp. 309–10.
[4] ibid. p. 311.   [5] ibid. p. 475.   [6] ibid. p. 325.

experience, and of the manifold feelings to which this detachment can give rise. We value the event in so far as we choose to regard it in a certain light relating it to ourselves. Thus our present, which is turned from itself, becomes a *presence* in the sense indicated above. The present object constantly escapes us, but we need to detach ourselves in order to gain that 'présence de l'esprit' which is our presence to ourselves.

THE FUNCTION OF TIME IN THE MAKING OF VALUE

From the point of view of value there are three aspects of time: becoming, duration and eternity; and these correspond respectively to three fundamental activities: destruction, conservation and creation. Becoming is presented negatively as the agent of change and of the inevitable loss of whatever is brought into concrete being. What strikes us most forcibly in the succession of time's moments, says Lavelle, is not that they introduce novelty into the world, but that they annihilate every given reality in which, so to speak, we had hoped to find a footing. Hence becoming is always the antithesis of being; we are less attentive to what it produces than to what it destroys.[1] Becoming is seen as what has just passed and entered into history which, for its part, is both the account of what is past and gone and, at the same time, of what has become our spiritual present. Lavelle amplifies this in the following words:

> It is necessary to distinguish, in the present, the image which relates exactly to the superseded event – although it is now detached from that event and has no further place in time – and the spiritual significance of such an image, which must free itself from that image and be changed into a permanent possession always at the disposal of consciousness. Becoming is, then, the means by which consciousness is constituted, but it is also the means whereby it is purified.[2]

Becoming is, he goes on, the content of time, which is indispensable to participation. But time carries the same potential danger to spiritual life as the object does, in being liable to

[1] Cf 'The instant is the place of participation', p. 353.   [2] ibid. p. 366.

dominate consciousness instead of serving it, and become the 'place' (*lieu*) of spiritual life instead of its instrument. This is very like Alquié's emotional 'refusal of time'. The terminology is diametrically opposed, but in both cases the writer sees with apprehension an enriching past becoming a dead hand.

Duration (*durée*) contrasts with becoming in being the means of conservation: perhaps one should add, in view of what has been said in the last paragraph, that it is the sole legitimate means of conservation, which is not merely spuriously value-producing, i.e. which does not merely offer, as valuable, an embalmed and lifeless past. Memory, writes Lavelle, does not preserve the present just as it has been; there is no mummification, on the contrary it is the living act which enables us to take possession of ourselves.[1] Mind is always 'en acte', and trying to actualize things, but it succeeds only by conferring on them a character of duration by which they survive bare change (*devenir*) and take on, in face of the actuality of the instant, a paradoxical character of inactuality.[2] It is a mistake, furthermore, to believe that duration preserves the totality of the past.[3] Duration represents a choice, but not a haphazard one. The self builds itself up by a process of progressive enrichment; but there is also a parallel process of stripping away (*dépouillement*) and it is through this elimination of what is not required that the highest forms of being are attained. Duration is always the result of the mind's resistance to becoming. It is inseparable from eternity, but not identical with it; it is part of time, which, as a mixture of becoming and duration, is the instrument of participation.[4]

Duration has two aspects, logical identity and moral fidelity. Logical identity is what we create by denying change, or recognizing it merely as something relatively superficial. The terms duration and identity are applicable respectively to the spheres of life in general and, more narrowly, reason. The all-important common feature of identity and duration is that both seem to stand outside the transitory course of events or thoughts, and introduce into time an extra-temporal element; so that time, instead of merely bearing all its creations away, appears to express some eternal

[1] ibid. p. 392.   [2] ibid. p. 383.   [3] ibid. p. 386.   [4] ibid. pp. 387–8.

essence by means of its very diversity. Just as life provides the clearest example of duration by integrating within itself constant change, so reason, far from starting from homogeneity, discovers identity in, and only in, the varied material on which it works. Time is, of course, necessary to its operations, but this time, says Lavelle, is not the time of becoming. It is a logical rather than a chronological time, in which all the particular ideas or events which we rationally link together are theoretically (*en droit*) simultaneous (even though they have in fact a temporal order of occurrence) in that, without forgetting their phenomenal order, we can retrace their logical order in reverse, with or without taking account of the amount of time they took to happen.[1]

Now Lavelle appears to adhere to the voluntaristic tradition of Renouvier, since he says that the identity which is often regarded as a demand made by the rational mind is rather an effect of the will; we do not think without willing to think. Logical identity, therefore, he goes on, in its relation to will and not to intelligence, is an act of fidelity to oneself. The word 'fidelity' he finds appropriate for designating the creation of that spiritual duration which allows us to control becoming instead of submitting to it. Identity and duration are thus forms of fidelity, which is a refusal to succumb to temporal change.[2] We have arrived once more at the threshold of a discussion of authenticity, which must again be postponed.

Passing on to the concept of eternity, Lavelle shows that eternity stands in the same relation to duration, as duration does to becoming.[3] Time and eternity, in other words, are interdependent, and are linked together by our freedom.[4] If, says Lavelle, time and eternity meet in the instant, it can be said that the instant is the 'place' where our liberty operates, since we choose between becoming or pure change, in which things are thrown up and carried away, and eternity, where spirit constantly enlightens, sustains and inspires us, *conferring upon each moment of becoming its particular meaning.*[5] This raises the question of the nature of the instant, which will have to be discussed when we

[1] ibid. pp. 396–7. Cf Alquié's 'intellectual eternity'.
[2] ibid. pp. 399–401.   [3] ibid. p. 403.   [4] ibid. p. 411.   [5] ibid.

come to consider the writing of Jankélévitch. It is obviously a more complicated idea than that of a minute fraction of time, and is more related to qualitative judgement and quasi-Gestalt psychology than to any mathematical conception of time. Eternity thus becomes in effect an activity, and an aspect of the 'act' which is intentional and sense-giving, but not the sense given. It is a kind of for-itself, 'a perpetual beyond which prevents time from ever coming to a stop',[1] or the never-ending requiredness which elicits a never-ending series of concrete answers. It is the simultaneity of an act, not with all its parts seen in one theatre of action, but with all its possibilities which require time for their expression.[2] This is what Lavelle calls the eternity of the 'by' as opposed to the eternity of the 'in', which latter is conceived as a totality in which time is contained.[3]

Summing up the relations between the three aspects of time,[4] Lavelle shows eternity as the motive force. Whereas duration is a process of enrichment, eternity is one of stripping off. This time the expression 'stripping off' does not simply refer to the selective process by which duration operates through memory. It refers to a liberation of the self from its creations – just as duration is a liberation from passivity to an imposed becoming – and its identification with the creative act. Eternity is, in other words, the cutting edge of sense-giving activity, never at rest, always ahead of the forms which it engenders. As duration is the accumulation of spiritual possessions (*having*, in Marcel's language), eternity accumulates nothing and is the purified form of *being*. Time as becoming simply produces and then destroys actualized events, but in the form of duration the events are resuscitated in a second actualization, this time spiritual. But the eternal is the impulse, the act behind the whole of participation and one which is 'unaware of its creation'.[5]

CONCLUSION

This philosophy evidently aims at greater inclusiveness than Sartre's, in so far as it tries to allow for more characteristic, not to

[1] ibid. p. 419.   [2] ibid. p. 422.   [3] ibid. p. 420.
[4] ibid. pp. 428–9.   [5] ibid. p. 434.

say inevitable, psychological experiences and their associated ideals. For instance, Sartre and Camus both see life as a matter of hurrying into new experiences, living both exhaustively and exhaustingly, so that at the end of it all, in hell or heaven, we shall not have to offer excuses for the little we have made of our opportunities, and for our failure to perform *our* acts, which is the unfortunate lot of Garcin in *Huis-clos*. We must be able to feel that we have lived, quantitatively, as full a life as possible. We have seen, on the other hand, that Lavelle does not stigmatize some degree of attachment to the in-itself as an infallible sign of bad faith. Without consenting to any objectification of the spiritual act and the eternity which is its source, he allows a more fruitful role to the in-itself. Of course he uses different terms, and what he talks about is the dual process of enrichment and elimination (or purification) of the self by the conversion of change (becoming) into duration, and duration into eternity. What Lavelle is doing is giving due emphasis to the integration of past experience into our present. In a sense Sartre does this too, in recognizing the dependence of the for-itself on the in-itself, but he stresses feverish restlessness and search for novelty, while Lavelle is not unwilling to dwell on the aspect of conservation. The difference lies in what these writers emphasize rather than in what they recognize, for in this they are not as far apart as they might seem. Sartre does not want the contemplative life to receive any sanction, whereas Lavelle is more sympathetic to the claims, often conflicting, of the different sides of our human nature, of which Sartre denies even the existence!

However, although an embodiment of greater wisdom, the *Dialectique de l'éternel présent* is much more open to criticism on the score of self-contradiction, use of false analogy and abuse of metaphor. Lavelle wants the best of all worlds; not wishing man to be the sole creator of his universe and its values, and thus independent of God, he tries to reconcile free spiritual activity with a preordained totality of being. The attempt at synthesis seeks to retain intact the value-creating act which is at the same time an act of participation, that is, a taking part *in* something and therefore a partial abdication of autonomy. I think that a writer who undertakes such philosophical tight-rope walking on such a very long tight-rope is courting disaster.

The fact remains that the central idea of Lavelle's work, that of participation, when carefully examined, is seen to keep constantly in view the virtual autonomy of mental act, any departure from this position being a concession to a traditionally religious idea of man's relation to his creator. The act, Lavelle insists, is never to be assimilated by analogy or any other procedure to an object, which, being inconceivable otherwise than as static, denies the dynamic essence of participation. This, as we have seen, is a perpetual response to an inner dissatisfaction with what is, and a demand for something else. From this it is clear that the 'is' is in a sense banished from reality except as a convenient scientific or other fiction; it is shown as derived from the 'ought', or, as the French would say (assimilating moral, and indeed rational judgements into the generally axiological), existence is a value-producing impulse which is never finally consummated. This is immediately recognized as in all essentials Bergson's position, and indeed it is typical of contemporary French philosophy.

There is in Lavelle a compromise between the purely creative idea of action and its objectification in the notion of spiritual possession. Sartre would, I think, absorb this latter into the in-itself, as what is built into our being by past living. And he would be quite justified in so regarding it. Lavelle is careful not to suggest that he recommends any kind of subservience to, and cult of, a totally memorized past life, a passivity which would destroy our autonomy in relation to what, of our being, is already *there*. He points to what is manifestly true, namely that we choose our past as we choose our future, and use both prospection and retrospection in making ourselves. Again this freedom in retrospection is what Sartre is, presumably, referring to when he says that we can change our past life by choosing to change the significance it now has for us. But Lavelle, unlike Sartre, leaves us with the impression, I feel, that a spiritual possession can be intrinsically valuable, and enjoyed as well as exploited.[1]

[1] The best-known writings on being and having are those of Gabriel Marcel, though his tendency to rush his readers into Christian theological

fields is disconcerting. He has some interesting things to say in his *Etre et avoir* ('Esquisse d'une phénoménologie de l'avoir'). The word 'having' has, in all its uses, several implications. It suggests a container and content; and content in turn suggests enclosing, preventing, resisting the expansion or escape of something.* Hence the idea of repressed dynamism. There is also implied a *possible* externalization inherent in the situation of having, as in having a secret, which we can keep to ourselves or reveal. All having has this quality of relating to something which can be exposed. The possibility of externalization mentioned is particularly dangerous when the things possessed are spiritual possessions. In this case what, in Lavelle's philosophy we have seen as dynamic *being*, is conceived as *having*, and this is the death of spiritual life. We are henceforth more possessed than possessing, and thought which, again in Lavelle's language, is in essence reflective and dialectical act, becomes mental anchylosis. Something of our self, of our being, has become alienated and made into a thing, a transformation which genuine thought is always seeking to avoid. The thinker is perpetually on guard against this alienation, says M. Marcel, this possible petrification of thought; he remains in a perpetual state of creativity, his whole thought is at every moment called into question.†

In relations with others this alienation (which in Sartre is the basis of 'inter-subjective' relations and almost naturally takes the form of possessing or being possessed, that is, of sadism or masochism)‡ is, for Marcel, transcended by love and charity. This means that for the impersonal 'he' (corresponding to *das Man*) is substituted the reciprocity of 'thou', which seeks a relationship and not a subjugation.

---

* *Etre et avoir*, Aubier, 1935, p. 231.
† ibid. p. 242. Cf *Homo Viator*, p. 30.
‡ This is further criticized by Marcel in *Homo Viator* in the examination of *Being and Nothingness*.

PART TWO

THE ROLE OF REASON
AND THE CONCEPT

4

As **mediation** between subject and object. Alquié

'Participation' turns out to be a somewhat obscure and self-stultifying concept, in so far as it tries to combine the characteristic modern French conception of mental activity as by nature creative, with the traditional view of an objective reality, including objective, 'given' values, providing a pattern to which our actions are required to conform. The necessary implication of 'participation' is that one should participate in something, and this is already a step towards concrete analogies between being and reality.

I think it can be said that these are almost completely avoided by M. Ferdinand Alquié in two of his books: *Le Désir d'éternité* (1943) and *La Nostalgie de l'être* (1950). I shall deal with the second of these two first, since it concerns the more general question of being. Alquié begins by stating his position clearly. He is concerned with 'the eternity of philosophy' which is to be sought, not in the content of its formulas, but in the constant re-enactment of the procedures which bring these formulas into being.[1] He goes on to point out the danger of historical realism, a danger which he thinks is too often overlooked. He indicts Hegel specifically for neglecting philosophy in favour of a cult of history. He rejects, moreover, as unphilosophical any attempt to present the history of thought as quantitatively constituted through retention of the 'essence' of the work of individuals, which is made to form a patchwork mosaic of ideas. One can prefer Descartes's to others, but one cannot refute them and yet claim that their contribution is part of a valuable heritage, part of a progressive groping towards the Truth. Such a course involves the confusion of science and philosophy. Philosophy is not a collection of objective

---

[1] *La Nostalgie de l'être*, p. 3.

truths or errors, but the outcome of the total response of a mind to the objective conditions it encounters. A philosophy can be accepted or rejected, but not absorbed into an impersonal body of thought.[1] The progressive or dialectical conception of the history of ideas is here repudiated. And in answer to all those who try, in general, to see the past as in any way purified, preserved and in some manner redeemed in the present, Alquié points out, with a commendable clear-sightedness and sincerity, that people, for example, who lose those near to them whom they love, know with a conviction impervious to the claims or persuasion of any system, that time too often means privation and not dialectical transcendence.[2] As Santayana wrote:

> Ignoring that pain will not prevent its having existed; it must remain for ever to trouble God's omniscience and be a part of that hell which the creation too truly involves.[3]

Examining the character of metaphysics, Alquié maintains that it has traditionally shown, not the nature of man in the light of his history, but that through his liberty man escapes *from* history.[4] The motive dominating a good deal of contemporary philosophy of all kinds is one of vague apprehension that somehow philosophy is destined to be reduced to concerning itself with a completely vacuous absolute, to a concept of being as that which all things have in common, namely nothing. This apparently imminent removal from philosophy of all tangible content, making philosophers into marginal people who have no influence on the world's affairs and the development of history, results in a tendency to value force and fact. The result is that philosophy takes its criteria from what it should be judging, and elects to base itself on the object to which it is assigning a place in the scheme of things. Marxists and a number of independent individual philosophers are criticized for having allowed their idea of philosophy to become 'contaminated': Bergson, Brunschvicg and Merleau-Ponty. In contrast Cartesian doubt, Kantian criticism and even the introspection of Maine de Biran begin with the basic act of

---

[1] *La Nostalgie de l'être*, p. 3.   [2] ibid. p. 4.
[3] *Reason in Society*, p. 106.   [4] *N.E.* p. 5.

mind seeking a relationship between spirit and object, recognizing that the latter can be known, whereas the former is 'known' only through awareness of its absence. 'Pure metaphysics encompasses nothing and supersedes nothing: nor does it presuppose anything as anterior to it.'[1] Alquié, as we have seen, is severe on Lavelle's contamination of the notion of being.[2] Lavelle is taken to task for over-familiarity with Being, for claiming that we are 'on a level with it'.[3] There is a good deal of obscurity in the last paragraph criticized, but it is noticeable that towards the end of it Lavelle says: 'I detach myself from being only in order to establish my own limitations which I am constantly trying to overcome.' I wonder whether Alquié would regard this as so very exceptionable. After all, in his *Le Désir d'éternité*, about which I shall have something to say, self-detachment from an impersonal spirit is what constitutes the act of rational thought as distinct from any search for its source.[4] However, it is probably the case that in philosophy expression is all, and that if one is to talk, literally about nothing, one had better not employ analogies which reify it. Perhaps if one insists on writing a work of some 1,200 pages on nothing, one will be unable to avoid the trap of making something of it. At all events Alquié's examples of more obvious cases of the contamination of the concept of being by objectification cannot be defended, and it must be conceded that Lavelle is too often extremely unclear.

The starting point of philosophy, for Alquié as for others, is the 'écart' which was mentioned earlier. For whether one considers, with Spinoza, that some final synthesis can be achieved, or whether the way appears to be rather in separation and analysis, the fact remains that philosophy begins as awareness of transcendence, hence of value in the seeking rather than of a reality possessed.[5] Being is 'absent', and the distinction must always be observed between 'derealization' in relation to being and explanation in relation to the One.[6] In other words, between philosophy and science. Descartes's doubts, expressed in the *First Meditation*,

[1] ibid. p. 9.   [2] ibid. p. 11.
[3] *De l'être*, p. 13. 'Nous sommes de plain-pied avec l'être.'
[4] *Le Désir d'éternité*, p. 143.   [5] *N.E.* p. 13.   [6] ibid. pp. 19–20.

as to whether he is awake or whether a malignant demon is mis-
leading him, have nothing in common with the beginnings of
scientific investigation and could not conceivably be verified;
similarly Berkeley's contention that perceived qualities cannot be
self-sufficient, but demand the existence of God, has nothing to do
with explanation. However, as a concession to human frailty and
recognizing that, if we are to talk of a uniquely peculiar thing
which is not a thing, we may allow ourselves at least a symbol,
Alquié admits Descartes's substance and Kant's thing in itself as
'our sure shield against idolatry, which consists, not in seeing in the
object the sign of being, but of seeking being in the object'.[1] He
considers science to be pragmatical in the last resort, as 'desire in
disguise',[2] and the proper concern of philosophy as the power of
refusal which frees the mind from all alienation.[3]

In the *Symposium*, the *Meditations* and the *Critique of Pure
Reason*, philosophy is presented, declares Alquié, as a discourse on
absence, as a remedy for passion, which feeds on the refusal of
absence, on impatience and regret. To specify being is to define
it objectively,[4] and this produces the illusion that the distortion of
the problem's presentation is its solution. Failure is transformed
into success, and the problem into a solution.[5]

But science is not the only culprit in leading us into the temptation to 'contaminate' being. Just as being may be wrongly
assimilated to the object, it can be equally so to the subject. The
danger of idealism is that it ultimately finds everything in the
subject, which should be seen rather as the source of our privation
and inadequacy.[6] Similarly being cannot be regarded as interior
to any concept, and Heidegger is justified for this reason in
issuing the warning that being-in-the-world does not express an
objective relationship of the part to the whole, but a primary
relationship constitutive of both myself and the world.[7] All representation of being is inadequate, and this inadequacy is the reason
for the succession of ideas and systems through the ages. Thought
is not only separated from being – separation is essential to it, for

---

[1] N.E. p. 22.   [2] ibid. p. 25.
[3] ibid. p. 40. Gabriel Marcel uses the term 'alienation' in a similar way.
[4] ibid. p. 42.   [5] ibid. p. 43.   [6] ibid. p. 45.   [7] ibid. p. 48.

the subject is revealed always in the light of defect of being (*un manque d'être*).[1]

The haunting omnipresence of the concept of being is shown in the fact, for example, that doubt about the existence of the object appears as the assertion, in the *cogito*, of subjective being. *Cogito ergo sum* does not mean that I am a thought, but that since I think, I am. My thought is deficient in relation to being, for, says Alquié, to be conscious of sense impressions, e.g. of colours, is to gain an impression not of enrichment, but of impoverishment. This would not be so if, according to idealistic principles, the subject apprehended itself as being. To attribute a fresh quality to the subject-being would then amount to qualifying being. To discover that a quality is part of consciousness is to discover that consciousness is to that extent deficient. Here we seem to have again the suggestion that consciousness is necessarily bound up with requiredness; according to Sartre it secretes its own nothing-ness. According to Descartes, as Alquié interprets it, the 'I think' is grasped only in the 'I doubt', as insufficiency, anxiety and imperfection. It seems tempting at this stage to go on to say that being is some sort of totality of possible experience in which we participate in some degree, our participation consisting in con-stantly becoming aware of lacks which are made good only to reveal other lacks, the process being endless. This would bring us back to a position rather like Lavelle's, with the same appeal and the same snags. However, Alquié will have nothing of such con-tamination, though he himself seems to come close to it at times, as when he describes knowledge as 'a loss of being',[2] thus seeming to suggest that some pre-reflective naïveté is to be taken as one-ness with being, which must then be qualified as total, since what our reflection hews out of it is a partial view. Alquié would prob-ably allow this as an analogy, provided that it were borne con-stantly in mind that it is no more than an analogy, from the space-time world of experience to a sphere unimaginably free from such determination. The danger of imposing a sensible totality on to being lies more with time than space; we have seen how suspect historicism appears to Alquié.

[1] ibid. p. 50.   [2] ibid. p. 51.

He seems to occupy a position somewhere between Lavelle and the existentialists. He criticizes Lavelle for his objectivization of being, and the existentialists (and Marxists) for 'making man into a principle by denying the transcendence of God' and 'recognizing none but man-made truth'.[1] His own position is difficult to sustain discursively, so that he is led to say that 'human liberty is a second-order activity and makes its appearance in a world of beings and *values* which precede it'.[2] This mention of pre-existent values seems to justify M. Raymond Polin in placing Alquié's among the 'objectivist axiologies'. Here we have something more in the nature of traditional 'eternal values'. It is necessary to see Alquié's values as potentialities for a certain kind of mental activity, namely valuation. As we shall see when we come to *Le Désir d'éternité*, these potentialities differ from their Sartrian counterparts in not being possibilities of individual persons. Alquié often appeals to the authority of Descartes and Kant in putting forward this impersonal source of action, which he calls spirit (*esprit*). It is not always easy to see how such an intermediate concept avoids usurping the role of being.

It should be noted that Alquié's attachment to certain classical philosophers, particularly Descartes, leads him to make frequent reference to the ontological proof, but he is aware that the value of this is in relation to being, not primarily to any deity, Christian or other.[3] What this proof pre-eminently effects is, according to Alquié, to establish the primacy of being over the subject itself, permanently separating our ontological from our objective consciousness. He makes a shrewd remark when he suggests that the underlying motive of various forms of objectification, such as seeking the Absolute in totality as does Hegel, or in Bergson's *élan vital*, or, with Sartre, in the immediacy of human reality, really amounts to seeking a consolation, the recourse to a final despair being itself a sort of odd consolation.[4] His conclusion cannot be better stated than in his own words.

What reveals authentic consciousness is the dual relationship of man, firstly to objectivity which he posits and dominates, and

[1] *N.E.* p. 63. Gabriel Marcel uses the term 'alienation' in a similar way.
[2] ibid. p. 62. My italics.   [3] ibid. p. 65.   [4] ibid. p. 117.

secondly to being, on which he is dependent and to which he is subordinate. . . . Descartes and Kant regard the science of being as consisting in the knowledge that on the subject of being nothing can be said. . . . This negative ontology is properly speaking a metaphysic. . . .[1]

Philosophy is analysis and separation. The history of philosophy shows no progress, only a ceaseless recall to being.[2]

In *Le Désir d'éternité* Alquié is concerned with a less generalized nostalgia than in the book we have been considering. *La Nostalgie de l'être* deals with philosophy as negative ontology, in the sense that its aim is to make explicit that being is quite inaccessible to experience, and that the greatest of snares and delusions is the belief that it is to be sought in either subject or object.[3] It transcends both, so philosophy is not creation, but discovery, or, since this discovery is negative, then making explicit the nature of its quest: it is the messenger of transcendence.[4]

It seemed expedient to deal with this book first, since in other works Alquié examines more specific mental activities which are, of course, manifestations of being, or, as he might prefer to say, derived from it, though their 'quodditive'[5] nature is such that to speak of their being derived seems equally wrong. In *Le Désir d'éternité* we are shown two kinds of objectification of what is essentially act, or, as it is expressed here, two kinds of refusal of time. Alquié's conception of time is in a way less complex than Lavelle's, so that what the latter calls 'becoming' is here time's only mode, and can be either refused to our ultimate cost, or accepted, thus making distinctively human existence possible. The quest of eternity is shown to be vain and harmful.

The refusal of time is possible in two ways, emotional and intellectual. The emotional refusal presents itself as passion, which is defined as in some sense a preference for the present over the future. But in this case the present, in turn, derives its strength as a determinant of thought and action from the past. Much passion is owed to habit, which is the past weighing down on the

---

[1] ibid. p. 149.   [2] ibid. p. 152.   [3] ibid. p. 132.
[4] ibid. p. 148.   [5] vide supra, p. 62.

present.[1] Memory in its involuntary, obsessive form is habit of this kind. It is unconscious and imposes itself upon us; the past is diffused into our mentality, so that it becomes dispositional rather than the clear and deliberate recollection of an episode by 'healthy' memory. Habit presupposes a detachment of action from its appropriate occasion, and thoughtlessness as to its origin and application. Localizing memory, on the other hand, is action, constructive, interpretative and affirmative, and is the enemy of eternity. It places the recollected event deliberately in the past, and clears the decks of the present for coming action. There is some reluctance to do this, because it involves the recognition that a part of oneself is irrecoverable, that it must be denied and terminated. The common attitude to death exemplifies this reluctance. We put flowers on graves in the belief that the solitude of the dead will thereby be lessened, and that some pleasure can still be given to those who have ceased to exist.[2] Remorse is an even clearer case of feeling that has no legitimate object, since we cannot undo the deed which has caused it. It is not a punishment, since a punishment cannot be merely the direct, causally produced effect of an act; moreover, for the person stricken with remorse, it is felt not as a punishment but as a demand for punishment. So it lies outside the sphere of morality, and is to be regarded as vain passion. Moral conscience is turned towards the future, not the past.[3] But the truly harmful effect of remorse is to paralyse action, and to hinder the assumption of fresh tasks. The loss of independence consequent upon remorse, and the feeling that what is in fact outside us is somehow inside, is the mark of true passion. This is illustrated by Sartre in Les Mouches, where the people of Argos are obliged by custom, on one day a year, to receive into their homes the ghosts of their dead, whom they have in some way wronged by sins of omission or commission, and towards whom they have a permanent feeling of guilt, which cannot be removed because the sufferers are no longer alive to see their wrongs righted. These ghosts symbolize the useless gnawing of remorse, which reduces the remorseful to superstitious and resentful pas-

[1] Le Désir d'éternité, P.U.F., 1943, p. 24.
[2] ibid. p. 38.   [3] ibid. p. 39.

sivity and cowardice. It is against this paralysed attachment to a dead past that the existentialist Messiah Orestes revolts. He follows the activist precept to apply all his energies to what he is capable of affecting, and ignoring those things for which he is not responsible, which are *given*: the essence of his nature or his character. Time buries our states in the past, and carries forward our selves. It demonstrates that the self is superior to, and independent of, its states. When time is accepted, availability (*disponibilité*) replaces mere habit, and we are morally free.

Why should we want to cling to a past event or events and allow time to slip by without carrying us with it? Why, in short, are we tempted to refuse time? Because whereas the past is a possession and is determined, the future is only in part dependent on our own actions; it excites fear because it contains possible danger, and certainly our death. The acceptance of the future is acceptance of risk; and the idea of its uncertainty is always accompanied by 'dread' (*angoisse*). The scientific organization of life aims to mitigate this dread by determining the future for us, but no organization can include in its closed system every detail of contingency, nor, so far as can be seen, can it postpone indefinitely our personal extinction. Time will eventually defeat us (*le temps à venir aura raison de nous*).[1] The future contains our death, the past our being.

> The individual seeks to make himself eternal: he fears a future which holds his own death in store for him, and he tries to cling to the shreds of his past, refusing to consider them lost, and coveting them through the present. Thus does he express his will to live and his refusal to die. But thus too does he let slip away the only being truly accessible to him, condemning himself to love only what has passed away.[2]

By loving the past we are forced to love only our own past and our own self, for we cannot love another's past. Love should be forward-looking in order to be other than self-love, and in order to be capable of securing the well-being of a loved one, which alone is true love. Passive love is egoism, active love forgetfulness

[1] ibid. p. 48.   [2] ibid. p. 60.

of self and of what one was,[1] and advance into the unknown. This involves risk, but not total risk if there exists an eternity enabling us to foretell the future at least in its general shape. Reason is the key to this eternity, but it too has its traps for the unwary.

RATIONAL DEMAND AND THE TRUTH OF ETERNITY

If refusal of change is a form of passion, must we therefore reject all permanence? asks Alquié. The reply is no, because not only do we not reject all permanence by submission to the instant: we are incapable of doing so. The Heraclitean denial of permanence, which is reduced to pointing to things because they are too transitory to be even named, is a travesty of rational behaviour. Such an attitude may be based on something conceivable, but not 'livable'. Every action, however small, presupposes an end which transcends and guides the instants which go to perform it. But this end which dominates action is not thought of as slavery or a passional negation of the instant. It seems, on the contrary, to conform to the demands of the mind, which stands above time and is able to subject it to thought. Reason can initiate a refusal of time, for it is not compatible with the notion of either absolute beginnings or endings.[2] Hence such Greek ideas as that of eternal recurrence.

Causality attempts to reduce the heterogeneity of the terms of a succession. Causal explanation sets out to substitute for the mutual transcendence, that is, separateness, of these terms, some kind of immanence.[3] For science this may be mechanism, which postulates the preservation of movement: for philosophy the notion of substance, of what remains beneath and through apparent change. Modern thought generally is inclined to abandon the search for an undiscoverable identity[4] in favour of functional law. But a law too exists in virtue of its constancy, its introduction of an element of permanence into diversity; and its applicability, unchanged, to different sectors of time. Like Plato's ideas, scientific laws provide a non-temporal order.[5] Determinism leaves heterogeneity un-

[1] *Le Désir d'éternité*, P.U.F., 1943, p. 67.   [2] ibid. p. 74.   [3] ibid. p. 77.
[4] In recent times Lalande and Meyerson have attempted to show reason as a process of assimilation and as a search for identity.
[5] *Le Désir d'éternité*, p. 81.

touched and shows us only the invariability of succession. The attempt to establish the logical necessity of sequence is abandoned as impossible, and time is acknowledged as dividing rather than joining; whence Descartes's postulate of continuous creation, and Hume's analysis of the concept of causality. From this Alquié concludes that the refusal of time, which on the one hand is the source of our emotional delusions, is, on the other, the very condition of a thought[1] which links disparate instants to each other, and raises us above the bewilderment of pure succession.

But there is more to be said about causality and determinism. Determinism is a partial negation of time, causality its total negation. The old idea of causality denied time from within, and tried to see the effect as part of its cause. In the framing of scientific laws, the search is for a constant relationship outside change; determinism, therefore, leaves part of reality to change, and involves a certain dualism. Modern thought has been forced to an increasing recognition of contingency, and a further step in this direction is the principle, or suggestion, of indeterminacy, which restores value to the notion of 'real' time. Philosophy of history also tends to do this, so that the eternal recurrence of the Greeks is broken, just as, one may add, though Alquié does not say so, the terminus of rectilinear change in the shape of Christian salvation, or the earthly millennium of believers in progress, tends to be scrapped. Are we then to share the conclusion of many contemporary existentialist philosophers, and see eternity as something to be eschewed, and every aspect of mental life involved in the adventure with which time confronts us?

Philosophers, however, dislike dualism and are tempted to seek unity. Thus Bergson makes duration the source of knowledge, and regards the obstacle to knowledge, not as temporal dissipation, but as intelligence, which is impotent outside the solidified stages which it imposes upon every process.[2] It is true that duration is at first conceived by Bergson as an object of contemplation, but later it is seen as created by the self, the gaining of knowledge being explained phenomenologically as coincident with the act which brings reality out of nothing; and psychology

---

[1] ibid. pp. 84–5.   [2] ibid. p. 89.

becomes cosmology.[1] Alquié's complaint is, in effect, that such an approach retains the synthesis of the eternal and temporal which is immediately given, and which it is precisely the office of thought to separate out into its components, otherwise we merely endorse the confusion of naïve experience.[2] It is natural that Alquié should be even more critical, as he invariably is, of the synthesis of real and ideal proposed by Hegel. The triad of thesis, antithesis and synthesis transcends becoming, and the idea of a consummated history implies a mind capable of apprehending it. Eternity here appears not in the form of an extra-temporal and abstract relationship, but as totality.[3] What is required instead of these monistic distortions is the positing of a separate 'eternal subject' outside the instants of time, these latter being self-contained and successive, the former being the agent of their unity.

Time and eternity are complementary in forming the world. If we ask whether eternity is in the subject or object we find that any consideration of its relation to the object leads to the demand that it should be outside that object, transcending appearance. After mentioning how Hume showed that every relationship presupposes the permanence of the subject (causality, for example, being dependent on our expectation of a habitual sequence) without being able to conceive the identity of that subject without introducing a second subject observing the first, Alquié says:

> It is clear indeed that if we try, after having convinced ourselves that we are eternal, to say in precisely what this subject, allegedly descried in us, consists, we can give it no content. No sooner is any content whatsoever thought of as belonging to it, than we are forced to admit that this content is not eternal. For nothing that I think is present, or remains present. All that I think is objective, and every object is characterized by at least possible absence. To assert that the self is eternal is to declare one's inability to form any specific idea of it, to say in what its nature consists, it is to posit it as radically different from experience, as being one while experience is manifold, identical while experience is always changing.[4]

[1] *Le Désir d'éternité*, p. 90.   [2] ibid. p. 97.   [3] ibid. p. 97.
[4] ibid. p. 105.

Alquié confesses to a liking for the Platonic distinction between the subjectivity of the given, and the transcendence of the eternal object: the objectivity of the idea being opposed to the subjectivity of appearance. This distinction ensures that the principle of knowledge is not confused with the self (*le moi*). The self, which dominates time and allows us to conceive it, is impersonal. For this concept the term *esprit* is used, which here had better be translated as 'spirit'.[1] Spirit is that by which I am adapted to things. It is not individual; the individual self, like everything else given to spirit, is subjected to time and enclosed by it.[2] It is here that Alquié dissociates himself from the view of the thoroughgoing upholders of the creative theory of values, for he sees wisdom in Descartes's postulate of time as God's creation, not man's. Man's task, we are told, perhaps a little surprisingly, is reconstruction and rediscovery, not creation.[3] The aim of spirit or mind is the discovery of the eternal, though by this statement we are not to understand the acquisition of some possession. It is more in the nature of a liberation of something which too often tends to be dammed up, with the result that our acceptance of time and the change it brings are resisted. The mind cannot engender time, but it can dominate it, arresting its dispersal of things, forming syntheses, in short, acting. 'The refusal of the pure multiplicity of time is spiritual action.'[4] The intellectual and emotional forms of the refusal of time are, respectively, activity and passivity. Reason is the 'faculty of the eternal',[5] and its function is to adapt us to the future, to make action possible, and it alone is the means whereby consciousness can be progressively orientated.[6] Alquié points out that, whilst spirit is directed to life, the individual self is beset by intimations of mortality and is therefore emotionally backward-looking. This, as is immediately seen, is very different from Bergson's teaching, which stresses how fundamentally alien to life are the processes of reason. Lalande, too, would, I think, see in the words 'l'Esprit et la vie qui l'exprime' a curious association of ideas.

[1] One is tempted to translate it as *mind*, since it is, after all, the ghost in the machine.   [2] ibid. p. 110.   [3] ibid. p. 111.   [4] ibid. p. 117.   [5] ibid. p. 117.   [6] ibid. p. 118.

The opposition between the self and spirit, which is available to it as a kind of organ-obstacle, causes some uncertainty of the will – and this is surely the uncertainty of existential 'dread'. The forces in action are, on the one hand, spirit for which there is no risk, and on the other affectivity which brings fear of suffering and death. So voluntary action involves both certainty and peril: the knowledge that such a value will retain its force, or such a law its validity, but also the knowledge that in realizing the value or causing the law to operate our self may perish, since the future remains unpredictable. The individual sees at one and the same time the value of the act and the threat to the self. Obscurely realizing that to lose one's life is to gain it, we remain hesitant before the dilemma with which eternity confronts us,[1] either attachment to the self which means cherishing a possession, or instead to what can be cherished only as a source of action. This latter is, however, not the *en-soi* of Sartre, which rather than being compared to a source is better imagined as a spring-board. The intellectual eternity of Alquié is a power which we carry in us and is infinitely adaptable, but easily degraded from a creative force to a thing.

This degradation is liable to take the form of rationalization (if we may adapt the psychologist's term), or the disguise of the desires of the individual self as eternal spirit. We need to distinguish between habit and reason which, Alquié alleges, empiricists confuse. Now I think that this distinction is less difficult to make than some recent French philosophers seem prepared to admit. André Lalande establishes the distinction very adequately in his 'raison constituée' and 'raison constituante',[2] or the works and achievements of reason as opposed to its processes. Religion presents the commonest case of the 'rêve passionel' which degrades the spirit, animating it into a mere object of pious contemplation. Religion is characteristically concerned with eternity; but this concern more often than not produces a situation in which such objects as sacred stones, totems, myths, superstitions and rituals which relate in some way to the past, preserve a relevance

[1] *Le Désir d'éternité*, p. 120.
[2] *La Raison et les normes*, Paris, Hachette, 1948, pp. 16–17.

for the present: indeed that relevance is bound up with their traditional character. So, says Alquié, it will always be legitimate to ask what part of religious belief is owed to the requirements of the self, and what to those of the spirit.[1]

Philosophy is a method, not a possession. Descartes and Kant are the models proposed for our admiration, the philosophers of analysis rather than synthesis. The renunciation of eternity is to be our attitude of supreme wisdom, laws never being things upon which, but from which, we act. This idea is elaborated on deductive lines, and it is stated that thought does *not* pass from the concrete and particular to the general, but makes sense only through the order which it imposes on things. Science always goes from the universal to the concrete and applies to particulars 'the exigencies of thought'. This is a phenomenological view of science as being a product of the intentional activities of mind, and it is not entirely wrong since scientific truth is not arrived at by simple enumeration, but to some extent by the application of a preconceived hypothesis to the reality before us. We are now back at Lavelle's idea of the given as something which the mind *gives itself*. Simply because constituted reason is being made afresh, we are not entitled to objectify the constituting reason and this is really the message of Alquié's book. Thought is, and should be, *behind* us, and not its own goal. All search for eternity is a denial of human nature, 'revolt of the self, therefore renewed passion'. We may betray our humanity either by trying to petrify it, or by a vain aspiration to self-deification, which is as foolish as seeking our lost childhood. Both desires are overweening, and the accomplishment of our daily human task requires us to turn our back on eternity.[2]

Alquié gives some final consideration to attempts made to mediate between the passional and active consciousness. Art is a sort of mediation, but a spurious one in the last resort, and all the better for that. It tries to perpetuate the concrete, and the temporally localized feeling or situation. Baudelaire is satisfied to think that he has retained the form and essence of his 'amours décomposés'. Art, however, is distinguishable from the emotional

[1] *D.E.* p. 129. [2] ibid. p. 141.

refusal of time earlier considered; it does not deceive those who create or enjoy it into accepting its false mediation as a true one. It co-exists with science and clear thought, and its object is not presented, but represented, or presented as absent.[1] Compared to the moral attitude, however, it is passional, for morality is a principle of concrete action. Its values may be universalizable and in a sense existing and static, but they are not there to be contemplated and enjoyed as a spectacle; they are there to make a demand that must be met in action. Religion is more complicated. It too may encourage its adherents to seek a mystical co-presence with, and contemplation of, the eternal, but there is a corrective tendency in most religions which emphasizes the importance of works, and an active charity turned outwards rather than a self-sufficient communion turned inwards.[2] Metaphysics too has its 'mysticism', and Alquié criticizes Spinoza on this ground, since the individual is assimilated to substance as one of its modes, which is a version of the vain attempt to make man into God. Turning to the metaphysicians of the temporal, Alquié finds that Hegel and Bergson fare little better. Bergson tries to preserve the past and make time a totality in which man is absorbed. Proust's integral memory ignores the fact that memory is highly selective and schematic, that the emotional content of the past is largely lost, with the result that the past can appear only as past and gone. Hegel conceived history as ultimately consummated, this consummation being a spectacle for a transcendent mind, but not for ours. If we are to accept time we must renounce totality as we do eternity. This renunciation is what Descartes teaches us; in his philosophy the mind, the object of mind, and the method of attaining this object are distinguished.

> Eternity for him is not what can be contemplated or in which one can lose oneself, but what ensures that tomorrow we shall not be defeated by the course of events.[3]

Descartes seeks to widen consciousness; all eternity is unconsciousness, both in the form of passional eternity and spirit, which

---

[1] *D.E.* p. 147.   [2] ibid. p. 149.   [3] ibid. pp. 153–4.

leads to knowledge but cannot be known. Our life is not our history, but our renewal at every moment by act of will.[1] The ontological proof is to be seen less as the understanding of the infinite than the understanding of the necessity of the infinite and of the domination which it exercises on the mind.[2] Values and laws are eternal and yet they are realized in time. So we are not faced with a choice between the temporal and the eternal, but, as men, with the necessity of action which *derives from* eternity. Reason mediates between time and the eternal.

PAUL VALÉRY AND REASON

The possibility of a dynamic reason, capable of being applied to tasks normally thought of as outside reason's province, is one which intrigued and exercised Valéry. He also realized that the principle of constituent reason is one which cannot be objectified,[3] or identified with the thinker himself. It is in fact, for Valéry as for Alquié and Descartes, an impersonal self which directs, or should direct, the action of the empirical self or personality.[4] Unfortunately Valéry, at least in his *Monsieur Teste*, allows his 'derealizing' enthusiasm to run away with him, so that the preposterous marionette Teste becomes a negation incarnate of all commitment. This vacuity is as objective in its way as a set of fixed and immutable ideas. But happily Valéry produces something more interesting and significant than Monsieur Teste. What he produces is not thinkers thinking about thought, but speculation on the nature of the creative activity which is orientated not towards a vain quest of pure form, but towards the ordering of reality.

This process of ordering is not problematical so long as it confines itself, in Cartesian fashion, to the geometrical sphere of spatial arrangement, but it becomes so when the temporal and emotional are involved. The world of duration is that of art and is, according to Bergsonian principles, inaccessible to rational methods, which are applicable only to what can be analysed into states. Valéry, however, is not content with this account of reason

[1] ibid. p. 154.   [2] ibid. p. 155.
[3] See F. E. Sutcliffe, *La Pensée de Valéry*, Nizet, 1955, pp. 40 ff.
[4] ibid. p. 35.

and tries to see its domain as much wider than that mapped out by traditional 'Cartesian' rationalism, thus laying himself open to the attacks of such an antagonist of movement and fluid, 'feminine' states of mind as Julien Benda. In the dialogue *Eupalinos*, the architect is presented as the type of creator whose work derives most directly from mathematical relationships, but what is more interesting is the shipwright's achievement in constructing, by a more subtle and functional adaptation of means to ends, a vessel which shall not stand permanently like a building on solid ground, but ride purposefully on the ever-mobile sea, which has those attributes of which Valéry is so suspicious: movement, depth and darkness: 'Everything becomes more complicated with movement', and rational procedure here consists in 'disposing of forms and forces',[1] not of objects whose contact constitutes a durable situation, but of potential contacts and resistances in situations whose shape and occurrence can be only schematically foreseen. The organ-obstacle of the sea[2] has its permanence in the constant variability of the challenge which it offers to human ingenuity and contrivance. But for being incessantly renewed this ingenuity is none the less rational.

In *L'Ame et la danse* the art form of movement is discussed. Here in the dance is incorporated the activity of reason, but a dream-like activity this time, divorced from purposive action, its order not teleological but symmetrical; 'the statuesque progression which has only itself as its end, all variable impurities being eliminated, becomes a universal model'.[3] In what sense is it universal, however? If this dance is a ballet with set choreography, clearly it is a universal model in that it can be repeated indefinitely. But there is the possibility that the dance is improvised within the framework of the music, in which case its expressiveness has that peculiar appearance of necessity which is none the less spontaneous and not repeatable. I think this is the kind of creativeness with which Valéry is concerned, and which he wishes to show as a response to what is in some way required.

---

[1] *Eupalinos, L'Ame et la danse, Dialogue de l'arbre*, Gallimard, 28th ed., 1944, p. 110.
[2] ibid. p. 111.   [3] ibid. pp. 147-8.

Bearing in mind the important French voluntaristic current of the past century and a half, in which Renouvier, for example, made the will a crucial determining factor in the establishment of truth, we can see that reason will tend to appear as one value-producing activity among others. Therefore, if reason is to be put on the same footing as other servants of requiredness,[1] we are likely to find that its universalizability has to be conceived in a rather sophisticated way. I think we shall find, in fact, that the treatment to which Valéry subjects it destroys that universality, which depends upon the possibility of formulating a maxim or a law, this depending in turn on the likelihood of the repetition of a situation, therefore on some generality of that situation. If some event is highly individualized, its exact repetition is unlikely, and therefore the mere inevitable fact that there is a 'reason' for it does not make it significant as a model. The movements of the dance are expressive and hence not random, but neither are they rational. The moves in a game of chess, which is always unique, are rational in virtue of the atomistic character of the game. The precise nature of each move can be stated as a rule of the game, though the relevance of any one move is determined by the course of a particular game. The same is only trivially true of a dance, because the possibilities of movement are infinitely greater, because movement is not divisible, and because the nature of each movement as it is aesthetically appreciated cannot be precisely described, nor can its unique appropriateness be demonstrated. Valéry reaches no usefully universalizable entity when he sees the dance as the essence of expressiveness, or pure movement: 'movement and rhythm which are what is real in the real',[2] or 'the pure act of metamorphoses'.[3] But by this time he has forgotten about universality, which he jettisons rather unexpectedly. He goes on: 'Opulence immobilizes; my desire is for movement',[4] thus evoking 'having' and 'being'. What constitutes having and being for him is revealed several pages further on. In a discussion of the

---

[1] Hume said that reason is the slave of the passions, but not that it is a passion. Neither would he have conceded, I think, that it is an activity in the modern French sense. For him it was an auxiliary activity.
[2] op. cit. p. 158.   [3] ibid. p. 160.   [4] ibid. p. 161.

possibilities of escaping *taedium vitae* he says of men: 'Their concern is to *know*. What is to know? Surely it is not to be what one
is.'[1]

It is clear from what is said here that knowledge involves a
distortion of reality in the Bergsonian sense, and a 'divertisse-
ment' in the Pascalian sense.

> It is strange to think that Totality is not self-sufficient! Its terror
> at being what it is has made it create and paint for itself count-
> less masks. There is no other reason for the existence of mortals.
> . . . The idea adds to what is, the leaven of what is not. But
> sometimes nevertheless the truth will out, and is discordant in
> the harmonious system of phantasmagorias and errors. Im-
> mediately everything is threatened with destruction, and
> Socrates himself asks for a remedy for this hopeless case of
> clear-sightedness and tedium.[2]

Knowledge is the meaningfulness which one can impose on
reality, but which is not proof against the *ennui* which breaks
through, whatever we do, at the sight of 'human reality as it is'.
The remedy against absurdity is not knowledge, but action, particularly physical action, indeed Dionysian action.[3] As a principle
of 'absence', of not being what one is, knowledge is a poor substitute for action, which serves the true aim of the soul, whose
'sole and perpetual object is what does not exist, what was and is
no longer, what will be and is not yet, but never what simply
is'.[4] Paradoxically the body, which is what it is (and thereby
recalls Sartre's in-itself), tries to imitate the universality of the
soul, and tries to compensate for its identity by the multiplicity of
its acts, constantly emerging from itself and ceaselessly renewed
like a flame.[5] Though a thing, it expends itself in events.

It is perhaps worth while contrasting with Valéry's prose poem
another 'soul and the dance'; this time by Saint-Exupéry, for
whom they are antithetical. The passage occurs in *Courrier Sud*,

---

[1] ibid. p. 166. Valéry's italics.   [2] ibid. pp. 165–6.
[3] ibid. p. 179. The dancer Athikté says: 'Asile, asile, ô mon asile, ô Tour-
billon! J'étais en toi, ô mouvement, en dehors de toutes les choses...'
[4] ibid. p. 172.   [5] ibid.

where the pilot Bernis goes to a cabaret and watches a troupe of dancing girls, whose dance, far from being spontaneously expressive, is quite unambiguously the execution of a 'dance routine'. The girls are thought of by Bernis as going absent-mindedly through their act, one not feeling well, another thinking about a 'date', another about a debt, the whole thing, as a dance, universalized down to the last movement, but entirely without a soul. Here in 'the backstage of life' a show has been projected and contrived for the purpose of pushing a dancer 'hostess' into his arms. She, out of the dance, her element, is without any expressiveness at all; her only spontaneity was what was factitiously contrived for her.

What are we to make of Valéry's confused mythologizing? It is fairly clear, I think, that Valéry began by seeking the principle of meaningful change and action, of what is not random yet not fully within our powers of conceptualization, and realized ultimately that this change and creative activity is lived, not known, or lived prospectively and known only retrospectively. Movement is mysterious rather than problematical, in Gabriel Marcel's sense of these two terms.

But discontinuity presents difficulties, too.[1] In fact greater ones, since Valéry regards speculation as the attempt to widen the limits of continuity.[2] Now I feel quite sure that Valéry confuses the issues by using the concept of continuity, at least by implication, for two distinct and different things. Firstly there is duration in Bergson's sense, which is finally seen by Valéry as the stuff of the dance. Secondly there is rational assimilation, in Meyerson's and Lalande's sense: the identity which we discover beneath apparent difference, and which is the means of explanation. The result is that the difference between Bergson's duration, or reality, and reason, is blurred, if not abolished, and Valéry's arguments suffer in consequence. He finally recognizes, however, that the origin of creation is discontinuity, which is no origin at all, or quoddity. He does, of course, trace 'inspiration' back to sense impressions, but he is aware that that is only pushing chance back a step. In any case even the intellect seems dependent upon

---

[1] See Sutcliffe, op. cit. pp. 110 ff. [2] ibid. p. 114.

unconscious sources, such as sleep, for the consolidation of its symmetrically woven patterns.

> *Que fîtes-vous cette nuit*
> *Maîtresses de l'âme, Idées,*
> *Courtisanes par ennui?...*
> *Ne seras-tu pas de joie*
> *Ivre! à voir de l'ombre issus*
> *Cent mille soleils de soie*
> *Sur tes énigmes tissus?*[1]

But these constructions are rejected in favour of the more obvious hazard of sensual feeling.

> *Leur toile spirituelle,*
> *Je la brise et vais cherchant*
> *Dans ma forêt sensuelle,*
> *Les oracles de mon chant...*
> *Voici mes vignes ombreuses*
> *Les berceaux de mes hasards.*

In *Le Cimetière marin* it is the mortal body and soul which sustain the eternity of the enveloping world, not the familiar reverse, which derives movement from immobility.

> *Beau ciel, vrai ciel, regarde-moi qui change!...*
> *L'âme exposée aux torches du solstice*
> *Je te soutiens, admirable justice*
> *De la lumière aux armes sans pitié!*

The Eleatic world of permanence in which movement is an illusion is the vainly desired goal of the living mind, which is carried forward in spite of itself, and should be so carried forward 'dans l'ère successive'.

> *Brisez, mon corps, cette forme pensive!...*
> *Le vent se lève, il faut tenter de vivre!*

An even more perfect, though less familiar, expression of the disordering and destructive incursion of action into the placid

---

[1] *Aurore.*

world which is the object of contemplation, is the poem *Le Rameur*. Here the image used is that of the rower breaking with his oars the mirror-like surface of the water which reflects the greenery on the river banks. The act is almost vandalistic, but it aims at escape from the hypnotizing world of no change, of presence, which is no more than it is – a possession.

> *Le cœur dur, l'œil distrait des beautés que je bats,*
> *Laissant autour de moi mûrir des cercles d'onde,*
> *Je veux à larges coups rompre l'illustre monde*
> *De feuilles et de feu que je chante tout bas.*

> *Arbres sur qui je passe, ample et naïve moire,*
> *Eau de ramages peinte, et paix de l'accompli,*
> *Déchire-les, ma barque, impose-leur un pli*
> *Qui coure du grand calme abolir la mémoire.*

Finally the boat, resisted in its progress by 'toute la nymphe énorme et continue', plunges under the arch of a bridge into uncertainty and obscurity, leaving the clear sunlight which so often stands in Valéry for the temptation of an illusory eternity.

> *Quand, par le mouvement qui me revêt de pierres,*
> *Je m'enfonce au mépris de tant d'azur oiseux.*

Valéry is at first suspicious of the contingent, and nostalgic for the realm of necessity, but realizes that this realm can have no content, and that only the world of 'chance' leaves room for creativeness, and is a truly and fully human world. Moreover, the order which we create and take pleasure in contemplating is dependent upon us, creatures of 'l'ère successive', for its existence. Without the human imitation of eternity there is no eternity. I should be inclined to sum up Valéry's position in perhaps a rather unsympathetic way, but one not precluding full recognition of the beauty of his poetry. In so far as he is concerned with what one may call a retrospective search for the causes of creative states, and the works to which they give rise, he is seeking solutions to psychological problems, and his curiosity is scientific. When he tries to discover principles governing artistic creation which he hopes will be prospectively applicable to his work as a poet, he is trying to universalize rationally what is necessarily unique, and is mistaking the nature of art. The opposite of universality is not randomness or nonsense. The notion of aesthetic relevance does not include that of universality. From the fact that aesthetically something is required, it does not follow that it is universally required, in fact to say that it is, is vacuous, because the poem, picture, composition, etc., is not being put forward as a model for imitations, but purporting to stand alone.[1] We shall perhaps see that in morality the question is not so simple, but in aesthetics the attempt to universalize is doomed to failure. As Professor Stuart Hampshire points out,[2] the critic, unlike the moralist, can reject a work without being under any obligation to say what the artist *ought to have* done; and when, in aesthetics, we pass from the particular to the general, we are moving in the wrong direction. It is true that, as we have seen, Valéry comes to recognize and reluctantly accept the contingent nature of creation, and that it is only from a rather pedantically analytical point of view that one wants to question his hankering after universality, particularly since this hankering is in its expression an aesthetic fact and not a platform for philosophical argument. Nevertheless there are people who like to speak of Valéry as a 'precise and rigorous thinker', and he may well have liked at times to imagine himself as such. He was nostalgic for rationalism rather than an exponent of it. He yearned for a self-contained system of thought free from any intrusive element of discontinuity, and at the same time would not ignore the challenge of the contingent. His writings are variations on the themes of this dilemma, and show flashes of philosophical insight that arise from it.

My reason for dealing with the rationalism of Valéry along with that of Alquié is that Valéry tries to undertake the philosophic journey, from the rational act to its source, accomplished (or

---

[1] 'Association, or rather "affinity", in the Kantian sense, is the central phenomenon of perceptual life, since it is the constitution, *without any ideal model*, of a significant grouping,' Merleau-Ponty, *Phenomenology of Perception*, p. 53. My italics. Cf ibid. pp. 73–4.

[2] *Aesthetics and Language*, edited Elton, Blackwell.

should one say abandoned?) by Alquié, but without the acumen to understand fully the nature of his quest. He cannot see that the works of reason, which are orderly, and the working of reason, which is order-producing but not orderly, are quite different. Nor does he see that in the sphere of aesthetic creation or artistic ordering, a factor is relevant but is not universally so. A work of art is not a tool or formula for future use. Though we are inclined to see art, particularly certain kinds of art ('classical', for example), as composed of parts which can be said to be appropriate to the totality of the work, no useful generalization can be made on the basis of the relevance of an artistic part to an artistic whole. The relationship is not a manifestation of truth, but of beauty (or lack of beauty). Of aesthetics we can say what Bernard Mayo says when discussing ethics: truth is not the only kind of appropriateness.[1] Alquié sees the orderliness of thought as proceeding from an inaccessible eternity, and finding expression in action. Valéry wants the principle of necessity to be objectifiable and universally applicable, and when he realizes that this desire is doomed to disappointment, he evolves a cult of contingency.[2]

5

As an **assimilating** force within the world.
André Lalande

One might describe Valéry, in the terminology of recent English philosophical history, as searching unsuccessfully for a naturalistic

---

[1] *Ethics and the Moral Life*, Macmillan, 1958, p. 74.

[2] On the question of our immediate apprehension of rationality see Merleau-Ponty, *Phenomenology of Perception*, p. xx, 'Rationality is not a *problem*. There is behind it no unknown quantity to be determined. . . . We witness every minute the miracle of related experiences, and yet nobody knows better than we do how this miracle is worked, for we are ourselves this network of relationships.' Cf V. Jankélévitch, *Philosophie première*, p. 188, 'Ce qui fait n'est pas ce qu'il fait.'

concept of reason,[1] as trying to track down, capture and display it. A philosopher who produced a stimulatingly naturalistic form of rationalism is André Lalande.[2] His doctoral thesis of 1899 was entitled *L'Idée directrice de la dissolution, opposée à celle de l'évolution, dans la méthode des sciences physiques et morales.* This was republished in a revised form in 1930 under the title *Les Illusions évolutionnistes,* and is an attack on the wide nineteenth-century application of evolutionary ideas. The idea of progress is by definition the idea of movement in a desired direction, and with the tendency to confuse progress (or desirable change) and evolution (or differentiation), the latter, a fundamentally scientific notion, of limited applicability, came to acquire a normative colouring. Lalande points to a duality observable in things. Opposed to, and even more widespread than, evolution is dissolution, or, as he prefers to call it in his book of 1930, *involution,* since dissolution inevitably suggests some kind of degeneracy, and since it is as something desirable that he wishes to present the opposite of evolutionary change. His theory has ethical implications which are highly naturalistic. Involution is change in a certain direction and is widely exemplified in nature; reason brings about involution in the sphere of human affairs, and this is desirable and good.

Involution, or assimilation, as I shall often call it, is observable in the physical, inanimate world in the form of entropy, the tendency of levels of energy and pressure to become equal. There is a universal movement of energy towards homogeneity, towards randomness and unavailability, which purely negative aspect Lalande does not stress, preferring that of assimilation, which he sees, in the human context, as the predominantly civilizing agency. In nature entropy is a principle of despecialization and death, a movement from the heterogeneous to the homogeneous. The sea washes angular, irregular rocks of all shapes and reduces them in course of time to smooth and comparatively symmetrical pebbles. In autumn the leaves of the forest are shed and

---

[1] i.e. a conception of reason as reducible to something else, not as something autonomous and unanalysable.

[2] Born 1868.

gradually lose form and identity, mingling into undifferentiated mould.[1]

This universal tendency is not, Lalande maintains, one to be ignored or depreciated, but is highly significant and ultimately fruitful, despite its being the negation of growth. Every difference is a contingent fact, which demands an explanation, and perhaps some rectification. If we see two towers of different heights in a building, we ask why they should be so. But we do not wonder why the trees in an avenue of limes are of uniform height. The fact that physical changes usually, and in the last resort always, tend towards the production of uniformity is in accordance with the demands of human reason.[2]

Life is an exceptional, and in the widest context, an unnatural thing. It produces heterogeneity, and defies, at least for a time and in the interest of the unity of the individual, the more general laws of change, which, however, do increasingly prevail as the momentum and vigour of the vital force weaken. The separatist and deviationist drive is finally spent, and the parts of the decomposing organism go their separate ways to the same goal of assimilation with inanimate, unorganized matter. Lalande uses the trajectory of an object thrown into the air as the model of life's course, since this brings into relief the inevitability of decline and death. Most people are, in one way or another, killed, in the sense that some illness, which might theoretically have been prevented, brings about their death. Nevertheless it is in their nature to die, and no precautions can indefinitely stave off the downward dip of the parabola.

Lalande's thesis moves towards the conclusion that the vigorous development of physical life, the most striking and successful manifestations of the 'life-force', are *not* directly associated in many cases with flourishing intellectual and aesthetic activity. He maintains, as Bergson often did, that the brain is characteristically an inhibitor, leading to suspension of judgement, and that close attention is accompanied by a slowing down of bodily functions. The frontal lobes, which appear, he says, to be the seat

[1] *Les Ill. év.* pp. 27–8.   [2] ibid. p. 45.

of intelligence, are closely associated with inhibition.[1] Bain is quoted as saying that to think is to refrain from acting.[2] So in the beginning was action, and only through some incapacity which stood in the way of spontaneous action did thought, and a new kind of experience, appear. We must choose one direction or the other; thought, in so far as it is bound up with an organic body, is an obstacle to that body's evolution.[3] Perhaps Lalande's whole thesis is best summed up in the following words:

> It seems to me that any action, word or thought, when it is directed towards the three guiding categories of our conscious nature (logic, morality, aesthetics), causes the world to move in a direction opposite to that of evolution, that is, it reduces in the world individual differentiation and integration, and brings about instead assimilation and liberation. Their effect is to make men less different from each other, and to produce in each a tendency, not, as in the case of the animal, to absorb the world into its individuality, but to free himself, by becoming identified with his fellows, from the self-centredness towards which he is driven by his biological nature and the action of the organic structures in which life involves him.[4]

In the intellectual field reason tries to ensure that although people feel differently, they shall think in the same way.[5] They move towards this end, moreover, by seeing objects themselves as more alike. There is no science of the particular; the intellect assimilates by classifying. Lalande goes on to discuss assimilation in the realm of values, morality and art, but consideration of this must await treatment of the notion of authenticity. I am here concerned with that of reason.

It is well known that a closely similar philosophy, which presents knowing as a process of identification of differences, is that of Emile Meyerson,[6] expounded in his *Identité et réalité* and

---

[1] *Les Ill. év.* p. 122.   [2] ibid. p. 133.   [3] ibid. p. 134.
[4] ibid. pp. 142-3. It is, of course, obvious that this assimilatory process can become the opposite of a liberation, and this will be examined in relation to inauthenticity.
[5] ibid. p. 181.   [6] 1859-1933.

Cheminement de la pensée.[1] But there is an element in Meyerson's thought which anticipates the kind of 'open' rationalism which I am about to discuss. It is the search for that factor which keeps thought on the move, and explains why knowledge is not in fact a spreading pool of increasing homogeneity and quiescence to which assimilatory rationalism would seem to point. Meyerson does not lose sight of the bipolarity which persists between 'the need for rigour which forces the mind to mark time, and the need for progress which forces it, in its urge to invent, to be constantly breaking the circle in which identity tends to circumscribe it. The paradox of all reasoning is that the conclusion must in a sense be contained in the premises, and must in another sense outrun them.' [2]

LÉON BRUNSCHVICG

Another important philosopher who provides, so to speak, a bridge between an assimilatory and a developing conception of reason, is Léon Brunschvicg, known to students of French literature everywhere for his edition of Pascal's *Pensées*. In *La Modalité du jugement* of 1897 he puts forward an idealistic view of truth. A judgement is anterior to its constituent terms, and the copulative 'is' merely expresses the synthesis which the mind effects as its act of understanding. This means that the world is not in existence, and waiting to be apprehended. It is, in a sense, dependent upon the constituting reason for its emergence into objectivity, and this mutual dependence and inter-operation of mind and the given is reminiscent of Lavelle's view of 'the act'. What guides the formative activity pursued by intelligence is the general compatibility of a judgement with a system of judgements previously made. Thus there is a progressive and dialectical process going on between the mind and its material, producing new and varied forms, but not haphazardly. The directive force running through change is that of coherence, and its corollary, communicability. It is therefore mathematics which is the key human activity, and

[1] 1908 and 1931 respectively.
[2] L. Lavelle, *La Philosophie française entre les deux guerres*, Aubier, 1942, p. 217.

which, as for example in the advance from Newtonian physics to relativity, provides the means whereby the real can be assimilated into concepts and relationships which are more homogeneous and intelligible.

Le Progrès de la conscience dans la philosophie occidentale traces this general process historically through western thought. Furthermore, just as Lalande, in his *Les Illusions évolutionnistes*, extends his survey from the life and work of reason to that of ethics and politics, so Brunschvicg here moves on from mathematics and science to the altruism of love and generosity, which he sees as inseparable from the intellectual virtues. Just as reason establishes intelligible and communicable relations, so consciousness in general 'is a capacity for creating values of truth or justice', and there arises naturally, 'at the heart of human consciousness, the law of reciprocity which is the basis of justice, and that disinterested virtue from which springs the generosity of intellectual love. The mind will therefore be a capacity . . . for transcending itself. Every stage of this inner progress will be marked by a break, a tearing away. It will be a matter of freeing oneself from errors associated with narrowness of thought, and prejudices stemming from self-centredness.'[1]

This ethical and religious theme is developed in *De la connaissance de soi* (1931) and *La Raison et la religion* (1939). The first is not a treatise on introspection, which holds no attraction for Brunschvicg, nor is it the search for an abiding Self (*in itself* as Sartre would say). Brunschvicg sees self-knowledge as the exploration of a developing being: 'To know oneself is, true enough, to scrutinize one's past in the hope of bringing it to life again' – here is the contemplative, Lavellian tolerance of one's being in itself. But 'it is also, and indeed more, to question one's development (*son devenir*) and one's destiny, it is to lay a wager upon oneself (*parier sur soi-même*)'. This means, in effect, challenging oneself to transcend one's animal nature – or, as Lalande might say, one's purely vitalist and evolutionary drives – and to be equal to the demands of an altruistic morality.

So far, then, we may summarize Brunschvicg's thought by

[1] *La Philosophie de l'esprit*, P.U.F., 1949, 16th lesson.

saying that I understand myself and the world through self-identification with what I seek to apprehend. I synthesize the world in terms of my human reason. This assimilatory force is in its element in the domain of science, and in so far as it is also the basis of spiritual communion, this too must partake of rationality, abstraction and impersonality. Brunschvicg himself does not shrink from the implications of this for the religious man, but others do. Lavelle, in his *La Philosophie française entre les deux guerres*, anxiously asks: 'Can the communion of minds be regarded as the effect of science? . . . M. Brunschvicg would not be prepared to maintain that the law of love waited upon mathematical physics before taking possession of our conscience . . .'[1] Even more critical, from a Protestant Christian point of view, is Roger Mehl in an article[2] on contemporary religious philosophy. It is clear that the non-historicity and non-temporality of Brunschvicg's religion, in the form in which it is presented, is unacceptable to the Christian. The complaint is that there is here no personal God who will reciprocate his creature's love, no relevance of ritual, or anthropomorphic forms, to the life of the spirit, no exceptional significance in temporal occasions. It is a mathematician's religion, for, writes Mehl, 'truth for him is of the order of eternity, and the primary characteristic of eternity is, of course, non-temporality. . . . That the plenitude of eternity could have been given in a moment of time is what he categorically rejects.'

There is in Brunschvicg's notion of religion an 'openness' which recalls Bergson's *Two Sources*, but in Brunschvicg's case the drive is by its nature intellectual, and is indeed presented as the moral flowering of what is in essence the communion of rational minds. In this complex, scholarly and evocative philosopher we find anticipations or echoes of many and varied thinkers of recent decades: of Lalande, Lavelle, Meyerson, Poincaré, Bachelard, Merleau-Ponty. He brings together into a synthesis almost all the purely rationalist elements in the thought of our century.

[1] op. cit. p. 190.
[2] *L'Activité philosophique contemporaine en France et aux Etats-Unis*, Vol. II, pp. 273-5.

6

As a **dissimilating** force. Gaston Bachelard and E. Morot-Sir

The view of reason and understanding as the reduction of differences to identity is not shared by certain more recent philosophers, notably M. Gaston Bachelard and M. Morot-Sir. I shall take, to illustrate the thought of these two men, *Le Nouvel Esprit scientifique* and *La Philosophie du non* of M. Bachelard, and *La Pensée négative* of M. Morot-Sir. What the assimilationists like Lalande and Meyerson wanted to show was that rational thought seeks more and more general resemblances between things and systems of things, and extends the field of human knowledge and power by this means. M. Bachelard stresses the discontinuity in rational and scientific thought which is brought about by the periodic bankruptcy, from the point of view of further progress, of a coherent rational system, and its replacement by a new model, involving a new synthesis. So scientific advance does not depend on any gradual and continuous process of the elimination of diversity, through the action of a mental substance which is simple in nature and tends to impose its homogeneity on its environment. On the contrary the world is seen as stubbornly plural, so that any synthesis is of limited validity, not only in space but in time too, since a constant discarding of useless moulds is necessary in the face of new difficulties which arise.

The belief that philosophy of science should be pluralistic, refusing to envelop everything, or a great number of things, in a convenient but specious unity, is entirely in the stream of empiricist philosophy, and marks a break with the *a priori* rationalistic tradition to which French philosophers have tended to remain faithful. Bachelard dubs his new philosophy 'dispersed' or 'distributed' philosophy, and considers it the only one relevant to the incredible complexity of modern science.[1] He criticizes and rejects the Cartesian doctrine of simple and absolute entities, and

[1] *La Phil. du non*, P.U.F., 1940, pp. 12–15.

holds that the gradual changes brought about in knowledge are attributable to the successive approximations to truth to which experience has led.[1] His anti-Cartesianism is explicitly shown in the preface to *La Philosophie du non*. A thesis which presents knowledge as an evolution of mind, he says, and which recognizes variations which destroy the unity and perennity of the *cogito*, must necessarily worry the philosopher[2] (as opposed to the scientist). The doctrine of an absolute and immutable reason is only one philosophy among others, and one moreover which has outlived its usefulness.[3] Science moves forward in jerks, and every significant step involves a conversion,[4] he says, using a word rich in associations outside the sphere of science. The new experience says *No* to the old.[5]

Because these changes in the state of knowledge involve the rejection of one model in favour of another entirely different,[6] the new situation being inconceivable as in any sense a continuation of the old, and there being no question of the anterior state's prefiguring the later, M. Bachelard talks of an *open philosophy*,[7] of *experimental transcendence*,[8] using words ('open' and 'transcendence') which are frequently met in other fields of contemporary French philosophy, and which will have to be examined respectively in relation to Bergson's 'open' morality and M. Raymond Polin's philosophy of values.

What calls forth this 'open' rationalism is the nature of modern science, which is not static but dynamic. As long as science was organized common sense, dealing in concepts which at least roughly corresponded to real objects, science could appear to be concerned with the concrete. But with the appearance of non-Euclidean geometries, corresponding to no tangible or even

---

[1] *Le Nouvel Esprit scientifique* (1934), 2nd ed. 1949, P.U.F., pp. 141–2.
[2] M. Bachelard does not appear to expect that he will be read by English philosophers!
[3] *La Phil. du non*, p. 145.   [4] ibid. p. 8.   [5] ibid. p. 9.
[6] Cf J. Z. Young's suggested replacement of the clock, as model for a living organism, by the whirlpool, which retains its form but constantly changes the matter of which it is composed (Reith Lectures).
[7] *La Phil. du non*, p. 9.
[8] ibid. p. 10. Cf *Le Nouvel sp. Esci.* p. 175, 'le rationalisme ouvert', and *La Phil. du non*, p. 104, 'un rationalisme souple et mouvant'.

imaginable reality, or theories of the world and its happenings expressible not in language but only in mathematical formulae, science is seen as concerned less with objects than with projects. 'Above the *subject*, beyond the immediate *object*, modern science is based on the *project*.'[1]

The project is an attempt to go beyond material data, and find, instead of things, relationships.[2] There is a 'dematerialization of materialism', a conferring of primacy on relationship rather than on being.[3] Bachelard might have used Alquié's word 'derealization' to designate the process whereby 'the instrumental product (electron, field, current, etc.) is adopted as a logical and not substantial element of theory; in so far as it remains a substance, it retains something which must be subjected to further abstraction: it retains an unwanted character of naïve realism'.[4] Why are we thus impelled to sublimate our realistic notions? asks Bachelard, and does not give a very satisfactory answer. Indeed he seems, at the end of the chapter on determinism and indeterminism, to be tacitly subscribing to the assimilatory concept of reason put forward by Lalande and Meyerson. He quotes the latter on the hydra of realism, which produces a new head every time one is cut off. Meyerson, of course, conceives derealization as the imposition by the mind of its own universalizable laws on individual circumstances, and some such idea seems necessary if the *project* is to be an agency of progress and not a manifestation of mere instability. But progress towards what? What is the teleologically conceived principle of change? Assimilation, says Meyerson. Bachelard seems uncertain, except to the extent of declaring that realism is not the cause of its own rejection. Between the rejection of the old model and the adoption of a new one there is an interval, an ephemeral instant of discovery, which is the essence of scientific thought: a crisis which necessitates a shift in the nature of the realism into which thinking necessarily degenerates. This revolutionary force has its source in the realm of abstraction, in mathematics.[5] Now this seems very like an *a priori* principle of assimilation. There seems to be no suggestion that mathematical concepts

---

[1] *Le Nouvel Esp. sci.* p. 11.   [2] ibid. p. 132.   [3] ibid. p. 67.
[4] ibid. p. 133.   [5] ibid. pp. 131–4.

and relations are models. They are rather represented by models. The abstractions themselves are, presumably, not directly taken from experience as objects, but are some basic and universal means of ordering, master-keys to the world's doors. But ordering, as Valéry discovered, is not itself ordered. It is to be discerned in what it brings about, and this may be no less *necessary* for recurrently becoming congealed in *real* forms. These forms are in a sense irrelevant, as Bachelard recognizes. What they trace may well be a kind of imperialistic activity of reason, which brings more and more of reality into a coherent system, despite the unstable and arbitrary models which have to stand as landmarks in the mapping of it.

Or the ordering may be not so much form-creating as pragmatical. Modern science substitutes for intrinsic clarity a sort of operational clarity. Instead of there being a situation where reality throws light on relationships, relationships elucidate being. The real value of the 'philosophie du non' seems to be that it inculcates an attitude of intellectual 'availability'. I have in mind the French word 'disponibilité', which Bachelard does not use, but his insistence on the need for periodical 'openings' in our views of reality suggests a constant readjustment or rearrangement of knowledge in readiness for renewed assaults on the unknown.

The derealization characteristic of open rationalism may have its dangers. Hannah Arendt, in *The Human Condition*,[1] warns us that the call to adapt our cultural attitudes to scientific thinking would involve condemning ourselves 'to a way of life in which speech is no longer meaningful'.[2] The language of mathematical symbols may originally have been no more than a shorthand account of relations expressible in words. But now a great many scientific truths are incapable of being translated back into ordinary language, and these truths are therefore communicable only among a few specialists. The knowledge which shapes and controls our world is entirely beyond the ken of ordinary people, because it cannot be expounded in a language which they understand.

There may be truths beyond speech, and they may be of great

[1] University of Chicago Press, 1958.   [2] op. cit. p. 4.

relevance to man in the singular, that is, to man in so far as he is not a political being, whatever else he may be. Men in the plural, that is, men in so far as they live and move and act in this world, can experience meaningfulness only because they can talk with and make sense to each other and to themselves.[1]

We can therefore only act or undergo the consequences of action; we are rapidly losing our power of collective discussion, and man as a political animal is in danger of becoming extinct. When we come to discuss authenticity and the open morality, we shall in effect be trying to talk about a derealized ethic, the province of which is one individual's choices, and considering whether any purpose can be served by attempting to treat such an ethic as if it had a universal relevance.

Morot-Sir, in his *La Pensée négative*, is concerned with comprehension and knowledge. He examines carefully and successively certain epistemological theories and concludes, in the anti-naturalistic way with which we are now familiar, and which is an almost universal characteristic of twentieth-century philosophy, that they try to define knowledge in terms of something other than itself.[2] His own contribution is on phenomenological lines and undertakes to 'describe the basic fact of knowledge'.[3]

This is seen to spring from a desire for a *tabula rasa*, and this approach inevitably leads to the rejection of the pure involutionary or assimilatory point of view advanced by Lalande and Meyerson.[4] Not unnaturally Morot-Sir cites Hegel's 'thinking is primarily denying' and Laporte's 'it is the *feeling of difference* which is prior to all others',[5] in support of his thesis, which is that 'the opposition of a consciousness[6] is governed by the consciousness of an opposition'.[7] On this depends the positive act of proposing a new model or theory. Hence knowledge is always provisional, since there is no possibility of the final assimilation of all things in an all-embracing system. Again, however, having expelled a criterion of progress (assimilation) which is at least in principle

[1] op. cit. p. 4.   [2] *La Pensée négative*, p. 50.   [3] ibid. p. 51.
[4] See ibid. pp. 62 ff.   [5] *Le Problème de l'abstraction*, p. 137.
[6] i.e. its rejection of the given, including given or constituted solutions.
[7] *La P. négative*, p. 65.

empirically verifiable, Morot-Sir, like Bachelard, cannot find anything quite so convenient to put in its place. There is unavoidable inability to understand, he says,[1] and the sole criterion of progress is the feeling that we have understood more and better.

But criteria of progress are less important than the periodic negation of the existing structure of knowledge[2] under the impulse of a feeling of its inadequacy. Retrospectively to affirm that progress has been made is less significant than prospectively to recognize that a frontier of knowledge has been reached,[3] and the dynamic march of consciousness arrested. This is quite typical of the kind of philosophy that I am treating, the 'open' kind which constantly, or at least fairly regularly, confronts one with choices to be made and readjustments to be contrived, and plays down the idea of permanence and lasting possession. Discontinuity tends to be stressed by Morot-Sir,[4] and the essential nature of analysis is seen to be in its pluralism and distintegrating activity.[5] At this point, however, a distinction must be made. Morot-Sir is concerned with two things in *La Pensée négative*. With the oppositional structure of comprehension within the simple act of understanding, and, on a larger scale, the breaking of the received mould of knowledge in the interest of a fresh synthesis. Analysis is part of the act of understanding and it *objectifies* its material by splitting it into its component and disjoined elements. These are held, so to speak, in provisional relationship by the unifying subject, who has to be invoked to prevent fragmentation from degenerating into utter unintelligibility.[6] It is, on the other hand, synthesis which creates new, *abstract* unifications.

Morot-Sir's emphasis, it must be admitted, is on the oppositional character of the single act of understanding; but this idea of a single comprehending act is rather artificial, and must be

---

[1] ibid. p. 69.

[2] 'structure oppositionnelle de la compréhension', ibid. p. 183.

[3] See ibid. p. 102, the italicized definition of the *compréhension-limite*.

[4] See pp. 103–5. A 'state of comprehension' retains great elasticity.

[5] Though, of course, Morot-Sir has constantly in mind the *double* 'oppositional' character of comprehension and does not neglect synthesis. Since, however, Meyerson and others have insisted on synthesis, his emphasis is naturally on analysis.   [6] ibid. pp. 189–90.

understood as being hardly distinguishable, in some of its forms, from the 'complete phenomena'[1] or 'superobjects'[2] of Bachelard. In other words, an atomistic theory of comprehension is hardly more satisfactory than atomistic psychology, since it is so difficult to identify the atoms. But the book is interesting and, in showing a positive and negative bipolarity in thinking, with an alternation between the two in the form of synthesis and analysis, its thesis is consistent with the general trend of French philosophy with which I am concerned. We never reach a state of equilibrium. All hope of a final truth must be abandoned, since thought is at any stage necessarily partial, and in its history a succession of partialities.[3]

It is not sufficient to invite consciousness to run risks. We must demand besides that it accept and maintain an awareness of intellectual insecurity. . . .[4]

7

The concept as **expression.** The extraction of provisional meanings from the permanently indeterminate. Merleau-Ponty

---

The writer who most successfully analyses experience in phenomenological terms, as 'open', is Maurice Merleau-Ponty, in his *Phenomenology of Perception* of 1945. It is a work which goes far beyond what its title would lead us to expect, and is in fact a phenomenology of experience and consciousness. Merleau-Ponty may be said to conceive man and his world as standing in a relationship of mutual 'participation', though he does not use Lavelle's term. Perception is a means of being in the world, and as such it is not necessarily an explicit and deliberately thematic act,[5] it is the background from which all acts stand out, and is presupposed by them.

[1] *La Phil. du non*, p. 17.   [2] ibid. p. 139.   [3] *La P. négative*, p. 388.
[4] ibid. p. 389.
[5] i.e. an act bringing something into the focus of consciousness.

This notion of perception as an activity which is in part non-thematic is the starting point of the analysis. Discarding the 'sensation' as an atomistically conceived unit of experience (which he identifies as an empiricist notion), he goes on to show that every identifiable sense-experience owes its existence to *others against which it stands out*, so that the figure-background structure is the essence of the perceptual field, and a kind of perceptual relativism replaces the idea of clear, and clear-cut, impressions.[1] The boundaries of the visual field itself are vague, a fact, he asserts, which psychologists have consistently overlooked, preferring to attribute the imprecision of the object to inattention. But, says Merleau-Ponty, 'we must recognize the indeterminate as a positive phenomenon', for 'we are concerned with expressive value rather than with logical signification'.

What is stressed in these first three chapters is the immediacy of perception, and its independence of various mental procedures which are allegedly, or supposedly, superimposed on what has to be postulated as a bare physical reception of impressions, with the object of interpreting or making sense of them. The crude idea of units of sensation somehow combining into aggregate shapes having been dismissed, Merleau-Ponty goes on to show even such comparatively sophisticated hypotheses as Wertheimer's laws of proximity, resemblance and good form as too associationist and atomistic.[2] To hold that the stimuli in closest proximity, or most similar, or which endow the spectacle with the best balance, are somehow the basis of the object or percept, is to manifest the 'préjugé du monde'. The objective, analytical findings of scientific thinking are surreptitiously brought in to explain the basic experience from which such thinking is derived. The unity of the object of perception is not arrived at by association, that is, by invoking relationships belonging to the objective world, but is the very condition of association. The identification of stimuli which combine to form the 'true' objects of our perception is retrospective, for perception always precedes the operations into which it can be

[1] *Phenomenology of Perception*, trans. Colin Smith, 'International Library of Philosophy and Scientific Method', Routledge & Kegan Paul, 1962, p. 4.
[2] op. cit. p. 16.

decomposed. Walking along a shore towards a ship which has run aground, I at first fail to see the upper part of the ship, which merges with its background. But gradually a tension is built up, and instantaneously the masts and funnel are seen. There is no perception of resemblances or proximities, but a sudden recasting of the sight before me in a manner satisfying to my vague expectation.[1]

The 'prejudice in favour of an objective world', underlying the mistakes which Merleau-Ponty purports to expose in these early chapters, has led psychologists and philosophers of an empiricist persuasion to put forward various products of sophisticated thought as bases for perception involving recognition, without realizing that these 'bases' can be arrived at only after perception and recognition have taken place. In referring the understanding of the 'cultural world' back to the 'natural world' which sustains it, empiricists revert to the wrong background.[2] It is true that every cultural object refers back to the natural background against which it appears, but what this natural background is not is one of stimuli and qualities, which are themselves cultural objects, evolved by a tradition of objective thought. The natural world, whatever it turns out to be, is not that of the scientific object. Just as we may make the mistake of assuming that schematized objects somehow underlie and sustain the objects of perception, so we may be misled into imagining that the operation of perception is helped out by certain occult intellectual activities such as attention and judgement. In effect Merleau-Ponty accuses the empiricist of betraying his own principles and multiplying entities beyond his needs. Judgement and attention, which are held respectively to correct and interpret erroneous and rudimentary perception, are shown as otiose notions, 'since the least significant vision outruns the pure impression and thus comes under the general heading of "judgement" '.[3] Perception is thus not a fruitful physical passivity

---

[1] op. cit. p. 17.
[2] It must be admitted that Merleau-Ponty is attacking a rather old-fashioned empiricism. He seems to be aware of this when he concedes that science conceived as organized common sense is no longer the science of the scientist.   [3] op. cit. p. 34.

which has to be fertilized by some mental act obscurely but necessarily connected with it, but 'just that act which creates, at a stroke, along with the cluster of data, the meaning which unites them – indeed which not only discovers the meaning *which they have*, but moreover *causes them to have a meaning*'.[1] It does not rest upon pre-existing norms issuing from an intellectually or chronologically prior source. It is not the 'sensation', which is atomistic and always in need of some auxiliary element of experience to make it meaningful, belonging as it does to the 'domain of the constituted and not to the constituting mind'. It is, on the contrary, sense experience (*le sentir*).

However, although sense-experience is not the same thing as the 'constituted' sensation of the empiricist tradition, neither is it wholly the work of the 'constituting' mind, as 'intellectualism', or psychological rationalism, would have it. In his chapter entitled 'The Phenomenal Field', Merleau-Ponty presents sense-experience as lying between the pure sense quality and the object, as 'an experience in which we are given not "dead" qualities, but active ones'. Thus the perception of objects carries a kind of functional colouring, being perception in the light of possible action, or, in the language of the phenomenologist, intentional. A wheel lying on the ground is not, *for sight*, the same thing as a wheel bearing a load.[2] It is the mind which identifies the two; but the percept is not the concept; it precedes the concept and is the material from which objective thinking extracts its knowledge – 'the intentional tissue which the effort to know will take apart'.[3]

Having established that perception occurs on the basis of a focus-background, or object-horizon, structure, which is that of the perspective, the inquiry moves on to consider how the 'absolute object', or notion of a thing as determinate or in principle wholly explorable, emerges from this.[4]

A house, seen at any moment necessarily from one angle, is open to the endless exploration which could be undertaken by moving round it and looking everywhere inside it. But each

[1] ibid. p. 36.   [2] ibid. p. 52.   [3] ibid. p. 53.   [4] ibid. pp. 67 ff.

perspective provides only one appearance of the house, and we may be tempted to say that the house *itself* is none of these appearances, but the perspectiveless view from which all the empirically viewable aspects are derived: in other words, the house seen from nowhere. But this is hardly satisfactory, and Merleau-Ponty says that in supposing *the* house to be essentially the house seen from nowhere, we are trying to express a certain manner of approaching the object, that manner being the gaze, and that what we must do is 'to try to understand how vision can be brought into being from somewhere without being enclosed in its perspective'.[1]

Our awareness of the actuality, though limited accessibility, of other perspectives comes about through our ability to choose which shall be the focus and which the horizon of vision, and our ability to convert one into the other at will through the mobility of the gaze. This spatial transferability and interdependence has its temporal counterpart, since the present must have its hold on the past and the future for the object to be constituted. I do not expressly identify the detailed object before me with that which I viewed a few moments ago, in order to construct a spatio-temporal synthesis of co-ordinated aspects. I am obliged to *remember* only if I am artificially deprived of the horizon of a lived-through perceptual field. For example, if in a film the camera suddenly moves to a close-up view of an object, a hand or an ashtray, we recall that this is the hand we have just seen, perhaps without noticing it, in the context of the whole body, or the ashtray in that of the whole room. This is because the screen has no horizons. But in real perception the sector of the visual field which is relegated to the marginal role does not cease to be there. It is not so much a permanent possibility of sensation as an actuality of peripheral sensation, and as such is part of the significance which is disclosed by the gaze. 'The horizon is what guarantees the identity of the object throughout the exploration.'[2]

The horizon, however, is imprecise. We have seen that the indeterminate is in itself a phenomenon, and in consequence the object is never posited with all its unexplored aspects in time and

---

[1] op. cit. p. 67.   [2] ibid. p. 68.

space made explicit. Its synthesis remains forever presumptive, and we are left with an object the substantiality of which is always slipping away.

> If it is to reach perfect density, in other words, if it is to be an absolute object, it will have to consist of an infinite number of different perspectives compressed into a strict co-existence.[1]

But of course this absolute density is never achieved, though it is almost inevitably posited as the goal of thought. The object is never absolute, but always open to further exploration, not to say to change in itself. Thus our positing of objects is always an approximation. This may seem to do little more than reaffirm that we never step into the same river twice. Rather than being an assertion that reality is perpetually subject to change, however, Merleau-Ponty's inquiry, at least in part, is into how change becomes reality.

Thanks to the expressive power of the perspective, with its horizons, we are made to go beyond the limits of our actual experience and posit an object. 'Obsessed with being, and forgetful of the perspectivism of my experience', I tend to objectify it too, and its ostensible source, my body, which becomes an object in geometrical space, not essentially different from other objects. Similarly my world, which is an open situation of indefinite extent and implication, becomes the 'universe' at this moment, which is a closed and consummate totality. 'I detach myself from my experience and pass to the *idea*.'[2] The whole life of consciousness takes the form of constantly positing objects, 'yet the absolute positing of a single object is the death of consciousness', for it has the effect of congealing the whole of existence. This description of existence as a series of acts which in effect arrest existence is the antithesis of Sartre's, which presents a perpetual vain effort towards a definitive consummation, an in-itself-for-itself, which he picturesquely and characteristically terms self-deification. Sartre's experience draws us on towards a fulfilment which is destined never to be realized; in Merleau-Ponty's view the fulfilment must be constantly realized for consciousness to exist, since consciousness

[1] ibid. p. 70.   [2] ibid. p. 71.

is always consciousness of something, but this something is necessarily incomplete and open, by reason of its horizon of ambiguity. There follows an analysis of the object, and the body as primary object, conceived as 'partes extra partes': conceived in such a way, that is to say, that only external and mechanical relations can exist between its parts, or between it and other objects. But modern physiology, says Merleau-Ponty, no longer links the different qualities of one and the same sense, and the data of different senses, to distinct material instruments.

The difficulties inherent in any causal theory of mind-body relationships, thought of as determinate and one-to-one interactions, are set forth in an examination of the phantom limb, and anosognosia, or failure on the patient's part explicitly to take account of a disability.[1] The illusion of still experiencing sensations in an amputated limb is seen to be in part dependent on personal history, memories and volitions, and to be more persistent in the educated than in the uneducated patient. The fact remains, however, that the severing of the afferent nerves abolishes it. So one must concede that it lies in some ambiguous, intermediate zone between the physical and the psychic. A similar case, lying outside the alternatives of final and mechanistic causes, is that of the insect which substitutes a sound leg for one cut off. It is not a case of being aware of some specific act, explicitly posited, nor is some stand-by device being automatically brought into play. The insect is 'in the world' and belongs to that world, which under the circumstances makes a certain demand on it, a demand which is met in the most effective way from the total resources at the creature's disposal. The situation is a practical situation which 'requires' the insect's movements, as the first notes of a melody require to be continued and resolved in a certain key. We may thus say that the phantom limb is an incipient response of the organically integrated, though accidentally disabled, person to the world which continues to make its demands on his whole dynamic being. The severance of the nerves from the stump to the brain, which causes the phantom limb to disappear, presumably further contributes to putting the body out of the normal circuit of being

[1] op. cit. pp. 76 ff.

in the world. It would seem to be, on the physical side, a factor corresponding (but of course in the reverse direction) to that, on the psychic side, of having the circumstances of injury recalled, or being temperamentally resistant to the idea of disablement.

Our actions, even reflex actions, express our orientation towards a 'behavioural setting', and answer, from a distance, to the general structure of the object or situation, and not to any partial stimuli within that situation. Both the reflex and perception are modalities of a pre-objective view, which is being in the world. Prior to stimuli and sensory contents we have to recognize an inner force which determines what our reflexes and perceptions are to 'aim at' in the world, and this force is variable from person to person. Some subjects can come near to blindness without losing their 'world'; they stumble against objects and remain apparently unaware of their deficiencies. Others, on the other hand, anticipate the loss of their world and become premature invalids, already cut off from vital contact with their surroundings while sensory contact is still available to them. This means that there is not an objective world which makes an invariable impact on all individuals, but one which is variable in accordance with what Sartre would call an original project or existential choice. 'What it is in us which refuses mutilation and disablement is an *I* committed to a certain physical and inter-human world, who continues to tend towards his world despite handicaps and amputations, and who to this extent does not recognize them *de jure*.'[1] The phantom arm is a kind of implicit will to remain in the world of unrestricted living.

It is nevertheless a failure to adapt oneself to the present situation, and Merleau-Ponty, in this connection, speaks of the 'customary body' and the 'body at this moment'. The ability to perceive objects as manipulatable when I can no longer manipulate them implies the existence of a customary body which is the body as an object, and the source of external things as objects. The manipulatable is not what I am now manipulating, but what *one* can manipulate, what is manipulatable *in itself*. The residual behaviour represented by the phantom limb is analogous to a

[1] ibid. p. 81.

repressed experience, since it is what persists into a present which can find no use for it. At this stage Merleau-Ponty's argument runs parallel to that concerning the two eternities put forward by Alquié. One present among all presents acquires a privileged status, impersonal time flows on, but personal time is arrested, the traumatic experience does not survive as a memory or a representation, 'dated' and at the disposal of the autonomous subject in an open situation. The subject has forgone his power of providing himself with 'worlds', and abdicated in favour of one of them. Yet, though emotional repression and the objectification of affective experience can amount to mental derangement, we are constantly engaged in a kind of 'repression' which is the condition of our having experience, and indeed a *body*, at our disposal. All repression is, then, the transition from first person existence to a sort of abstraction of that existence, which lives on a former experience.

> Just as we speak of repression in the limited sense when I retain through time one of the momentary worlds through which I have lived, and make it the formative element in my whole life – so it can be said that my organism, as a prepersonal cleaving to the general form of the world, as an anonymous and general existence, plays, beneath my personal life, the part of an *inborn complex*.[1]

This prepersonal cleaving is the expression of our need of a common world, of that acquired reality which provides counters for factual communication and intercourse. We cannot respond with ever-renewed spontaneity to every instant of our experience. If man is to be aware of the world 'as the common reason for all settings', then forms of stimulation from outside must not be for him the totality of being. Nor must his responses be for ever at the centre of his existence, but must be relegated to the periphery, in order that he may remain the subject in control of his world through them, and not be the object of them.

Thus it is by giving up part of his spontaneity, by becoming involved in the world through stable organs and pre-established

[1] op. cit. p. 84.

circuits that man can acquire the mental and practical space which will theoretically free him from his environment and allow him to *see* it. And provided that even the realization of an objective world is set in the realm of existence, we shall no longer find any contradiction between it and bodily conditioning: it is an inner necessity for the most integrated existence to provide itself with an habitual body.[1]

What emerges from this is that the phantom limb is an even more ambiguous entity than Merleau-Ponty makes explicit in his interesting analysis. It is part of the customary body, though physically non-existent, so that as an 'acquisition' it tends to 'be available' in circumstances calling for a real limb. Thus the phantom limb symbolizes the ambiguity (ambivalence would perhaps be a better word) of sedimentary and objectified being: it saves us from being lost in the novelty of every unique situation, but, as here, is liable to offer itself for use, where it is no longer relevant. This latter aspect is the one which obsesses the extreme existentialist, who sees the parasitic nature of sedimentary being as in itself a sufficient indictment of 'objectivity'. But Merleau-Ponty realizes that it has a fruitful side, indeed a necessary side. He sees the organ behind the obstacle. There is the 'commonplace and cyclic side' of experience; and there is the 'open and unusual side', which may be called *history* (personal and collective), since it brings novelty into the world. But the figure in history is seldom, if ever, *entirely* new: Nicolas II repeats the words of Louis XVI, which typify the situation of traditional power faced with a new order, and translate the *a priori* of reaction and revolution, just 'as our reflexes translate a specific *a priori* . . . So history is neither a perpetual novelty nor a perpetual repetition, but the *unique* movement which creates stable forms and breaks them up.'[2]

Examining further the ambiguity of the body's role we are led to consideration of the *body image*,[3] which is not an associative compendium of interacting parts, but essentially dynamic and integrated. Its spatiality is not that of objects arrayed in space, but

[1] ibid. p. 87.   [2] ibid. pp. 87–8.   [3] ibid. pp. 98 ff.

a spatiality of situation, which means that it is a 'laying down of the first co-ordinates . . . the situation of the body in face of its tasks'.[1] These 'polarize' the body, and the notion of the body image provides a way of stating that the body is in the world. It is, moreover, related to the figure-background structure, of which it is the 'third term', so that the figure 'stands out against the double horizon of external and bodily space', stands, in fact, in 'orientated space'. Now orientated space is not the same thing as geometrical space nor, what is more important, is it extracted from the latter. On the contrary homogeneous space is the explicit expression of orientated space, and conveys the latter's *meaning*, but in a misleadingly rigid way. 'As soon as I try to posit bodily space or bring out its meaning, I find nothing in it but intelligible space.'[2] We 'live' bodily space, but when we are obliged to treat it in any way discursively, we cannot avoid speaking as if there were an absolute set of basic directions and spatial relationships underlying it.

It is in action that bodily space is clearly seen as different in kind from abstract space, and the body image as a dynamic and intentional power. Merleau-Ponty gives a detailed account of the abilities and limitations of a patient, Schneider, who has suffered brain injury, in consequence of which he is unable to perform 'abstract' movements, that is, movements not relevant to any immediate need or everyday context, though he can perform actions quite well which are habitual, or occupational, even though they may be highly complicated ones.[3]

An analysis of the contrast between pointing as an abstract movement and grasping as a concrete one follows, and this draws on the experimental psychology dealt with in Goldstein's *Zeigen und Greifen* (1931). The patient cannot, with his eyes shut, perform movements to order, such as moving his limbs, nor can he describe the position of his head and body during these movements. He is able to perform abstract movements of this kind only if he can watch the required limb or go through preliminary movements designed to give him his bodily bearings. Yet he can, even with eyes closed, do the manual work involved in his former job as a leather worker quickly and without any preliminary movements. He cannot simply point to a part of his body, but he can and does move his hand to a point where he is pricked, which shows that 'concrete movements and acts of grasping enjoy a privileged position'. Why is this so?

The question is answerable in terms of the body image, which in turn implies a spatiality other than that of objective space. Traditional psychology, says Merleau-Ponty, takes no account of a consciousness of place which is not a positional consciousness, a representation or *Vorstellung*. The patient is conscious of his bodily space as the setting of habitual action, not as an objective setting; 'his body is at his disposal as a means of ingress into a familiar surrounding, but not as the means of expression of a gratuitous and free spatial thought'.[1] Now the distinction between the instrumental and the expressive is crucial. The instrumentality of the handicapped man's body is, we might say, acquired expressiveness, since its flow is owed to the action's being habitual. When, however, he is required spontaneously to 'grasp' a new situation in its totality and give expression to it in action; when, that is, he has to perform an action not rigidly required by a familiar context, but merely has to 'act' it, projecting himself into an arbitrary or imaginary situation, he has recourse to the kind of laboriously synthetic procedure which the normal person is forced to adopt only in the face of some task of great intellectual or physical complexity; and indeed for the same reason, namely that he is working at the limit of his capacity. For melodic flow to be present, the situation must be 'assumed' or grasped, and not 'worked out'. What is worked out is, as it were, atomistically elaborated by piecing together the objective, or acquired, fragments of more or less habitual living. But the normal person's grasp transcends the literal reality of acquired thought and action, and projects itself into what is merely possible or imaginable. The patient cannot do this. He must have recourse to preparatory movements in order to 'find' the relevant limbs and attitudes. Placed in front of a door, he can knock at it as if seeking admission, but put out of reach of the door he cannot *pretend* to knock.

[1] ibid. p. 104.

He needs all the elements of his situation presented to him, or already built into his experience, otherwise he can do nothing. In habitual action he has established channels of activity provided for him, in the form of bench, scissors, pieces of leather 'to be cut up', linings 'to be sewn'. His intentionality, or power of resolving a situation, is of course here fully operative, but his limitation consists in its being operative within a system of closed and objectified elements. These he can grasp, but he cannot grasp the possible melodic flow of a new situation. Or, more precisely, he cannot 'point to', or trace in outline at a distance and without total involvement, what is not within his 'grasp'. 'The normal person *reckons with* the possible, which thus, without shifting from its position as a possibility, acquires a sort of actuality. In the patient's case, however, the field of actuality is limited to what is met with in the shape of a real contact, or is related to these data by some explicit process of deduction.'[1]

What the patient lacks is any 'motor intentionality'. He either evolves an ideal formula for the action, or else launches himself into blind attempts to perform it. The normal person, on the other hand, performs every movement against a *background* which is its envisaged completion. He anticipates his aim, and his 'plunge into action is, from his point of view, an original way of relating himself to the object'.[2] If his movement is a 'concrete' one, he is acting within his habitual bounds, but, unlike the patient discussed above, he is further able to project a background which is not wholly immanent in his action, and hence execute an 'abstract' movement. Strictly speaking, 'abstract' movement is divorced from a living context, and makes its appearance when we 'play at' doing something, or do it for its own sake. Intermediate between this and habitual movement there is the open gesture which is required by the situation, but is not entirely conditioned by it. When, for example, I beckon a friend to come nearer and receive no response, I may vary the gesture, with the same intention, but more insistently, in the light of my friend's hesitation or unwillingness. Or I may perform 'the same' gesture to order, for its own sake, in which case the motor project is no longer directed to-

---

[1] op. cit. p. 109.   [2] ibid. pp. 110–11.

wards someone in the world, but towards the use of the limbs themselves, or towards an entirely imaginary situation.

It is, in a sense, the 'imaginary' element in the imaginary situation which is the condition of consciousness, since to be handicapped in such a way that one can deal only with closed, invariable situations, is to be virtually unconscious, and certainly to be able to act only 'absent-mindedly'. For pointing, as distinct from grasping, is conferring meaning, identifying, objectifying, adopting the 'categorial attitude'. We have seen that abstract movement is related to pointing out, since it operates at a distance from its intentional object, and, as Merleau-Ponty says, 'it consists in placing beneath the flow of impressions an explanatory invariant, and in giving a form to the stuff of experience. Now it is not possible to maintain that consciousness *has* this power, it *is* this power itself.'[1] Existence is a generalized intentionality, abstract movement is 'for itself', and the stimulus is not its cause but its intentional object. Concrete movements in illness might seem to be movements 'in themselves'. Yet the difference is only a matter of degree; there are, strictly speaking, no 'automatic' movements which do not announce themselves to consciousness, and in both concrete and abstract movement we know where our body is without having to look for it.

What the analysis of grasping and pointing illustrates, in a case like Schneider's, is in the first place that a stimulus is a motive and not a cause, which means that a purely physiological explanation is inadequate to account for behaviour, whether deficient or normal. It also shows that conceptual thinking, or step-by-step reasoning, in a way displays a lack of that anticipation of the goal aimed at which is the mark of normal perception and action. The 'assumption' of situations, and their transcendence towards new unities, whether of perceptual objects or values, is not characteristically effected by stringing together habitual or sedimentary elements, but by instantaneously drawing upon them, without being explicitly aware of them, for the creation of the new situation. There is an existential and a general intelligence, and it is the former which is wanting in such complaints as 'number blindness',

[1] ibid. p. 121.

which may reduce calculation to counting on the fingers. 'Consciousness holds in reserve, behind itself, completed syntheses.' In the laborious synthesizing of Schneider there is certainly an intentional core, otherwise his actions would be random, but they impart to movement, behaviour and perception a certain flaccidity. Authentic action has a tension within its intentionality, which can operate even where truth is hard to win. In scientific hypotheses there is a tension built up within the established mould which is broken by a new vision. If the acquired looms too large in the process of finding new meaning, and cannot be thrust into the background to which it belongs, then the new meaning is obscured by the old, and knowledge remains stagnant. For new objects to be brought into being, there must be a free-ranging consciousness not bogged down in its own forms, but working in open situations. Consciousness, perceptual or axiological, is not 'I think' but 'I can'.[1]

An open situation is one in which our bodily and acquired being flow spontaneously towards a possible resolution in the musical sense, and this is demonstrated in various fields of experience, of which speech is perhaps the most significant.[2] Language is presented as a more sophisticated kind of 'gesture', rather than as a set of signs with fixed and imitable thought-equivalents. It uses sedimentary material for expression, which means that it uses acquired meanings for the purpose of realizing new ones. Language is not essentially constituted, but constituting, if it is authentic language. It 'secretes' its own meaning, which is always new, even though the individual words may have dictionary equivalents. The fact that the elements of language are acquired obscures the expressiveness of speech, and makes us tend to see it as the manipulation of a set of linguistic permutations, 'because we have the illusion of already possessing within ourselves, in the shape of the common property meaning of words, what is required for the understanding of any text whatsoever. . . . But it is less the case that the sense of a literary work is provided by the common property meaning of words, *than that it contributes to changing that accepted meaning.*'[3] It is true that phonetic 'gesticula-

[1] op. cit. p. 137.   [2] ibid. pp. 174 ff.   [3] My italics.

tion' must use acquired forms and meanings, but authentic speech puts up a new sense, just as gesture endows the object for the first time with human significance, if it is initiating gesture. The intention to speak can reside only in an open experience, expressing the demands and springing from the tensions of a certain concrete situation.

The speaking subject does not visualize the words which he is using. His vocabulary is at his disposal as are things behind his back, or as the horizon round his house. He reckons with it, as in perception we reckon with what is peripheral and auxiliary to our sensory focus. It is comparable to whatever is 'stored' in experience and yet 'generalized, and detached from its empirical origins'. It is therefore comparable to the acting body itself, which is conceived and described by Merleau-Ponty as an 'inborn complex'.[1] But it is a complex which is fruitful, as, indeed, a pathological complex may no doubt be. I reach back towards the word as I reach for the part of my body which is being pricked; the word 'has a certain location in my linguistic world, and it is part of my equipment'.

The distinction between word or concept, in its obstructiveness on the one hand and its fruitfulness on the other, is established by the terms 'la parole parlée' and 'la parole parlante'. The latter shows speech as 'the surplus of our existence over natural being', because, 'like a wave, (it) gathers and poises itself to hurtle beyond its own limits'.[2]

Passing from his long analysis of the body which, as an initial, ambiguous object, is the source of all objects, Merleau-Ponty

[1] We have seen that the body is an 'inborn complex', which means that it is a repository of acquired experience and habitual action. To describe it thus is to draw attention to its obstructive aspect, to its tendency to be an obstacle as well as an organ. But by its ability to throw up, either by its own expressive movement, or by the instruments of its cultural world, objectifications of experience, it has the function of endowing 'the instantaneous expressions of spontaneity with a little renewable action and independent existence'. Through its 'renewable' creations it is seen as a source of norms.

[2] op. cit. p. 197.

considers the world as perceived, and examines such factors in perception as space and lighting.[1] What interests him in relation to space is that certain orientations are tolerable while others are not. What degree of obliqueness in placing makes a thing unintelligible or incapable of being dealt with as the familiar object which intrinsically it is? What is 'upside down'? Is the body or the visible world ever strictly upright, and if not, what degree of tilt can we make allowance for without undue effort? The answer to these questions is that spatial level is always related to action (in which recognition is included), in other words to *sense*.[2] What counts for the orientation of the spectacle is not my body as it in fact is, as a thing in objective space, but as a system of possible actions, a virtual body with its phenomenal 'place' defined by its tasks and situation. We always have an acquired spatiality, but it is never absolute: there is no level of all levels. In the same way lighting is a level, which is noticed when it changes (from daylight to electric light, for example), but, in assuming the function of lighting, it tends to become anterior to any colour, tends to be absence of colour. It tends to be ignored, and to be the background and mediator of colours.

Because being in the world is bipolar, being partly constituted and partly constituting, the treatment of illusion is particularly interesting. We can all be victims of illusion, but if we are 'in the world' really and truly, then we can always correct it, not so much by attention as by the natural evolution of a situation which will make further and more searching demands upon us.[3] A large shadow appears in my field of vision, and a moment later I 'correct' this impression, or rather make more satisfactory sense of it, by seeing a fly which had come near to my eye.[4] We can never be sure of our perception. We simply elect to believe provisionally in a world, the provisional nature of which is perpetuated by its permanently indeterminate content which we are always liable to

[1] op. cit. Part II, Chaps. 2 and 3.

[2] Much play is made with the convenient ambiguity of the French word *sens* (sense, meaning, direction). Cf ibid. p. 310.

[3] Here we already see the importance of the temporal aspect of perception, which will be discussed presently.

[4] op. cit. p. 279.

verify, without ever having *finally* verified it. The present never guarantees the future. Truth is never more than a precarious hold on a world in which the indeterminate is a phenomenon. The world is always open to further exploration, because being in a situation always prevents us from constituting instantaneously an absolute object, as Merleau-Ponty calls it, that is, prevents us from constituting something which displays to us all its aspects simultaneously. We are never faced with absolute absence of sense, nor do we ever finally and definitively understand. In Merleau-Ponty's language, the world is always opaque, never transparent; but, of course, never *absolutely* opaque either.

The alleged illusory perception of victims of hallucination and mentally deranged people is not perception at all, even for them.[1] Merleau-Ponty reports experiments which involve creating real situations corresponding to hallucinations. A man who thinks the doctor's hand is a guinea-pig has a guinea-pig actually placed in his hand. One who thinks he sees a man standing in a certain attitude in the garden is asked to look at someone who has actually been placed there in the appropriate clothes and attitude. A woman who complains of powder in her bed has some talcum powder shaken into it. All these people immediately recognize that the real situation is not their hallucination. Their illness is not so much defective perception as deficiency of being, analogous to Schneider's. For the schizophrenic 'everything is amazing, absurd or unreal, because the impulse of existence towards things has lost its energy, because it appears to itself in all its contingency and because the world can no longer be taken for granted'. Hallucination is not 'in' the world, but 'before' it. Hallucination is comparable to Schneider's closed situation when he is engaged on his leather-work.

> The world has lost its expressive force, and the hallucinatory system has usurped it. . . . The patient's existence is displaced from its centre, being no longer enacted through dealings with a harsh, resistant and intractable world which has no knowledge of us, but expending its substance in isolation, creating a fictitious setting for itself.[2]

[1] Cf ibid. pp. 334 ff.   [2] ibid. p. 342.

The normal person is 'equally afflicted with this gaping wound through which illusion can make its way in'. But he is not content with subjectivity or eternity, he is concerned with being in the world, and his hold on time is consequently direct, and he does not shirk its perpetual challenge.

In discussing the possibility or impossibility of guaranteed experience, Merleau-Ponty follows the phenomenological fashion and, perhaps anachronistically, talks about the *cogito*.[1] He says that the *cogito* is neither psychological immanence, the blind contact of sensation with itself, nor transcendental immanence, the possession of clear thought by itself. It is, he says 'the deep-seated momentum of transcendence which is my very being, the simultaneous contact with my own being and with the world's being'. The situation in which this transcendence, or evaluation, operates is always in need of further exploration. But we do throw up provisional objects on the way. As we have seen, where Merleau-Ponty differs from Sartre is in recognizing that we do achieve significant contact, that is, meaning-giving contact, with our world, even if the moulds are always being broken and reconstituted. Sartre's drive towards the 'in-itself-for-itself' is always 'un Dieu manqué', and we are a useless passion. But for Merleau-Ponty this process, which he more prosaically describes as sedimentation, or objectification, is normal experience, ceaselessly re-enacted. There is nothing tragic in the fact that the perceptual synthesis has to remain incomplete, since if it is to be a thing, it must have sides hidden from me. It cannot present me with a reality otherwise than by running the risk of producing error.[2]

But what of mental states?[3] Can I not be certain that when I think I love, or will, I really do? Surely everything is true within consciousness, and there can never be illusion other than with regard to an external object. But we can be mistaken about being in love. In distinguishing true love from misguided love, Merleau-Ponty invokes the notion of authenticity, or total commitment of the whole person. In mistaken love only one aspect of the whole persona is concerned: 'the man of forty' in late love, 'the traveller'

[1] op. cit. Part III, Chap. 1.   [2] ibid. p. 377.   [3] ibid. pp. 378 ff.

in the case of exotic appeal, 'the child', where the mother is recalled. But only retrospectively, when I have explored myself more deeply, can I be expected to make the distinction about myself, so that the inner life too is 'open', and its experiences never definitive and guaranteed. My existence is neither in full possession of itself, nor fully estranged from itself, because it is action or doing. I can effect the *cogito* and be assured of genuinely willing, loving or believing, only if I actually do will, love or believe, and thus fulfil my own existence. Self-possession and coincidence with the self do not define thought, which is the outcome of expression. The most intimate experiences are never indubitable, but become so only when constituted; in the constituting they were a matter of exploration.

Everything is historical, and nothing eternal. The acquired is often treated as eternal, but this is an abdication of our powers of innovation. Even rational truths have their day, and Euclidean geometry is a cultural object with a certain facticity about it, a certain arbitrary character possessed by any historical object. The ultimate reality of a self is that of a *field*, a possibility of situations.[1] In other words, just as perception, and behaviour in the world, are processes of endless exploration, positing provisional objects or concepts, so on the subjective side, existence is correspondingly a process of self-discovery.

Merleau-Ponty's constant insistence is on meaning-giving, or expression, on the basis of a focus-horizon structure of experience. This meaning is never the simple outcome of causal relationships or the piecemeal construction of objects, by juxtaposition, out of discontinuous elements. The senses supplement each other, 'levels' are constituted in terms of the tasks confronting us, and finally time is shown as the essential ingredient of meaning and expression. The free-ranging gaze can range and constitute its object only in time, and even in the perception of depth[2] which Merleau-Ponty calls the most existential of dimensions, we have a meaning conveyed which is implicitly temporal. The smallness of a distant object expresses (all the more so if it is approaching or

[1] ibid. p. 406.   [2] ibid. pp. 254 ff.

receding) my separation from it, within the context of a remembered or anticipated proximity.

The actual present moment is, like every other setting of experience, no more than a 'field'. Just as we bring a 'personal field', consisting of our history and acquired attributes, to the sensory fields which the world offers, so my present is a 'field of presence' which is strictly indeterminate. I may arbitrarily extend the term 'the present' to cover anything from the passing instant to the period of history in which I live, according to the amount of time, in past, present and future, I need to take as relevant to my situation as I envisage it. The immediately preceding part of my day is still with me, I 'have it in hand', and though my evening to come is not yet here, its general outlines can be seen already. Even the present, in the narrowest sense, is not posited; it consists in the availability of the objects which I need for my task, and I do not so much perceive these objects as 'reckon with an environment'. Our attitude to time, as far as it is lived, is of the nature of 'greifen' rather than 'zeigen', for if the past were available only in the form of express recollections we should have to be constantly recalling it, and be like the patient who was forever turning round to make sure that the world behind him was still there. Thus time is for each of us a form of indivisible expression, as a gesture unconsciously includes all the muscular contractions necessary for its execution. The whole of time, like the world, is an individual, 'a single concrete being, wholly present in each of its manifestations, as is a man in each of his spoken words'.

Time is something into which we are born, and in which we are carried along, whatever we do or do not do, and our defence is conceptualization. Establishing a concept or taking a binding decision, or even, Merleau-Ponty might have added, perceiving an object, 'withholds me from what I was about to become, and at the same time provides me with the means of grasping myself at a distance, and establishing my own reality as myself'. This is not unlike Alquié's conception of eternity in its rational (i.e. objective) aspect as that which leads us on to action and the assertion of the subject. If we were not able to arrest change by creating durable and identifiable objectifications, we would be conscious neither of the world nor of ourselves. The subject and his world are in mutual dependence.

The examination of temporality leads on to that of freedom, which is dealt with within the framework of behaviour as self-expression. If what we do is characteristically meaningful, it is necessary that the content of one instant should bear a relation to that of the next. 'Each instant, therefore, must not be a closed world, one instant must be able to commit its successors, and . . . I must have something acquired at my disposal, I must benefit from my impetus. . . .' Descartes realized that conservation is as great a miracle as creation, yet creation does come about, and in the instant, which is not a philosopher's fiction. It is, says Merleau-Ponty, the point at which the gaze is transferred from one objective to another, the *Augen-Blick*. But for the reorientation to take place the two spans of time must be of a piece or, to put it better, there must be movement in a determinate direction.[1] There can be choice, but never on the basis of nothing, never an initial choice, which means that we need a real situation in which to exercise freedom. An imaginary one is of no use, since dreaming, as Sartre says, is incompatible with freedom, because in dreams the objective is achieved without any intervening obstacles, so that there is nothing to *do*.[2] Our transactions with the world are conducted almost entirely by means of obstacles, which present themselves as 'to be taken', 'to be climbed over', etc., and which constitute the 'autochthonous significance' of the world, and are the ground of every sense-giving act.

The instantaneous extraction of significance from the elements of an acquired world, from a world *in itself*, is simply an example of *being* as continental philosophers generally present it. The situation is the organ-obstacle of its successor. Our freedom does not destroy our situation, but gears itself to it; as long as we are alive, our situation is open, which implies that it calls up specially favoured modes of resolution, and also that it is powerless to bring one into being itself. Our life for itself is similar to our perceptual life. There is an acquired and sedimentary self, which

[1] This power of initiation is what fascinates Vladimir Jankélévitch.
[2] op. cit. p. 438.

is what Sartre calls our being *in itself*. It is our provisional essence, because it is amenable to conceptualization, and formulation in terms of opinions formed of us, on our own part or on that of other people. But we are always free, and liable, to change it and give some new orientation to it. It is I who give direction, significance and future to my life, but we are not to understand these as concepts: they spring from my present and past, and from my present and past co-existence. In the case of an intellectual turned revolutionary, his decision does not arise out of a vacuum; it may well follow upon a prolonged period of solitude and, by imposing social solidarity upon him, act as a remedy for his self-centredness. Or he may yield to a convincing overall view of history which he finds in Marx; or his decision may be deliberately motiveless and 'gratuitous'; but this act of 'pure' freedom would be a certain way of being in the social world, and one which only an intellectual might be expected to adopt. In other words, the choice which we make of our lives is always based on a certain givenness, and in so far as it draws our life away from its existing course, does so only by a series of unobtrusive deflections, not by any absolute creation. If I made myself into worker or bourgeois by an absolute initiative, and if in general 'nothing ever courted our freedom', history, personal or social, would display no structure. We choose our world, and the world chooses us.

8

The rejection of 'expressionism'. The 'logos' as the 'rule' of thought. Brice Parain

An examination of language, in some ways related to Merleau-Ponty's, is undertaken by Brice Parain in *Recherches sur la nature et les fonctions du langage*.[1] This is a study of the relation of language to truth, and it traces the history of the philosophy of language from the Greek beginnings to Hegel. This book is roughly con-

[1] Gallimard, 1942.

temporary with Merleau-Ponty's *La Structure du comportement*, and yet its general conclusion appears to run counter to the historical development which it outlines, and which might be said to culminate in the phenomenology of Merleau-Ponty. In fact it seems to restore some kind of essentialist nature and normative function to language.

He deals first with the refutation, by Socrates, of the earliest Greek theory of the rigid correspondence between words and objects in the sensible world. The adoption of the theory of Ideas was the consequence of this refutation, since the act of naming was seen by Socrates to be in itself inductive, in so far as it implies the recognition of a kind, and not merely of one particular object. In modern times Descartes took language to be the representation of intelligible truth, but this led to too many difficulties, for, as Pascal pointed out, the confusion and distortion brought into clear thought by the passions is too great and too pervasive. A crisis and *impasse* was thus brought about by what was, in Brice Parain's view, the bankruptcy of French philosophy towards the end of the seventeenth century.[1]

It was the Germans who found the way forward with their dialectical philosophy,[2] which turned its back on sources and sought an explanation of language in terms of its outcome as an enterprise, an 'adventure'. In place of any idea of a linguistic representation of objects, 'sensations' or clear ideas, we have here what is called 'expressionism': 'language is no longer limited, as in Cartesian idealism and English nominalism, to embodying intellectual representations, but takes in the whole of our affective and active life'.[3] Our consciousness is, then, 'participation'[4] in the world, and our language is the expression of what in more recent terminology would be called our 'projects'. It is not surprising that, though Leibnitz and Hegel are presented as the philosophical mainstays of this new historical thinking, Brice Parain should find more vividness in Goethe, Nietzsche and Marx as its spokesmen. 'Im Anfang war die Tat', says Faust. The world is no longer to be interpreted, but transformed, according to Marx. Interpretation

---

[1] op. cit. p. 110.   [2] 'orientée vers la preuve par l'accomplissement'.
[3] op. cit. p. 138.   [4] ibid. p. 111.

brings knowledge of what exists, but the outcome of transformation cannot be known as long as it is still to be realized: as
Nietzsche says, knowledge and becoming are mutually exclusive.
'In all our judgements we must take the future as our *norm*, and
not look behind us for the laws governing our action',[1] which,
as Brice Parain correctly adds, means taking no norm at all.

Now Parain's book deals, historically, with the development of
that duality of acquisition and invention which is the theme of this
study. We are shown realistic theories of language proving their
inadequacy, and the 'expressionist' breakthrough following upon
the 'representational' deadlock. This development is, of course,
further exemplified by Merleau-Ponty's phenomenological analysis
of language (and indeed all behaviour) as expressive, that is, as in
part acquired, but pre-eminently available to the man confronting
his tasks, and, therefore, responsible to his creative will. Parain,
however, does not conclude, as he might, that the nature of
language is always provisional, and that its function is to be self-
transcending in accordance with human transactions with reality.
On the contrary, he appears to revert to an 'essentialist' view, by
maintaining that language is 'the rule of our human thought and
action'.[2] In describing it thus he seems to be stressing the compelling force of the word, which we utter on pain of commitment.
It may be, for example, a declaration of love, of which we are
nevertheless unsure. But the word is spoken. 'Il faudra désormais
que je passe par tout ce qu'il signifie.'[3] The peculiarly conclusive
force of expressions of love is understood by Count Mosca, in
La Chartreuse de Parme, when he jealously watches the Duchess
Sanseverina and Fabrice together.

> Il devenait fou: il lui sembla qu'en se penchant ils se donnaient
> des baisers, là, sous ses yeux. Cela est impossible en ma pré-
> sence, se dit-il; ma raison s'égare. Il faut se calmer; si j'ai des
> manières rudes, la duchesse est capable, par simple pique de
> vanité, de le suivre à Belgirate; et là, ou pendant le voyage, le
> hasard peut amener un mot qui donnera un nom à ce qu'ils
> sentent l'un pour l'autre; et après, en un instant, toutes les
> conséquences.

[1] *The Will to Power.*   [2] op. cit. p. 168.   [3] ibid. p. 169.

What we utter cannot be unuttered, and once spoken, words are added to the world and its events. We may undo their effects, but we cannot so order it that the words were never spoken. Now if the implication is that we should keep our thoughts to ourselves for fear of their consequences, this would perhaps amount to a useful social precept, but would hardly be of philosophical significance. I think we must assume that for the author all articulate thought is a commitment which, in making it articulate, we impose upon ourselves willy-nilly. We are impelled to articulate – publicly or privately, it makes no essential difference – what we can. Our 'secret wish, which urges us to destroy language',[1] may be for silence, but by naming that silence, we shut ourselves off from it. To speak, however, on impulse, prematurely, on half-understood desire, and subsequently to regret it, is the way to the kind of committal against which he is warning us. It is in fact the kind of judgement which is led astray by passion, away from the clear and distinct ideas upon which alone true action is founded.[2] Brice Parain thus rejoins Descartes.

Now this compulsion of the Word is something which we undergo. The 'rule' of language is external to us and transcends us, because it is the abode (le lieu) of the universal and of the reflective will.[3] Now Merleau-Ponty accuses Brice Parain of conceiving language as 'the obverse of an infinite Thought', an 'absolute thought',[4] which, of course, could not be more alien to the analysis of language put forward in Phenomenology of Perception. It seems to me that Merleau-Ponty is right, though one need not accept the implied censure. I want merely to draw attention to this further example of one pole, this time the essentialist pole, of recent French thought. We have seen that reason and the logos are amenable to either a static or dynamic conception, and we shall go on to see how far this dualistic tendency operates in the field of moral and aesthetic values.

[1] ibid. p. 175.
[2] Merleau-Ponty does not make the commitment of utterance wait upon Cartesian certainty. We may be mistaken in love, or in any inner state, but that is no reason for emotional paralysis, any more than the possibility of error in perception is a reason for not perceiving.
[3] op. cit. p. 168.   [4] Phenomenology of Perception, p. 392.

PART THREE

NORMS AND VALUES

9

Closed and open evolutionary morality. Bergson's *Les Deux Sources de la morale et de la religion*

The dualism of intellectual security and insecurity, of assimilation and the philosophy of negation, of closed and open rationalism, has its counterpart in the ethical sphere.

Bergson's *The Two Sources of Morality and Religion* was published in 1932, and is one of the major French philosophical works of this century. In it the main dichotomy of existentialist ethics is foreshadowed. Following the earlier French philosophers Maine de Biran and Ravaisson in his preoccupation with habit, he shows the affinity between habit and everyday morality, and begins with what is, in effect, an account of what has more recently been referred to in French as the 'quotidien' (the everyday). Generally speaking, throughout his work, Bergson identifies habit with reason, which, in the context of my subject, I want to narrow down to 'closed' or 'constituted' reason, because this is really the only kind of reason which Bergson recognizes. He does not feel any need to draw the distinction between closed and open rationalism that he draws between closed and open morality and religion. I should, indeed, be inclined to assert that recent French rationalistic philosophy has developed a distinction suggested, but left unexplored, by Bergson, whereas much post-war existentialist philosophy (in which ethical considerations are latent) has done no more than elaborate the dualism put forward in *The Two Sources*.

Bergson begins by examining the idea of law, and the way in which the double use of the word 'law', for natural regularity of phenomena on the one hand, and for the means of maintaining order in society on the other, are confused in most people's minds. The scientist normally maintains the distinction, remembering that a law promulgated by society is backed by force, and that this threat, it is hoped, will induce the waverer to conform, although of course he *can* disobey. A human law is an expression of the collective will, which seeks to prevail over the aberrations of individual wills. A law of nature, however, is not the outcome of anybody's will; it is merely an account of the order and manner in which things happen. But just as people tend to think of such natural laws as dictated by a higher power, so inversely do they come to think of the decrees of society as having the unquestionable force of the natural order. 'The law borrows from the command its prerogative of compulsion; the command receives from the law its inevitability.'[1] This appearance of inevitability is the commonest characteristic of any single obligation. Consequently people usually do their duty without question and almost without thought; hence obedience to duty is 'a form of non-exertion, passive acquiescence'.[2] This, Bergson rightly insists, is often overlooked by moral philosophers, who represent obedience to duty as involving tension and a struggle with oneself. This can occur, of course, and since morality becomes interesting only when some such self-conscious effort, arising from inner strife, is present, it is not surprising that the idea of obligation is associated with that of self-discipline and self-compulsion. But basically the sense of obligation is 'a tranquil state, akin to inclination'.[3] This form of response to obligation is very similar to the semi-automatic performance of any non-moral act, and its resemblance to the 'quotidienneté' of more recent writers is brought out when Bergson, remarking that only rarely do acts involve a moral struggle, adds that 'consciousness is this hesitation itself, for an action which is started automatically passes almost unperceived'.[4] Here the French word 'conscience' cannot be rendered adequately, since it means both 'awareness' and 'moral awareness' or 'conscience'. Except where there is effort which makes its impact on consciousness, our mental life proceeds in a kind of lethargic passivity.

[1] *The Two Sources of Morality and Religion*, translated by R. Ashley Audra and Cloudelsey Brereton, Macmillan, 1935, p. 4.
[2] ibid. p. 10.   [3] ibid. p. 11.   [4] ibid. p. 10. Cf supra pp. 103-4.

The rules which we observe and the duties which we perform in accordance with the species of social requirements so far discussed are not in any way sources of inspiration or exaltation. They could not be so without changing their nature. We do not feel proud or gratified to have paid our income tax or parked our car clear of the Fire Station exit. These are hypothetical imperatives which society imposes for its own preservation and the furtherance of its interests, and complete adherence to these aims, though it may constitute the good citizen, does not suffice to make the good man, at least by the highest standards. Between the nation and humanity lies the distance separating the finite and the indefinite, between the closed and the open.[1] Bergson shares the view of André Lalande, that attachment to family, party or nation does not show so much an ever-widening sympathy, liberating us from the demands of egoism, as a partiality and limited loyalty, even perhaps a sublimated self-love which is different in kind from the universal love of humanity, the *agape* which is the true negation of all power-seeking.

What difference can be found between the closed and the open moralities?

Whereas the former is all the more unalloyed and perfect precisely in proportion as it is the more readily reduced to impersonal formulae, the second, in order to be fully itself, must be incarnate in a privileged person who becomes an example. The generality of the one consists in the universal acceptance of a law, that of the other in a common imitation of a model.[2]

This states unambiguously the opposition between universalist and existentialist ethics: the one belongs to the world of legislation, the other to that of inspiration. Closed morality is social, open morality is what Bergson calls 'human',[3] and the use of the word 'human' here we must understand in the sense in which Sartre uses it in the expression 'human reality': a morality or a reality in which the person is the origin and measure of the world which he bodies forth by his own participation. The social is

[1] ibid. p. 21.   [2] ibid. p. 23.   [3] ibid. p. 23.

restrictive, tending to dehumanize, the human is expansive and moving constantly away from the objectified values embodied in maxims and universal, impersonal ordinances. 'Whereas natural obligation is a pressure or a propulsive force, complete and perfect morality has the effect of an appeal.'[1]

There is no natural progression from one to the other. As we have seen, a limited loyalty, however intense, is of a different nature, and the move from the closed to the open is by way of what existentialists would call a leap, or conversion. There is absolute discontinuity between the two worlds: 'it is not by a process of expansion of the self that we can pass from the first state to the second'.[2] What force, at least, corresponds here to social pressure? asks Bergson, and concludes, reasonably enough, that apart from instinct and habit, only feeling can exert a direct action on the will. Strong feeling, passion in fact, has something in common with obligation; it exerts a compelling force on its victim, who is not necessarily under the illusion, at the outset, that he is pursuing his own pleasure. His future may be fraught with tragedy and he may be aware of this, but it makes no difference. The tragedy of passion in conflict with obligation resembles the situation of the man faced with a truly 'costing' moral choice. So creative activity in art, science and civilization, says Bergson, is owed most often to new feelings, felt and communicated through the force of great personality or ability, or both.

It is interesting to observe that Bergson, in his conception of the open morality, stands at the end of one tradition, and at the beginning of another related one. In regarding open morality as owed to a model who is imitated, and who initiates a new way of feeling, Bergson looks back to the philosophy, and more particularly the Christology, of the quasi-Hegelian tradition of Strauss, Feuerbach and Renan. Divinity is incarnated through history in exceptional individuals. Jesus, said Renan, brought into existence a new manner of feeling, and this is the novelty of Christianity. Humanity puts the best of itself into its gods and heroes; such is the message of these incarnationists. Now more recently, although of course we have had the philosophy of per-

[1] op. cit. pp. 23-4.   [2] ibid. p. 27.

sonalism and of the concrete situation, the existentialist emphasis on transcendence makes the repetition or imitation of a model or example almost a betrayal, and I think we shall need to look beyond the cult of the moral hero for the nature of authenticity.

Bergson examines the working of creativeness, and points out that emotion can be either owed to an anterior idea or representation, its status being then that of an induced or secondary experience, or it can relate to an idea which it brings about, thus becoming a cause and no longer an effect. The spontaneity of emotions, which in most people await the stimulus of something outside them, is the prime requirement of the creative artist, and Bergson draws no significant distinction between artistic and moral creation. Such intellectual power as is needed to provide moral revolutions is infused with feeling, and the amalgam is 'the intelligence which invents', and which is to be distinguished from and preferred to 'that intelligence which understands, discusses, accepts or rejects – which in a word limits itself to criticism',[1] and is what (literally in a word) Bergson always understands by reason.

From this point Bergson's distinction between the closed and open ethic is very similar to M. Raymond Polin's between norms and values in *La Création des valeurs*. Bergson says that the idea that the social order exerts a pressure on the individual must seem reasonably obvious, but that many people will find it difficult to understand how creative morality can exert the attraction of an emotion which we desire to share. And this, he adds, is because we cannot usually rediscover the original emotion in ourselves. But (and here he is close to M. Polin) we can find 'formulae which are the residue of this emotion'[2] (Polin would say: norms which are the residue of this value). Bergson constantly presents the closed value as something solidified and immanent in material reality, in contrast with the open or true value which is transcendent and derealized in the fire which burns in creative activity and its communication, and there alone. The original French brings out better than the translation, excellent as this is, the antithesis of real and ideal, of material and spiritual, which I

[1] ibid. p. 33.　　　　[2] ibid. p. 37.

wish to emphasize.[1] He characteristically reduces the distinction to that 'between repose and movement',[2] and this accounts for the ease with which closed morality, compared with the other, can be described and formulated. Intelligence and language deal with things, but are less at home in representing transitions or progressions. 'The morality of the Gospels is essentially that of the open soul.' In the Sermon on the Mount Jesus contrasts the universalized social ethic (Ye have heard that it was said . . .) with his own message (I say unto you . . .). The conventional morality is not discarded but comes to be seen as comprising so many particular instances of a dynamic teaching. We have, says Bergson significantly, a comparable relationship between pagan and Christian morality as between the mathematics of the ancient world and the differential calculus.

Still more interesting than Bergson's consideration of Christianity is what he has to say about Socrates. Here is a man whose teaching contradicts his personality. The teaching is the apotheosis of the activity of reason, and for Bergson, of static reason. The aim of the dialogues is the production of concepts amenable to definition. Furthermore he applies this logical approach to ethics, and makes a science of virtue itself: 'he identifies the practice of good with our knowledge of it',[3] and aims to absorb moral life into the rational function of thought. Yet this supreme apostle of reason has a mission enjoined by the oracle of Delphi; he is poor, and must remain so; he must be a man of the people and speak their language; his teaching is an oral one because his words must be a living force; he is capable of enjoying the good things of life, yet he can also withstand cold and hunger; he is guided by his 'daemon' to the end.[4] In short he is a mystic, whose 'teaching, so perfectly rational, hinges on something that seems to transcend pure reason',[5] and this can be detected in parts of his doctrine. Socrates may be described as an open soul who set the feet of philosophy firmly on the path of closed rationalism and

[1] See *Les Deux Sources de la morale et de la religion*, F. Alcan, 12th ed. 1932, p. 46.

[2] *The Two Sources*, tr. Audra and Brereton, p. 45.

[3] ibid. p. 47.   [4] ibid. p. 48.   [5] ibid. p. 48.

morality, and may not this, I wonder, still be the path of true virtue, taking everything into account? It is a question which I shall discuss.

It is interesting to note that the words 'repetition' and 'creation' are used of the two moralities; we shall encounter them elsewhere, notably in M. V. Jankélévitch, where they designate key concepts. Bergson says that somewhere between them lie detachment and contemplation, which have attracted some of the greatest minds, among them Plato and Aristotle, and which are a meeting ground for thinkers of many persuasions. Nevertheless this detachment is no more than a 'half-virtue'. The belief that complete virtue is inseparable from action, and the deprecation of detachment and contemplation, are typical of a thoroughly modern attitude, perhaps regrettably.

Justice is pre-eminently the field in which the dual morality manifests itself. There is the justice which is dispensed in law-courts, where existing legislation is interpreted and applied. This is closed justice, quantitatively established, and represented as holding the scales for the precise apportionment of what the law lays down. Equity here signifies equality, and originates in exchange and barter, which involved the exact assessment of the value of the objects exchanged. This concept of justice relating to objects is eventually extended to cover intercourse between persons, in which the idea of obligation attaches itself to that of equity in the exchange of actions. So injury naturally seems to demand an equal reciprocity.

What bridge is there from this justice which, sophisticated though it may be, is 'none the less faithful to its mercantile origins',[1] to the justice expressing the inviolability of rights and the impossibility of measuring the human person in terms of any values whatsoever? Retrospectively we think we see the gradual evolution of justice from a primitive state of injustice. The possible is conceived as pre-existing in the real, and awaiting its inevitable turn to come on to the stage of history. But Bergson rejects this and takes a forward-looking viewpoint. It is easy to be wise after the event and see a progression in what has happened.

[1] ibid. p. 56.

At some point, however, there is discontinuity; a 'leap' has occurred which in prospect was unforeseeable. It is clear that this must be so, for the state of mind of a community cannot be in process of constant evolution towards, for instance, the 'rights of man'. From time to time exceptional individuals must come forward and persuade society to change its attitude and its institutions. There is, set over against the closed morality of law, 'a series of appeals made to the conscience of each of us by persons who represent the best there is in humanity'.[1]

Now at this point a serious difficulty arises. I have had occasion to point out its counterpart in discussing open rationalism,[2] and shall show how it bedevils the concept of existentialist authenticity, as this affects the individual's moral choices. What is 'the best in humanity'? There seems to be some question-begging here. Bergson appears to conclude, in spite of himself, that there is a 'pre-existing entity' corresponding in some way to the ultimate goal of open morality, into which 'reality is . . . eating its way, . . . incorporating into itself, bit by bit, the totality of eternal justice'.[3] Bergson is practising what he has condemned when, having read the ideal of universal brotherhood into the historical succession of prophets, Gospels, American Puritans and the men of the French Revolution, he assumes, or appears to assume, that this ideal is the *absolute* ideal to which future mankind is committed further to approximate, even though that future is unpredictable! There seems to be the implicit assumption that something like assimilation is the guiding force of human destiny, that it must triumph, and that it must be good. But this is surely an example of the naturalistic fallacy. Any evolutionary or involutionary ethic must be a source of confusion, since it will have to ignore or misinterpret any moral backsliding in history, of which there is plenty by any standard. There will also be an almost inevitable tendency to transfer 'goodness' from the outcome of progress to progress itself.

It may be said in reply that Bergson conceives open morality not as something progressive, but as enunciated early in history

[1] *The Two Sources*, tr. Audra and Brereton, p. 68.
[2] See supra, pp. 110–13.   [3] op. cit. p. 63.

and periodically reiterated subsequently, so that men are from time to time being reminded of an eternal excellence to which they must try to conform. This ideal was capable of being stated early because 'there was no question here of clear-cut wisdom, reducible from beginning to end, into maxims. There was rather a pointing of the way . . .'[1] Since maxims could be dispensed with, no heed had to be taken of particular circumstances, historical, geographical or sociological. The open morality aims to inspire, and once inspiration is at work, the relevant means will be found and will form the newest embodiment of the eternally valid truth. But restatements of a general moral appeal can be subtly varied to the extent of producing historical results bearing no relation to each other. Some of the most tightly closed systems of morality have been ostensibly based on the open appeal of the Gospels. The revolutionary tradition, which springs from individualistic urges, has produced not a few repressive régimes. Even what is surely the basic general precept of all civilized life: Do to others as you would wish them to do to you, is liable to be stultified in practice by the extent to which people are prepared to be treated in different ways. The amounts of discipline which people are willing to put up with, and the sources from which they wish to see it come, vary enormously. One has only to consider the persecution of non-union workers, who resent tyranny from their fellows, by union members, who resent tyranny from their employers. In the army one man takes the hectoring of his superiors as a personal insult, another sees it as a comical affectation.

There is probably in the last resort no wisdom which is not reducible to maxims, since the difference between the closed and open morality is the difference between straightforward orders relating to one specified kind of behaviour (e.g. Thou shalt not kill), and what one might call *dispositional* recommendations which cover a great variety of actions and attitudes, and the relevance of which it is the moral agent's business to judge and act upon (Blessed are the poor in spirit). But the second category of dispositional precepts is further reducible to specific orders, which are always implied even if they are not stated.

[1] ibid. p. 62.

RELIGION

In proclaiming a morality either of the closed or open type we are concerned to influence action. We may do this by direct precept, or we may do it in a second-order fashion by means of indirect or dispositional exhortations; in either case we make some sort of appeal to human initiative, whether in others or, as when we act 'on principle', in ourselves. Moral influence is turned inwards towards the human.

When our initiatives are turned outwards *from* the human we have, objectively, scientific activity, and subjectively, magic or mysticism, the two poles of religion, to which Bergson turns his attention in the second part of his book. 'Static' religion is first dealt with. Just as static or closed morality consists of set precepts with which to meet types of action or situation, so static religion consists of formulable beliefs and rites; it is the body of doctrine to which people subscribe and the forms of worship or propitiation through which they go, and by which they provide evidence of their adherence to such and such a faith.

Bergson looks for the origin of the need thus satisfied, and from this point his treatise takes on, it must be admitted, more the character of primitive psychology than of philosophy. The characteristic of primitive religion is myth-making, and the social function of this is to provide a barrier against the disruptive activity of intelligence, which at all levels works against instinct, and which at this level is likely to bring a discouraging realization of individual limitation, without conferring much practical power to counteract such discouragement. To be dispirited in face of the irremediable is bad for the individual, and, by weakening, however little, his will to live, is also against the interest of the community. It is for this reason that suicide may be a crime, and that belief in immortality, which counteracts a sense of the futility of life, is regarded as beneficial. 'Religion is then a defensive reaction of nature against the dissolvent power of intelligence.'[1]

Intelligence is inseparable from conscious action, and in primitive societies much of what is done in the interest of all is done unquestioningly and even by force of habit, and it is to some extent

[1] op. cit. p. 101.

desirable that this should be so, for to question law would be to weaken it. Any distinction between laws and customs is blurred, and the compelling force of one, as in the case of natural and man-made laws, is confused with that of the other. What is expected of the individual in relation to the group assumes a religious significance, and, Bergson adds, it becomes clearer, when we study primitive cultures, what relation religion bears to morality.[1] Originally morality is co-extensive with custom, which is con-secrated by religion; thus an attempt to separate morality and religion in primitive societies is vain. In such societies morality is closed and aims at the protection of the community, which is conceived as the preservation of the social *status quo*. The danger is that the individual may come to think of himself as significant as an individual, and question, for example, the value of his life in the light of his mortality. Religion and morality then become 'a defensive reaction of nature against intelligence'. It is interesting to recall that Renan, in later life, was worried by the prospect that the majority of people might abandon their religious belief, and that human destiny might, in consequence, be controlled by un-trammelled intelligence! If the analytical and critical activity of intelligence were allowed free play it would reveal the hollowness of 'ultimate' aims and values, and the will to act would be thereby weakened. It is possible, says Renan, that dead planets are planets where life has defeated itself by the excessive cultivation of the intellect. This, of course, is a pessimistic version of the assimilatory view of intelligence and reason put forward, optimistically, by André Lalande. Renan stresses the affinity of reason and entropy, Lalande that of reason and altruism. For primitive man, however, as Bergson and Renan see him, reason is the way towards anti-social temptation, and the social significance of myth-making is seen in the fact that the myth always bears traces of its origin, in that 'it will never clearly distinguish between the physical order and the social and the moral order, between intentional orderliness due to the obedience of all to a law, and the orderliness manifested in the course of nature. . . . Does not the word "order" signify both system and command?'[2]

[1] ibid. p. 102.   [2] ibid. p. 103.

Bergson then enters on a discussion of the rudimentary creations of the myth-making function, and shows how these appear
virtually unchanged in civilized man. The myth, with its
humanized figures, is, after all, already a sophisticated product.
But the taboos and reassurances which are needed to reconcile
the individual's behaviour with the needs of his group are more
numerous than can be built into coherent accounts or made into
the content of ritual. We have in consequence a kind of fragmentary myth-making function which produces *ad hoc* bridges
between reality as it is and as we would have it. Such are, not only
the belief in immortality which is required in a society which
consists merely of individuals, without any material structures
which withstand the ravages of time, but also the animist tendency
to invoke individual spirits, friendly or hostile, which inhabit the
objects and places of everyday life. These fill up, so to speak, the
unmanageable gaps in experience, presenting an element of personality which can be propitiated, or at least in some way ration-
alized as continuous with those other parts of experience which
are under human control. Man thus inhabits a world which is
'physiognomic', as Werner terms it, and has a kind of animated
responsiveness, real or imagined, to our requirements. Phenomenology, with its 'intentional' world, is, among other things, a
reminder of the role of this physiognomic realm in civilized man.

Bergson emphasizes that this fabrication of intentional entities
is the work of intelligence, which thus erects a barrier against the
depressing incursion into human life of inanimate, meaningless
and random reality (the concept of which is itself the work of
intelligence). It becomes clear, I think, how a sympathetic study
of 'primitive' mentality throws light on modern misgivings about
the 'dehumanizing' potentiality of science which, it is feared,
will reduce everything to mechanism, even human feelings and
motives. These anxieties can fairly be described as constituting a
neo-primitivism in that they call for the maintenance of an area of
extra-instrumental reality which it is felt proper not to try to
dominate, and which calls rather for propitiation. Bergson will
have nothing of the attempt to find the true origin of science in
magic, for he says, rightly I think, that they have essentially

different functions and different provinces. Science deals with natural causality, which both primitive and civilized man accept and use; magic deals with supernatural causality which is analogous to human will and has to be induced, just as men are persuaded, or even threatened.[1] It seems strange that Bergson should see the myth-making function as a case of nature's turning intelligence against itself. Most of us would disqualify superstition from any identification with intelligence in any form. It is, however, consistent with Bergson's dualistic tendency to classify any non-intuitive mental activity as intellectual. We should realize that this 'primitive' dovetailing of the two orders of causality into a well-articulated picture of reality is, however unscientific, at least a piece of synthesis. Closed religion has this in common with closed morality, that it can be described. What Bergson contrasts with it is mystical communion with reality.

Interesting examples are given of the eking out of causal by magical connection, and of the ways in which nature fills the 'discouraging margin of the unforeseen'. A man aims an arrow, taking account of the relevant physical factors and forces. But once the arrow is released the man's control over it is at an end, and postulated forces, hostile or friendly, take over, which either speed it to its target or deflect it. A chain of causes and effects is begun, and at first everything depends on oneself; only when one can no longer affect the situation is one tempted to invoke an extra-mechanical power. Human activity is associated with events both predictable and unpredictable, and the tendency, among savages obviously, among civilized men less obviously, is to import some kind of purposive force into the domain of hazard which then acquires a kind of self-contradictory nature. The gambler sees luck or ill-luck as an occult intention.[2] He has made an initial choice and on this he superimposes a choice similar to, but independent of, his own. Soldiers in the First World War, Bergson reports an officer as saying, feared bullets more than shells, though shells caused more casualties. The reason for this

---

[1] There are cases of savages belabouring idols which have not served the tribe well.

[2] op. cit. pp. 121–2.

was that they felt that bullets were aimed at them, whereas it was realized that shells fell at random; one's own death could not be caused by a blind force, but only by something intentional. The fact is that absence of intention is almost inconceivable. The very word chance exists only because 'some human interest is at stake'.[1] A tile falling to the ground is simply a mechanical event; if it kills someone we see the event as having human significance, so that 'chance is then mechanism behaving as though possessing an intention', but, seen in detachment, it is an intention 'emptied of its content'.

These intentions present themselves to us as incomplete personalities. Bergson cites William James's description of his experience of the San Francisco earthquake.[2] For science the word 'earthquake' is the name of the collective phenomena; for James at the time, the 'earthquake' was the *cause* of the tremors; it was a kind of maleficent personality, but of a peculiar kind: it was incomplete, a mere element of personality. This incompleteness of personality consists in its lack of the potentiality, which a complete human personality would possess, to produce anything different from the set of acts which it does in fact perform. It seemed that the earthquake was *behind* the phenomena as an agent is *behind* his acts.[3] Yet the agent is the earthquake itself and has no independent activity or property, it is what it does. Such an entity, whose being is one and the same as its appearance, whose intention is immanent in its acts, is what Bergson calls an element of personality.[4] The earthquake was 'an individual with no body of its own, for it was nothing but a combination of circumstances, but it had a soul, a very elementary one, hardly distinguishable from the intention apparently manifested by circumstances'.[5] Now the kind of animism by which an accident 'carves itself out a place in the continuity of the real', has a function. It makes fear tolerable by conferring a certain human quality on the object of fear, which

---

[1] op. cit. p. 124.   [2] ibid. pp. 129 ff.

[3] Is he? A behaviouristic philosophy of the kind propounded in *The Concept of Mind* shows how complicated the notion really is. Bergson sees intention worked into blind reality. Professor Ryle sees even intentional action as merely what it is.

[4] op. cit. p. 131.   [5] ibid. p. 133.

is viewed as 'a bad lot', no doubt, but nevertheless as one of us, something in a sense understandable, and with which a kind of fellowship is possible. This reduces terror and gives to the most alien forms of experience a familiarity, and to the weak human individual a feeling of being at home in a universe much of which is hostile to him and beyond his control. The euphoria which can be extracted from misfortune may even include a feeling of gratification at being singled out, and thus flattered by fate. That an accident, if sufficiently sensational, should happen to me rather than to another seems to imply some preference for me personally. Thus the universe, if not exactly comparable to Prospero's island, which was full of noises that give delight and hurt not, is at least peopled with pseudo-intentions, with which we contrive to place ourselves on a footing of 'familiarity which puts us at our ease, relieves the strain, and disposes us quite simply to do our duty'.[1]

The function of myth-making is thus a moral one.[2] The difference between magic and science is the difference between desiring and willing. Science deals with what can be manipulated, magic reconciles us to the world. Bergson says that the myth is the creation of intelligence working, under the pressure of instinct, against its own overweening pervasiveness. It might be truer to say that it is imagination taking over where intelligence leaves off, but owing its existence to the glimpses of the greater power which the manipulative successes of *homo faber* afford. Static religion is what makes good any deficiency of attachment to life brought about by inadequate power.

Now this escape from limitation has its 'open' counterpart, which bears to it the same relation as open morality to closed. It is mysticism, the identification of the human will with the divine. This may, of course, be socially unfruitful, in which case it is hardly preferable to the myth-making of the primitive mind; it is then merely escapism. Such was the mysticism of Buddhism, which was not a 'complete mysticism',[3] for this would have to comprise 'action, creation, love'. The traditional Hindu mystic was a pessimist; he did not believe in the efficacy of human action, for he felt himself 'crushed by nature';[4] disease and famine were

[1] ibid. p. 134.   [2] ibid. p. 138.   [3] ibid. p. 192.   [4] ibid. p. 193.

evils against which he was powerless to fight effectively. Complete
mysticism, however, is dependent on a faith which moves moun-
tains. When occidental inventiveness and energy have been
harnessed to it, it has produced, within Christianity, Bergson
maintains, a religion of humanity committed to the active transformation of life. It is a vision with the will to produce the means
to its realization. What is certainly questionable is Bergson's
further assertion that 'its direction is exactly that of the vital
impetus; it *is* this impetus itself'.[1] This is, of course, to put forward
an evolutionary ethic, and we have already considered, and shall
consider further, the case against it.

Whether or not it is true that the 'élan vital' is a force tending
to promote universal and indivisible love, which Lalande would
deny quite flatly, Bergson sees such a movement towards universalism as good. Moreover, like Lalande, he sees the widening
of the field of human sympathy as progress, but whereas for
Lalande this movement is a continuous process of assimilation,
for Bergson there is absolute discontinuity between the open and
the closed society. They are not of the same essence.[2]

Yet to some extent Bergson is obliged to contradict himself,
otherwise his book could have no unity. At the beginning of
Chapter 3, devoted to dynamic religion, which is 'open' religion,
he asks whether one is justified in using one word, religion, for
two activities which are so different in nature; and his answer is a
qualified affirmative. Religion is what sustains in man the will to
live which, in animals, is purely instinctive. Through a superfluity
of intelligence, which involves and makes explicit foresight, man
sees clearly his position and potentiality; he realizes his mortality
and is exposed to a sense of futility. He is even more in danger of
succumbing to egoism, which is counselled by intelligence.[3] Intelligence, as Bergson sees it, then comes to its own rescue and fills
in the gaps which man the artificer has left. I have already criticized
the assertion that myth-making is an activity of intelligence, and
it is already clear also that the view can be plausibly advanced that
the evolutionary drive is diametrically opposed to the work of
reason. What leads Bergson to attribute such limited and curious

[1] op. cit. p. 201.   [2] ibid. p. 230.   [3] ibid. p. 179.

functions to reason and intelligence is that for him it is static, and opposed to dynamic *duration*. Therefore whatever can be formulated, whatever 'carves itself out a place in the continuity of the real'[1] and has a shape in the *Gestalt* sense, receives thereby an objective existence and must be considered the outcome of intellectual effort. This, I think, is overstraining any legitimate meaning one can attach to the word 'intelligence', but it permits Bergson to throw into the desired relief the intuitive character of open morality and religion, which cannot, except retrospectively, be formulated and objectified. Perhaps the nature of myth-making 'intelligence' is best expressed in these words:

> We know that all around intelligence there lingers still a fringe of intuition, vague and evanescent. Can we not fasten upon it, intensify it, and above all, consummate it in action, for it has become pure contemplation only through a weakening in its principle,[2] and, if we may put it so, by an abstraction practised on its own substance?[3]

Whatever the origin and nature of the myth-making function, however, its office is comparable at the static and dynamic levels: it is the restoration to man of active conviction. In static religion, however, it is attachment to life on the part of the individual for the benefit of the group which is at stake, whereas in dynamic religion anxiety for the future and apprehensive self-centredness have been left behind; 'now detachment from each particular thing would become attachment to life in general'.[4] One can say that security and serenity are here achieved, not by propping up the apparently faltering purposefulness of life, but by seeing one's own life and everybody else's as intrinsically valuable, by arriving at a view of existence as something worthwhile in itself. This kind of conviction in the form which Bergson has in mind, a feeling of mystical oneness with what is intuitively seized as the absolute, is rare. It is supremely valuable and ensures the humanity of man. Static religion is by comparison a poor thing, yet it is dignified by being a guarantee of the dynamic kind, however debased the

[1] ibid. p. 133. [2] Presumably intelligence's. [3] op. cit. p. 180.
[4] ibid. p. 181.

forms which it may occasionally assume. Warring nations profess
to invoke the aid of a God of humanity whose cause they are in
fact betraying, since their appeal is merely to a tribal god.[1] Yet
this is merely a failure, grave though it may be, to rise from the
letter of religion to its spirit; it should not discredit the reality of
the ideal. And as long as the formula is retained, it may play the
part of a truly magic incantation, and fire a spirit capable of understanding and acting upon it.[2] So an indifferent schoolmaster,
mechanically teaching the truths discovered by great men, 'may
awaken in one of his pupils the vocation he himself has never
possessed'.

The case which one is tempted to make in reply against closed
cults of all kinds is that they most often do their preordained work
only too well, and reconcile man to an imaginary world instead
of stimulating him to undertake the uncomfortable task of seeking
reality. 'Who knows that the truth may not be sad?' asked Renan.
Open morality, like open rationalism, is adventurous and generally proceeds by the discarding of old models which are seen to be
inadequate. The ethical conservative is the sole guide to the way
of comfort and consolation, as Bergson would have realized if he
had not become confused as to the nature of intelligence (which
is *not* what psycho-analysts call rationalization), and been in effect
unable to make up his mind whether mental activity and mental
inertia are the same thing or opposites. This much may be said,
however, in support of his presentation of static religion as the
servant of the dynamic, that ideals imperfectly lived up to are
better than no ideals at all, provided that the ideal remains a
genuine objective, and that failure to conform to it is not taken as
the necessary human condition, and a state of sin complacently
accepted and even flaunted.

The *Two Sources* is a stimulating book, but one in which Bergson
uses self-stultifying concepts. We have seen how the idea of
intelligence is one of these. Another, in this context at least, is the
élan vital, which appears to be a kind of evolutionary principle, yet
aiming at the triumph of spirit over matter, hence involutionary
rather, and yet also unpredictable, therefore surely random.

[1] op. cit. p. 183.   [2] ibid.

'Nature' produces man, the pride of creation, whose intelligence overshoots nature's intention. Nature therefore contrives that man shall, by a further exercise of 'intelligence' in the shape of the myth-making function, be reconciled to that purpose. But then, at a more evolved stage of humanity, mysticism, related to but different 'in essence' from the myth-making function, again turns the tables on nature by producing universal love and the democratic mood, 'a mighty effort in a direction contrary to that of nature'.[1] Bergson tries to achieve too great a synthesis of philosophical, psychological and sociological concepts. I consider that Lalande's *Les Illusions évolutionnistes* shows a more consistent argument. Bergson, however, has much that is relevant to my purpose. He clearly tries to show 'open' morality as what existentialists would call 'authentic'. It is dynamic, and dependent on constant vigilance and spiritual activity; it is opposed to 'objectified' precepts and rites, which belong to an inferior and more habitual morality. This closed morality, rooted in habit and day-to-day behaviour, prompts an automatic discharge of one's duty, while open morality in a sense transcends all individual duties, and prompts charity. Reason is the instrument by which habitual morality is evolved, intuition the force which produces the higher ethic. This latter differs, however, from Sartrian authenticity in being still linked to universalist values, and in not being an ethically neutral expression of individuality.

10

Involutionary mortality. André Lalande

Whatever the difficulties inherent in the conception of an evolutionary ethic, it might be thought that any involutionary morality must necessarily be 'closed', in the Bergsonian sense of the word. Reason, one might argue, will want to schematize situations and

[1] ibid. p. 244.

human responses to them, and will accordingly busy itself with the formulation of precepts. It will be easy to slip from this assumption to the further assumption that assimilation works against individuality and favours authority and uniformity. I think, in fact, that the existentialist complaint against reason and rationalist ethics amounts to saying that it stifles individuality and makes conformists of us all. But Lalande's thesis does not bear this out; his morality of involution is not the answer to a dictator's prayer. Indeed he attacks Renan's *Dialogues philosophiques* for the much-discussed passage in which Renan supposes the end of the evolutionary process to be the concentration of all matter into a single, all-embracing living organism.[1] This, of course, is genuine evolutionism (carried, it is true, on to a metaphysical plane) as Lalande has defined it, for a single expansive and acquisitive will is imagined as having prevailed over all matter and drawn it into its service. Moreover since, in Renan's image, we are presented with the apotheosis of assimilation, one being absorbing all things, it is desirable to clarify Lalande's conception of involution.

Renan's evolution carried to the extreme, with its 'dream of the whole universe integrated into a single organism', is not what Lalande understands by progress towards identity. At this stage of his book he has already shown society as evolving in all its aspects *away from* a state in which human beings are subordinated to a function, as the organs of the body exist merely in order to ensure the body's general health. Specialization is not a manifestation of progress, but of a material need; progress consists in mitigating this servitude to biological necessity, and in freeing ourselves from the function whereby we maintain ourselves and the society to which we belong.[2] The family has gradually weakened, to a large extent under the attacks of revolutionary principles, from being the tightly knit patriarchal unit of former times, women have won their emancipation, do work previously regarded as men's, and think and behave more like men. People bear to a lesser extent in modern times the stamp of their occupation, and certainly reduce to a minimum the distinctive dress and external signs of their profession or trade. In short, people, if no

[1] Cf *Les Illusions évolutionnistes*, p. 367.   [2] ibid. p. 273.

less functional, are less dominated by function, they have more leisure in which to escape from it, and more time to do what they want to do. So we see that the involutionary process has weakened society, in a sense, but freed the individual. Formerly, in Renan's words, the majority enjoyed life vicariously, and served the artistic and decorative life of society which was enjoyed by only a few. Now everyone can take pleasure in science, art and the good things of life which, Lalande adds somewhat confusingly, 'deny and efface the individual'.[1] He is in fact here contrasting the cultural assimilation inherent in art with the aggressive forms of ostentation and self-display which are the less admirable sides of human nature. But in order to make the position clear I think we need to distinguish two aspects of involution, as far as its end-product is concerned. It reduces, through its action on society, the functional role and the consequent blinkered dependence of the individual, and frees him so that he can be himself. But, in his newly found freedom to mix, on a functionless basis, with his fellows, he will pursue, this time in a human context, the aim of assimilation, by seeking to communicate with them on a deeper level than that of casual, day-to-day intercourse, and in this the resources of art and the instrument of reason will be his medium.

I think it must be admitted, however, that Lalande has in mind, as the involutionary goal, some culturally – though not politically – functional role of intellectual effort. This impression is strengthened if one takes into account his own main life's work, which is his justly famous dictionary of philosophical terms.[2] His contribution has been an essentially assimilatory one, promoting the spread of ideas and laudably insisting on effective communication by means of a universally understood terminology, but it is not individualistic. He has indeed subordinated the claims of his own individuality to an ideal of collective enlightenment, and the ambiguity of his involutionary ideal,[3] which hesitates whether to be or not to be individualistic, reflects the dual character of mental activity: it communicates what one has to communicate and to

[1] ibid. p. 365.
[2] *Vocabulaire technique et critique de la philosophie*, edited by Lalande.
[3] See *Les Ill. év.* pp. 406–9.

contribute towards a common level of knowledge and understanding, and at the same time it imparts what one has it in one
to impart. The universalist stresses one aspect and points to the
ideal of the ultimate equality of the spirit, the existentialist is
uninspired by this and prizes the gifts of individuality and the
value of the person. Ultimately they are probably inseparable, and
in any case the threat of an onset of intellectual entropy, ending
in a dead level of knowledge and sensibility, seems small.

In the political and sociological fields, however, Lalande leaves
his position in no doubt. Moral values here are opposed to
organicism, that is, to the reduction of the individual to the role
of a cell in a body. Political authoritarianism which teaches that
the state is 'higher' than the individual is appealing to a popular
version, one may say perversion, of evolutionism, and its fallacy
is to carry merely one stage further the individual's quest of
power, in which he vainly tries to ignore mortality and the ultimate fate of all things and activities, which is to sink into eventual
oblivion. Plain imperialism and tyranny are easily seen to fall into
this category, but what of a would-be involutionary authority, the
state which by its laws and actions tries to promote equality,
fellow-feeling and fusion among its citizens? This, says Lalande,[1]
is a contradiction in terms. Persecution, pacification, forcible
unification are always doomed to failure, for they bring about an
equal and opposite reaction. Force, to whatever end, even war to
end war, defeats its own object. Communism, which began as an
involutionary force, as a protest, that is, against inequality,
economic anarchy, plutocracy and the exploitation involved in
'free enterprise', soon betrayed its own principles by incorporating
evolutionist theories which were in the air at the time of its birth.
It adopted the 'essentially monist' doctrine of economic materialism, which taught that everything, left to itself, moves in the same
desired direction. Originally equalitarian and assimilatory, communism taught that the classless society is to be brought about by
the class war, so that what is hoped for is the subjugation and
elimination of the enemy – an objective taken from the 'old dream
of hegemony'. It is therefore perhaps richer in 'inherent con-

[1] See *Les Ill. év.* p. 444.

tradictions' than capitalism, which has after all a certain militantly expansive, therefore 'evolutionary' coherency.

The truly involutionist society is the one which in a sense works against its own organicist vitality. Yet it does not gain, any more than the individual, from being suicidal. As in the individual, its power for good is to some extent inherent in its organic cohesion.

> Would it not be a great loss to the cause of involution on earth if the most civilized nations should destroy themselves in an excess of involutionist zeal? All spirit of renunciation of individuality is good; all immediate renunciation of life is bad.[1]

Too much education and thought beyond the elementary stage, Lalande goes on (writing of course before the last war), is good in itself, but may have a debilitating effect upon a nation, bringing a reduction in the birth-rate, and causing discouragement among people who may well think themselves, perhaps justifiably, worth more than life has offered them. But all is not loss, for such a nation may, by its influence, exert 'a strong dissolving action' on its more bellicose neighbours, in which case its extinction is not useless, for it has played a part corresponding to that of the saint's heroic individual self-denial. It is only fair in passing to point out, since Lalande has criticized Renan so severely in this book, that Renan said precisely this, namely that France, the land of Joan of Arc and the first country to display militant nationalism, might well lead the way, in her 'decadence', to a higher ideal of international brotherhood. Those works of Renan written soon after the Franco-Prussian War do not show him in his best and most liberal light, and it should perhaps be remembered that the totalitarian visions to which he gave expression in such works as the *Philosophical Dialogues* stemmed from a mood of fear, resentment and pessimism caused by the war with Germany, to which land he owed much, and by the violence of the Commune, which seemed to confirm his worst misgivings about popular rule.

The important point which emerges from these books of Bergson and Lalande is, I think, this. Both evolutionary and involutionary moralities, as expounded by these two writers respectively,

[1] ibid. p. 446.

are incompatible with objectification. Bergson's open morality transcends precepts; it depends on models, on lives which are sources of inspiration, on experiences not amenable to discursive expression; it is dispositional. Lalande sees reason as the principle of involution, and, although his morality at first appears to correspond to Bergson's 'closed' type, it is in fact not so. It is not so much anti-individualistic as anti-organicist. It reconciles the human being to limitation and mortality, not by means of illusions or abnormal experiences, but by reminding him that the impulse to self-assertion and self-perpetuation is not the only fruitful one in human life, or even the more fruitful. It shows that men can be taught to collaborate and communicate, but that they cannot be made to do so, and that no sooner has an organization for the production of universal goodness and the millennium been set up, than the embodiment is seen to be not one of good but of evil. Finally, and surely not least endearingly for English philosophers, Lalande asks:

> For whom have we argued in the last resort, if not for those who already wished to live reasonably and intelligibly, and whose wish to do so was an act of pure good will, which no proof can bring into being?[1]

Now I think it is desirable to end my consideration of the philosophy of Lalande (whose long life has carried him through a number of philosophical climates) by dealing with a small, but significant, book published in 1948, *La Raison et les normes*. This, while reiterating the general argument of his thesis of 1899 and its revised presentation of 1930, does so in the form of a renewed challenge to twentieth-century philosophers of extreme individualism and 'open' thought.

Here the distinction between constituting and constituted reason is developed more fully. What is important is that constituting reason (and this provides a bridge between Lalande's earlier concept and that of reason as negation) is now presented as essentially *normative*. This means that it is not to be seen as hamstrung by a material reality which it exists merely to record, but that it

[1] See *Les Ill. év.* p. 416.

structures that reality. In so far as it is assimilatory, it is so through its *diverse* creations, and is therefore not fundamentally different from reason as Bachelard conceives it.

In presenting his position Lalande is fully aware of the course of recent French thought, and takes full account of it, while generally his argument runs strongly counter to it. Chronological, or homogeneous, or impersonal time is, according to Lalande, a legitimate *defence* against duration, or 'real' time, which we generally find uncongenial and are impelled to resist. This assertion of the superiority of objective time is parallel to Alquié's *intellectual* refusal of time which, if unresisted by the intelligence, degenerates into heterogeneous insignificance, or worse, into an endless passing away of things.[1] The recent tendency to seek, and approve of, such heterogeneity is evidence of a neo-Romantic search for colour, variety and surprise, which has a place in our emotional life, but is no basis for our scientific or even commonsense and everyday living.

The same general analysis is brought to bear on space. Lalande virtually summarizes Merleau-Ponty's arguments concerning the body image as the basis, not the outcome, of objective, geometrical spatiality. Whereas, however, Merleau-Ponty wants to reveal our heterogeneous, neuro-muscular 'spaces' as basic to our behaviour, though recalcitrant to discursive and theoretical description, Lalande is only too content with a situation in which the only space we can talk about is common property, and not that of the man confronting his tasks.[2] The appeal to the basic uniqueness of our behavioural space is, by Lalande's standards, retrograde, in so far as it may imply that this is a more 'real' space. His is a rationalistic faith in progress, measured by the increase of communicability, and of co-operative possibilities offered by the way of thinking which he recommends. He fastens unfailingly upon the ability of science to evolve models of reality in which unsuspected uniformity is shown beneath apparent diversity. Descartes earns particular praise because his bold identification of matter and

[1] 'Au contraire, quelle source de joie que l'Eternel Présent.' op. cit. p. 25.
[2] It is interesting to notice that Lalande refers his reader to discussions of these problems going back to 1901. Cf p. 37, note 1.

extension was in advance of his time. For in the following century scientists were busy drawing up an ever longer list of basic elements. In the nineteenth century and after, however, a more 'Cartesian' road is taken with involutionary hypotheses relating to atomic structure and the assimilation of matter to energy, so that not only were substances revealed as more alike, but more collectively amenable to conceptual and mathematical thought.[1]

One must recognize, however, that despite Lalande's skilfully and plausibly marshalled arguments, any approach to truth based upon a certain fairly arbitrarily selected, though respectable, criterion of validity, in this case universal communicability, has its limitations. Merleau-Ponty, by showing objective space and time as derivative and, because so much a part of our cultural world, so difficult to 'bracket-off' or circumvent, was enabled, paradoxically, to give an account of dynamic and exploratory consciousness, in terms of intentionality and the body image.

Lalande is particularly concerned in this book to emphasize that he too is an individualist, which means neither antisocial nor totalitarian. The antisocial individual goes his own way, hostile to any sharing of possessions or values. The totalitarian conceives society as the organism for which people exist, and to which they must sacrifice their potentialities for human fullness. The totalitarian carries further, with the help of the resources of collectivity, the imperialism and evolutionary drive of the relatively weak individual, but has in common with the Romantic individualist an exclusiveness which runs in the direction of instinct, not of reason. Real individualism, for Lalande, is self-expression serving increased understanding, and commanding spontaneous assent. Moreover, the kind of simplification or uniformization here achieved is simple only in its result, not in the bringing about of it. The working out of a more comprehensive and comprehensible structure may well be within reach only of the most exceptional minds at any time. This is equally true of all forms of creative thinking – political, scientific, artistic and ethical. They are not rigidly divisible into activities which are either factual or normative; they are all essentially normative in that they all require a

[1] op. cit. p. 75.

mind which dominates its material, and applies to it the ultimate
criterion of the superiority of similarity over difference. This does
not mean that all artists should create the same thing, or that all
people should behave in the same way, or that scientists should
promote their theories to the status of eternal truths, for these
are cases of constituted reason. It means that originality should
be at the disposal of all, even though it cannot be the attribute
of all.

It is, naturally, in dealing with scientific truth, and the notion
of fact, as normative, that the argument is most interesting.
Lalande begins by pointing out that though no imperative can
logically follow from an indicative, an indicative may well follow
from an imperative.[1] 'You must, therefore you can' is the type of
conclusion which derives a fact from a value. It is also true that
accepted values become facts, as Raymond Polin also maintains,[2]
but what is more significant here is that facts owe their guarantee
of truth to their normative character. A phenomenon may be
illusory, but a fact is part of reality, a part, however, which is the
logical product of a system of values upon which there is the
greatest measure of agreement, on the one hand with logical
norms, on the other among those most competent to judge. These
forms of agreement constitute objectivity. It is a 'fact' in this sense
that the planets, including the earth, revolve round the sun. The
heliocentric theory, on the other hand, is contrary to our perception, and our reason for conferring the status of 'fact' upon it
is that thereby, rather than by taking perception at its face value,
'do we make more things consistent, uniform or similar to each
other'.

Thus 'norms are more absolute than facts',[3] and the way is
opened for a consideration of the ethical field, and of moral
pioneering, in the chapter entitled 'Les Normes et les faits'.
Lalande begins by quoting persuasive texts which purport to
demonstrate the inherent contradiction in any idea of 'super-
normality' or supererogation. Durkheim, in his *Division du travail
social*, writes: 'Just as play is the aesthetic expression of physical
life, and art of intellectual life, so this activity *sui generis* is the

[1] ibid. p. 168. [2] Cf infra concerning Polin. [3] ibid. p. 170.

aesthetic expression of moral life,' and he adds that there is a
risk of undermining the sense of duty in recognizing a morality
expressed in free individual creation independent of any rule.
Lalande admits the logic of rejecting a morality which neither
accords with moral precept nor, in an ordinary sense, defines it.
Yet he remains unconvinced by this logic. Spencer's father of a
family who, by overworking for his children, shortens his life,
thus depriving them of any support at all, may lack judgement,
but the morality of his behaviour is not in doubt. He has done
more than duty required, and this, in itself, is virtuous. There is
a place for supermorality, which is *of the same nature as morality*,
since it pursues the same anti-vital ends. It is therefore not to be
confused with evil, at least in its intention, which is perhaps the
sole point of view from which morality pure and simple can even
be identified, let alone judged. Again morality, in its creative
aspects, is no different from other forms of originality; 'the in-
ventor lives in contradiction and obscurity as the doctor lives
among bacteria and sickness: in order to get rid of them'.[1] We may
well flout constituted reason in the greater interest of constituting
reason. The negation of order is provisional, and serves the pursuit of a greater order:

> Super-normal values are but strong and exceptional reactions
> in the face of those hostile and inhuman realities against which
> the current norms of justice, art and science teach us how to
> defend ourselves patiently and methodically in the small matters
> of everyday life.[2]

II

The creation of values. Raymond Polin

Now the evolutionary (and involutionary) approach to ethics and
value, which tries to show time as a factor which works, through

[1] op. cit. p. 186.   [2] ibid. p. 194.

one of its essential processes (whether conceived as the life-force or the death-force), is really a form of what English philosophers would condemn as the naturalistic fallacy, and is somewhat old-fashioned. The dichotomy of open and closed morality is, how-ever, still very much a live question, and I want to discuss a book by M. Raymond Polin, *La Création des valeurs*,[1] which takes it up in an existentialist rather than an evolutionist spirit. M. Polin deals in a much more detailed and precise way than Bergson with the difference between static and dynamic morality.

Polin anticipates his conclusion early in the book by stating that a phenomenological search for the essence of value is vain unless it leads to a philosophy of action.[2] He examines the possibility of discovering a basis (*fondement*) of values and quickly concludes that there is none. English-speaking philosophers of the 'emo-tivist' school argue that words are evaluative in so far as they express the 'attitude' of their user towards a thing, situation or action, and that by becoming descriptive, that is, by pointing to empirically observable attributes, they depart from their evalua-tive function. The attempt to dignify any attribute or origin with the status of a guarantee of value is naturalistic and displaces value from where it belongs: in the mind, or more precisely the feelings, of the person making the judgement.[3] Now Polin's position is not vastly different from this, and he certainly arrives at a similar conclusion though at first his argument appears to stress the pure contingency of evaluation. The idea of a *basis* of values, writes Polin,[4] has necessarily two parts. It presupposes firstly the in-trinsic validity of the basis which, to be a guarantee, must be *other* than, or 'transcendent' to, the value. But there must at the same time be the possibility of a comprehensible relationship between the basis and the value thus based. In other words he seems to be pointing out that no real or supposed origin or attribute confers value on a thing.[5] We are inclined to invoke authority as a

---

[1] Presses Universitaires, 1944.   [2] *La Création des valeurs*, p. 3.

[3] Cf A. J. Ayer, 'On the Analysis of Moral Judgements' in *Philosophical Essays*.

[4] *La C. des v.* pp. 12–13.

[5] Cf 'Value derives its being from its exigency and not its exigency from its

guarantee, particularly divine authority. But in invoking an authority we shift the value from the thing judged to the guarantee, and the problem is posed all over again. The authority may be compulsive, but then it is a force and not a moral authority; the very words 'moral authority' being in the nature of oxymoron, though of course we can find a use for them in certain everyday contexts.

In looking for the objectivity of values, then, we are undertaking a wild goose chase. M. Polin reorientates his argument, however, and removes it entirely from ground familiar to the empiricist. To the latter there is a world of things that are, and another, metaphorically speaking, of things that ought to be. To the phenomenologist there is, strictly speaking, no world of things that are, but only of things that are *for me*, that is, valuations. What is present is so loaded with possibilities of being otherwise, some of which will be inevitably realized, that it is in a sense not present at all.[1] Hence the Sartrian 'ambiguity' of our position. Reality is always intentional, which means that it is necessarily seen in the light of our demands. I think the phenomenologist, if forced to use the language of the empiricist, would say that of course a highly artificial abstraction, excluding the 'human' from reality, can be made and is made in scientific thinking, but this is a very specialized thing (one 'perspective' among many) and that 'human reality' is, strictly speaking, a reality in which there is no 'is' but only 'oughts'. This way of looking at things does away with the distinction between subjective and objective: 'the object has meaning only for consciousness. To think is both to have the object in mind as distinct and external, and also as of a piece with and identical to onself.'[2]

---

being'. *Being and Nothingness*, p. 38 (*L'Etre et le néant*, p. 76) '. . . *nothing, absolutely nothing, justifies me in adopting this or that particular value, this or that particular scale of values'*.

[1] Cf 'The For-itself is present to being in the form of flight; The Present is a perpetual flight in the face of being. Thus we have precisely defined the fundamental meaning of the Present: the Present *is not*. The present instant emanates from a realistic and reifying conception of the For-itself . . .' (*Being and Nothingness*, p. 123; *E.N.* p. 168; cf. *E.N.* p. 196).

[2] *La C. des v.* p. 20.

The 'externality' of the object is, therefore, now a relative concept and even a pseudo-concept, for it expresses only the relationship, or one aspect of the relationship, between consciousness and what we are conscious *of*. The general imagery of externality has therefore outlived its usefulness, and, along with the complementary one of coincidence and identity, could well be jettisoned, but instead it is re-applied in almost a diametrically opposed sense. The notions of identity and homogeneity are now made to relate to the static forms which the *intelligence* imposes on its reality in order to make that reality conform to its own nature.[1] This recalls, indeed reproduces, Bergson's theory of intelligence as a practical faculty which distorts the real in the interest of use. Adapting thus our representation of the world to the needs of the intellect is the process of knowing, not of evaluating, and the two are essentially distinct. 'Imagination . . . constitutes the necessary condition of evaluation; we do not directly evaluate the real, or evaluation and immanent knowledge would not be distinguishable.'[2] Evaluation is an operation of transcendence, and so we find the idea of externality re-introduced in a different way.[3] Evaluation is not mere representation, but the demand for *something else*.[4] It outruns the real, and in so far as it refers to reality at all, refers to the action required to fill the gap that is opened by the value-judgement.[5] There is no axiological reality, but only reality without qualification (*tout court*); axiology is exclusively concerned with a manner of conceiving reality in relation to action.[6] 'The transcendent has no present existence; it imagines itself in the future and cannot therefore be "known" by the imagination. The act of imagining is not an act of knowing, for knowledge is directed to the given and remains immanent in it. It is an act of creation.'[7]

The role of imagination in the 'transcendent' process of creation is best discussed in Sartre's *L'Imaginaire*.[8] Here the relations

---

[1] 'Theoretical thought aims, through immanence, at identity.' ibid. p. 109.

[2] *La C. des v.* p. 71; cf also p. 23.

[3] Value is 'external' to the given. p. 63.   [4] ibid. p. 67.

[5] 'The externality, the independence of the transcendent, that void created by negation.' p. 62.

[6] ibid. p. 76.   [7] ibid. p. 63.   [8] Gallimard, 1940.

between what he calls in *Being and Nothingness* the 'in-itself' and
'for-itself' are carefully and perceptively discussed. We are 'in the
world' in time, space and by reason of a host of other specific
relationships. They are the totality of the given, and necessarily
constitute the starting point for each one of us. Once we have
given a shape or sense to our situation we have simultaneously
apprehended by imagination the direction in which we are to
move; we have, so to speak, set time in motion. Theoretically we
might conceive a consciousness which did not imagine, and which
was in consequence completely bogged down (*totalement engluée*[1])
in present existence and incapable of extricating itself from it. In
this case the act of cancellation (*néantisation*) of the existing situation is paralysed, freedom, though there, is undiscovered, and the
individual is 'transfixed by reality and as near as possible to being
a thing'. This is the condition which Sartre calls elsewhere inauthenticity: valuation is suspended and any action which might
flow from it is frozen at its source. But the authentic human condition (if that is not a self-contradictory expression) is one in which
consciousness is achieved by apprehension of a situation and,
simultaneously and necessarily, a *lack*, a *void* is experienced which
the person is impelled to fill. A situation is not an abstract
condition of infinite possibility, but a 'concrete and precise
motive force producing one particular imaginary thing'.[2] Sartre
describes effectively the way in which evaluation is 'built into'
mental activity,[3] but his claim to have shown the 'liaison between
the real and unreal' seems scarcely justified. I find M. Jankélévitch's insistence on the pure contingency of creation more convincing. Perhaps it is this kind of claim made by Sartre which
causes Polin to accuse him of making value an object of knowledge.[4]

To digress for a moment, Sartre's descriptions of the processes
of evaluation and intention in *Being and Nothingness* are particularly
vivid. There is the example of writing by hand in which the writer

---

[1] *L'Imaginaire*, p. 237.   [2] ibid. p. 235.   [3] See ibid. pp. 238–9.
[4] See above, pp. 32–3. Cf Sartre's obscure reference in *B.N.* p. 625
(*E.N.* p. 719) to action which 'is to be considered simultaneously on the
plane of the for-itself and on that of the in-itself'.

is borne on by the 'passive exigency' of the unfinished sentence.[1]
There is the crescent moon which suggests the complete sphere.[2]
There are the values which 'spring up like partridges' as I move
forward.[3] The For-itself is the upsurge of negation.[4] The world is
peopled with demands,[5] each of which shows itself as a 'lack' or
absence.[6] It is through human reality that lack comes to things in
the form of 'potency', of 'incompletion', of 'suspension', of
'potentiality',[7] that, in short, value comes into the world.[8] The
question is: how do these partial representations, so to speak,
suggest their own completion? Taking Sartre's work as a whole,
he is as committed, in answering, to 'transcendence', to seeing the
creation of value as an unaccountable 'rupture with the given',[9] to
contingency in short, as anyone. The moral agent is 'the being by
whom values exist',[10] who brings to a situation something that it
does not contain and who, by action, leaves it behind him as a
part of history. This past is 'value reversed', 'the indicative from
which no imperative can be deduced.'[11] Similarly, in the purely
intellectual sphere, Descartes apprehended simultaneously his
doubt and the possibility of its being dispelled.[12] No content of
consciousness is strictly speaking *nothing but* itself. Husserl is
castigated for seeing consciousness as too self-subsistent: consciousness of reading is consciousness of reading *this book*, consisting of pages already read and others still to be read, not of this
letter, this word or this sentence. If we try to pin down precisely
what it is that 'spreads' consciousness beyond the instantaneous
impression (which is in fact the same thing as asking what *constitutes* such an impression), we must necessarily postulate something beyond the given which is not 'given', or 'present' or
objectifiable, yet which has a certain being, of a special kind. 'The
being of the self . . . is value. . . . Value has being, as value; but

---

[1] *B.N.* p. 36 (*E.N.* p. 74).   [2] *B.N.* p. 86 (*E.N.* p. 129).
[3] *B.N.* p. 38 (*E.N.* p. 76).   [4] *B.N.* p. 88 (*E.N.* p. 131).
[5] *B.N.* p. 39 (*E.N.* p. 76).   [6] *B.N.* p. 88 (*E.N.* p. 131).
[7] *B.N.* p. 196 (*E.N.* p. 246).   [8] *B.N.* p. 93 (*E.N.* p. 137).
[9] *B.N.* p. 478 (*E.N.* p. 558).   [10] *B.N.* p. 627 (*E.N.* p. 722).
[11] *B.N.* p. 120 (*E.N.* p. 164).
[12] *B.N.* p. 100 (*E.N.* p. 144). '...la possibilité toujours ouverte pour lui
qu'une évidence le "lève" '.

this normative existent has no being as reality.'[1] Value is con-substantial with the for-itself;[2] but we have seen that the for-itself too has no real being, this deficiency distinguishing it from the in-itself; it is a non-substantial absolute.[3]

Now a similar view of value is taken by Polin, who, however, finds a more explicit way of distinguishing between value and 'value reversed',[4] which he aptly calls the norm. For him too value manifests transcendence but does not merge with its pro-duct. It is the aim, the intention, but no sooner is it realized than it dies.[5] Just as for Sartre human reality is conceivable only as a 'rupture with the given',[6] for Polin the invention of values con-sists in a 'breaking of relationships', not a making of them, and in a 'refusal of identification and immanence'. Every transcendent move produces results irreducible to each other. Each value is unique and is a negation of all others.[7] This corresponds to Sartre's account of an equally infinite plurality of values, stemming each from a unique situation.[8]

As long as the general term 'value' is used, without qualifica-tion, the difficulties of this view are obscured. We may ask what kind of value displays in this way a break with the given and a negation of rational relationships, being transcendent and unique. We see in the first place, I think, that the general use of the word 'evaluation' would be preferable to that of 'value', since what is in question is an act, not a thing, and that the opposition of norm and value (or inverted value and value) creates the mystifying problem of distinguishing a thing from not-quite-a-thing, when what we are concerned with is a thing and an act. Even if, how-ever, we substitute the word evaluation for value, and say that each evaluation is related to a unique situation and is independent of every other, we need to recognize that this, while being a plausible assertion in aesthetics, would be a doubtful one in morals.[9] However, phenomenological and existentialist French

---

[1] *E.N.* p. 136. My translation (*B.N.* p. 92).
[2] *B.N.* p. 94 (*E.N.* p. 138).
[3] *B.N.* p. 619 (*E.N.* p. 713).   [4] *B.N.* p. 120 (*E.N.* p. 164).
[5] *La C. des v.* p. 123.   [6] *B.N.* p. 478 (*E.N.* p. 558).
[7] *La C. des v.* p. 98.   [8] See above, p. 174.   [9] See above, p. 100.

philosophers do not accept this distinction. Polin says that when value becomes ossified and fixed, that is, when an evaluation is regarded as repeatable in other contexts, it falls progressively from the status of end to that of norm, and subsequently to that of a work (*œuvre*) at which stage it is part of static reality and a historical fact. 'Evaluation resists every fixation . . . it is nothing; it creates.'[1] It is, moreover, a restless process of continuous creation, since 'scarcely has the *other* been created than it sinks into the realm of the given',[2] and a new 'other' is required to carry us still further. There is no end to this human activity of transcendence which is constantly reborn from its own ashes. It is as if, says Sartre, the world, man and man-in-the-world never managed to bring into being anything but a God who falls short of the divine (*un Dieu manqué*).[3]

There is, then, evaluation, which is a process of continuous creation. But there is no *attachment* to values, only attachment to goods or possessions. To become attached to reversed values or norms, under the impression that they are values, is self-betrayal (*abandon de soi*) and refusal to 'surmount oneself'.[4] What then of love and hate, about which – love in particular – Christian existentialist writers make much? I think Polin acts logically, from his own point of view, in rejecting them as factors in evaluation. He might perhaps have been tempted to regard love, a force not neglected by the Christian existentialists, as the motive force in the demand for the desirable, therefore as the essence of transcendence, but instead he clearly sees that we can love (or hate) only what is *there*, and therefore that the act of loving is not creative.[5] It is, on the contrary, 'born of values', that is, I take it, consequent upon evaluation, and what it clings to are 'goods' or debased values.[6] We may well have little emotional attachment to a value which we admire and wish to see promoted: we may, for example, admire charity but not feel charitable. On the other hand love may be irresistibly bestowed upon an unworthy object, and one known to be unworthy.[7] The result of this rigid exclusion of emotional

---

[1] *La C. des v.* p. 125. [2] ibid. p. 131.
[3] *E.N.* p. 717 (*B.N.* p. 623), 'a missing God'. [4] *La C. des v.* p. 146.
[5] ibid. p. 149. [6] ibid. p. 153. [7] ibid. p. 154.

attraction or repulsion from evaluation means that the creation of value is conceived as an adventure, a voyage of discovery, rather than as adherence to what is realized, or desire of eternity; in other words, as action and not as passion, and this is, I think, consistent with existentialist principles.

Certainty equally implies some sort of possession, or conversion of a content of consciousness to a static object. We are certain of a value in so far as we reduce it to the status of a fact.[1] Uncertainty on the other hand is a condition of action, which is always in the nature of an effort, a trial, an experiment, in life as in the laboratory, implying not certainty and knowledge, but a hypothesis.[2] We can see here one reason why existentialism tends to be anti-rational and anti-scientific. According to it, we do not want the future to be absolutely foreseeable, for such a future would deprive us of our liberty, which is conceived as an instrument for wagering rather than as one for insuring ourselves. Certainty paralyses action, while creation forces a way through the interstices of determinism and brings genuine novelty.

Once we have elected to have our actions governed by recognized principles, we have abandoned values for norms. Evaluation, Polin gives us to understand,[3] is irreconcilable with the formation of set maxims, and this, of course, is true if by evaluation we mean something essentially resembling criticism of works of art. This is borne out by implication when we read that the norm is recognized as requiring to be universalized.[4] It then becomes a basis for action rather than an end of action, yet it relates to intention and the future too, and thus has the paradoxical character of being transcendent yet given (*comme un transcendant donné*[5]). Whether or not the idea of values here presented is or is not characteristic of aesthetics rather than of morals, it is certain that society is the proper sphere of norms, as Polin says.[6]

Norms are what a man or a group imposes on others, which means that norms, unlike values, are enforceable by authority,

---

[1] *La C. des v.* p. 165.   [2] ibid. p. 167.   [3] ibid. p. 182.
[4] 'La norme se traduit par une exigence d'universalité', ibid. p. 210.
[5] ibid. p. 211.   [6] ibid. pp. 218 ff.

whereas values are not. There is of course the possibility that the authority may be self-imposed, in which case we have self-discipline. This is certainly the main basis of social life, where the creativeness which produces values finds a substitute in the conscientiousness which prompts an action because it is one's duty to do it. The distinction which Professor Nowell-Smith draws between virtue and conscientiousness[1] corresponds to that drawn in *La Création des Valeurs* between values and norms. As conscientiousness is second-hand virtue so norms are second-hand values, inferior but perhaps better than none. A value which gives rise to a norm tends to become universal, says Polin.[2] Does universalization then mean degradation? Existentialists almost always give the impression that they think so. What I think is true is that, since only norms and not values can be enforced, and more particularly self-imposed, the *feeling* of free response to a 'lack', the feeling in other words of free evaluation is not then present. We choose in both cases, of course, and so show ourselves free, as we must, by virtue of being 'condemned to be free'. But in spontaneously evaluating we choose our own value, whereas in conforming or acting according to a norm we choose, most often, someone else's. Or possibly we choose one of our own which has served on another occasion, and this repetition is of course equally second-hand. When we spontaneously choose a value, we *are* something, though this being involves act in the sense in which this word is used by Lavelle, for example. When we act according to a pre-established principle or norm we *do* something *as if* we were virtuous, courageous, etc., but without actually *being* so. It is clear that we can do little about fostering virtue, because we cannot order people to *be* anything – though through moral exhortation we may try to do so. We can, however, order them to *do* things and, by universal precepts, we can induce them to imitate virtue. We can give dispositional orders, but they are more likely to be listened to with an air of piety and then ignored than are real orders. We say 'Love thy neighbour as thyself' without thereupon expecting anyone to sacrifice one iota of his own personal interest, whereas 'Side-arms will be worn' is intended to be taken seriously

---

[1] *Ethics*, Pelican Books, 1954, pp. 258–9.   [2] *La C. des. v.* p. 218.

and can be enforced. Company orders are perhaps a more satisfactory form of injunction than the Gospels.

Polin, however, attaches more importance to the intention of an action than to its results, in which case a dispositional order is no doubt less inappropriate, since there is a salutary difficulty here in discovering whether or not it has been carried out. What counts for him is 'the activity of transcendence', and when this is neglected in the interest of the result, when 'the axiological consciousness tears itself away from its work and stands in opposition to itself, *sacred values* are imposed and appear in the light of an emanation from the transcendent'.[1] But 'sacred values' are really norms without values, whereas aesthetic values are 'values without norms'.[2] In recognizing this Polin shows that he is not unaware of the real nature of aesthetic values, which 'constitute a domain apart'.[3] Their distinctive feature, according to him, is that they do not require action and the transformation of the given; the world to which they point is an imaginary one. They are not normative or teleological. I think this is insufficiently precise. Surely what is said here about aesthetic values is true rather of the *criticism* of artistic performances, where the suggestion is rarely made that action should be taken to improve or re-do the work, or that a recipe has been devised for the production of like, but improved, works. On the other hand the *creation* of a work is indeed not relevant to action, but that is because it *is* action in the sense of being an 'activity of transcendence'. Values as here understood belong to the domain of the aesthetic, and norms to that of the ethical.

[1] *La C. des v.* p. 232.   [2] ibid. p. 233.   [3] ibid. p. 231.

12

The contingency of value. Vladimir Jankélé-vitch

The discussion in recent French philosophy of closed and open morality, of norms and values, of bad faith and authenticity, constitutes the field of twentieth-century French ethics, or by far the most important part of it. The question which forces itself upon us, and which may appear never to be answered, is: What are the springs of open morality, of value, of the authentic act? We are fairly familiar with the nature, in the form of action in a situation, of what one may call the existentialist Good, but perhaps only M. Vladimir Jankélévitch persistently and perspicaciously seeks its origins, or rather demonstrates its lack of origin, at the same time scrutinizing the nature of intention in both its phenomenological and everyday senses.

From his earliest works, which appeared in the early thirties, M. Jankélévitch is concerned with a duality of experience which consists on the one hand of a unity of being, unaware of itself precisely because undivided against itself, and on the other of various stages of explicit consciousness. To acquire knowledge is to divide the self, and destroy what others have called the pre-reflective stage of consciousness. Innocence is the condition of man 'intact', not 'split', not self-conscious, not therefore delivered over to 'the age of shame and bad conscience'.[1] But this state of innocence is precarious and ultimately, whatever we do, doomed to destruction in virtue of our human nature, because 'there is in us a principle of agility and universal anxiety', which prompts the mind to refuse coincidence with itself, in the interest of not being taken in by anything, even by itself.[2] This split produces what I have discussed earlier as the *écart* or gap opened up in experience between the individual and his world and the individual and himself as an object of consciousness. Of course, the inevitable

[1] *Le Mal*, Arthaud, pp. 89–90.
[2] *La Mauvaise Conscience*, P.U.F., 1933, pp. 1–2.

emotional effect is produced by this split: 'There is in the real something which demands to be justified.'[1] Detachment is the principle of pain and evil, and also of irony, which alleviates these.

Jankélévitch looks carefully at detachment and sees that only a certain degree of it generates anxiety and the desire to undo the initial act of dividing consciousness. This degree is what he calls 'half-consciousness' (*demi-conscience*). It is plain that complete detachment (*pleine conscience*) causes no distress. 'Practical intellectual consciousness'[2] frees us from the oppressive presence of the situation and from consequent urgent readaptations, and introduces us to disinterested contemplation. By using detached and transferable consciousness to compare and assimilate concrete occasions separated by intervals of time, by being rescued, in short, from complete immersion in the present, and by dominating time's flux, we are enabled to construct scientific 'laws' of trans-temporal validity. The other, and crucial, kind of consciousness is *demi-conscience*, or 'bad conscience', which is only half-detached from its content, and fails to reduce experience to problems, leaving it as a kind of incubus.

As a principle of evil, in so far as it reveals the world as unjustified or absurd, this half-consciousness is closely bound up with time's passage. We are prompted to question this passage, and generally to wish explicitly or implicitly that it did not occur. There is a 'desire of eternity' underlying our consciousness which seeks to perpetuate, not only positive pleasure, but any period of reasonable contentment. When we become aware that time's work consists in transforming the fleeting present into a solidified, immutable and irrecoverable past, not to mention bringing upon us a future of generally uncertain, perhaps fearful content (certainly so in the last resort), our lot is seen to have suffered through our widening consciousness. Present contentment has an air of eternity provided that it is unconscious of itself. As soon as the second, half-detached (which means half-adhering) self appears, our innocence and bliss are at an end. What are we to do? Can we, by an odyssey of consciousness, bring about a return to our

[1] *La Mauvaise Conscience*, p. 3.   [2] ibid. p. 11.

former unity?[1] Time is irreversible and so we cannot. Two courses are therefore open to us. The first is intellectual and the second may be called vital, although Jankélévitch does not use this term.

Rational consolation for irremediable ills takes the form of *conceptualization* or *banalization*, which consists in finding a way of denying the uniqueness of our predicament, in adopting a euphemistic fictionalism, and behaving 'as if' the irreplaceable loss of a loved one, for instance, were *a case of* death, the universal and inescapable fate of us all, and therefore in some way not as painful as it might seem. It is 'a consolation of resignation, a consolation for Spartan widows, which does not answer my need because it does not compensate for personal absence by personal presence'.[2] Whether this Stoical remedy is acceptable or not depends, of course, on individual temperament and outlook, and on the particular evil in question. It is surely true, however, that the consolation of banalization does play a widespread role, and a genuine one, in reconciling people with misfortune or disappointment, and that one's discovery that one's plight is the common lot makes innumerable 'quodditive' ills tolerable. Old age and one's own death *are* in most cases faced with comparative serenity because *nobody* escapes them, or at least if one escapes old age it is only at the cost of premature death. And to feel quite alone and unique in misfortune is almost certainly intolerable.

For Jankélévitch, however, consolation is 'a conviction of one's inmost self and not a matter of rational assent'.[3] The knowledge that every man must one day lose his parents does not console him, because it is irrelevant to the loss of his own, and has no common measure with it; it is merely an additional source of sadness. Christian *compensation* appeals to him more: Blessed are they that mourn, for they shall be comforted. But when? In an eschatological future, which makes the reparation 'somewhat metaphorical'. The intellectual solution, or solution of contrivance, which he examines with most insight and sympathy, but still without wholeheartedly accepting it, is *irony*. Irony, like art, is a

---

[1] Cf *L'Odyssée de la conscience dans la dernière philosophie de Schelling*, Alcan, 1932, p. 66.
[2] *La Mauvaise Conscience*, p. 79.   [3] ibid. p. 80.

product of leisure and the relaxation of the urgency of mere animal living. Where 'bad conscience', or semi-detachment, is a condemnation, because it holds us prisoners in the 'semelfactivity' of our own experience – its once-for-all-time occurrence – and at the same time offers that occurrence as an object of saddening contemplation, irony is complete detachment, good conscience, liberating us and conferring upon us mobility and the possibility of escape. To ironize is to leave the scene of action (*s'absenter*).[1] Irony enables us to prevail over our predicament, for though it recognizes the necessity of our limitation in time and place, it conceives the possibility of being elsewhere and later. It is essentially reflective and is turned in upon the self, as the intellect, which it employs, is usually turned outwards: upon a reality of which it is independent. It uses 'economy' and 'diplomacy' as its methods. Economy 'dates' our present, seeing it as part of a temporal process which has an infinity of moments, and thus reduces the intensity and obsessiveness of the Here and Now. Diplomacy is concerned not with 'justice of succession', but with 'justice of coexistence', and assigns to us our due place in the scheme of things. The discovery of plurality is to some extent humbling, for we must renounce our lordly solitude and share space and time with the multitude. But at the price of humility we gain reassurance. It seems that Jankélévitch is here presenting once more conceptualization, but coloured this time with something like humour. To bare consolation as a shared lot is added a certain feeling of freedom, in the form of awareness of necessity (which is true freedom[2]), and through this we are made 'available' without existentialist melodrama. Irony is absence and detachment, and its language is therefore non-committal. Indeed the ironist appears to take up a position antithetical to the one which he occupies; not, however, with the object of being believed, and

---

[1] Cf *Bergson*, 1931, p. 58. 's'absenter de soi et s'éparpiller parmi les concepts' (in relation to the passage from duration, or 'real' time, to chronological time).

[2] 'We can be said to be free in so far as we have a clear and distinct idea of the causes of our own states, physical and mental.' Stuart Hampshire, *Spinoza*, Pelican Books, 1951, p. 161.

making a victim of his interlocutor, but in order to be understood, and thus make a sort of accomplice of him. Irony is a kind of synthetic, intellectual consolation, but not quite a genuine one, according to Jankélévitch.

Perhaps there is no genuine one, no way by which the products of time – which hurries us on at its own speed, whether we want to hurry or tarry: regret, remorse, a sense of the irreversible, the irrecoverable or the irreparable – can be made no longer a source of distress, of the familiar existential 'dread'. All desire of immunity or deliverance from evil is shown to be a delusion. And, as befits the context of contemporary philosophy, which tends in various ways to stress the immediacy of experience, and the vanity of our demands for ultimate origins, objectives or explanations, the 'remedy' for living is shown to reside simply in living. We live on in hope, Christian-wise, but the hope is not now placed outside time, but resolutely inside it, so that, by undergoing it, we are homeopathically cured of its effects. Our recovery depends on both activity and passivity on our part. The activity consists in making a deliberate break with the obsessive past, the affective acceptance of time, and the rejection of the past experience or state to which memory has failed to assign a definite place in chronological time, and which tends to linger on parasitically, an eternity which we continue to cherish, or, in Sartrean language, an in-itself which vainly and disastrously pretends to have swallowed up the for-itself. The past, in the guise of regret, remorse, habit or repressed emotion, dominates the present, time is arrested, and what is then called for is wilful forgetfulness. This does not mean that the parasitical past is thrust into complete oblivion, but that it should be situated in its place and within its true dimensions, and not allowed to encroach insidiously and cancerously upon the active present. This kind of forgetfulness 'unfreezes the flow towards the future which remorse has congealed'.[1] Consolation is too quidditive in having recourse to ways and means,[2] to manœuvres different from living and designed as a

[1] *La Mauvaise Conscience*, p. 163. For 'remorse' read any persistent and obstructive feeling in relation to the past.
[2] ibid. p. 146.

substitute for it. This is why I have called the solution adopted a vital one. The event can be offset only by the event.[1] Living consists in taking the at least partially undesirable, the obstacle, as the means or organ of living. The attitude favouring this is 'le sérieux';[2] 'because it is the assumption of the obstacle, and neither the angelic nor Machiavellian will to achieve ends without means, but the comprehensive will to means and ends, because it is the rejection of purism, because it is the virtue of the modest, sincere and courageous man – it is seriousness which is the basis of true freedom from care. . . . The absurd is to be taken neither tragically nor lightly, but simply seriously.'[3]

Now the dyad 'bad conscience-irony' may be regarded as representative of a pervasive dualism in Jankélévitch's approach to human experience. He distinguishes between the instant and the interval, between creation and continuation, between the Quod and the Quid. And this distinction is the ground bass upon which the elaborate passacaglia of his books is worked out. We have seen that deliverance from 'bad conscience' by duration, by living through experience and living on past it, is better than consolation by economy or diplomacy. Now the characteristic of the latter expedients is that by locating an experience in space or time they give it air, so to speak, thus relieving the self of the oppressiveness of its presence. Moreover they banalize it and destroy its privileged status as *my* predicament. Thus the situation becomes one of many, one of a kind, with an assignable origin. Classification and detachment – the act of absenting oneself – place this approach firmly in the intellectualist category, which is that of the Quid, since it tells us *what* is in question. Now we have seen that Jankélévitch does not find this approach helpful in dealing with those emotional problems which are raised by the passage of time. The instants of time are not assimilable, but neither are they independent of each other; so that it is equally wrong on the one hand to pretend either that an experience is exactly, or even sufficiently,

[1] Cf ibid. p. 198.
[2] Not to be confused with Simone de Beauvoir's 'le sérieux'! Cf *Pour une morale de l'ambiguïté*.
[3] *La Mal*, p. 49.

like a large number of others for it to be in some way pigeon-holed and disposed of, on the other to allow it to overlay and smother the advance of present, living experience. The solution therefore is neither to behave *as if* it has not happened *to me*, nor to allow it to creep like a parasitical plant over my active life, but to integrate it into that active life. This is a quodditive solution. In adopting it, I stress the contingency, or gratuity, of what time brings into being, which means that I find it expedient to overlook its origin, even to deny for practical purposes that it has an origin, since the 'because' is usually, in human terms, only retrospectively obvious,[1] and we do not live in reverse. To account for something does not amount, morally speaking, to dealing with it, and our living is conducted on the basis of 'the fact that',[2] and not on that of 'would that . . .!' or 'if only . . .!' In other words, our past life is our facticity, from which we live, and not by means of which we evade the responsibility of living.

The dualistic philosophy of Jankélévitch, and of French phenomenology generally, tends to jar upon those who, almost necessarily in our time, have been brought up to accept a scientific monism according to which everything that happens is, in principle, causally determined.[3] Jankélévitch finds it convenient to postulate, in human terms, which are his chosen terms of reference, a *quidditive*, or causally accountable world, and a *quodditive*, or radically contingent one. I have tried to provide a preliminary illustration of these concepts in the foregoing pages, by taking a fairly simple problem of affective experience with which Jankélévitch deals in two of his early works. I shall go on to show, as best I can, how this distinction forms the basis of a

---

[1] 'I acquire certitude only when it is too late, when the secret of the future has become the reality of the present.' *Bergson*, p. 91.

[2] Cf *Philosophie première*, pp. 176 and 231.

[3] I think that it is unnecessary here to take account of the objections to the notion of cause, and indeed the demonstration that it is obsolete, contained, for example, in Bertrand Russell's essay 'On the notion of cause' (*Mysticism and Logic*). Nor do I feel able to discuss the loop-hole of the 'principle of indeterminacy'. I am concerned with the regularity of sequence, and the necessity of antecedent events, which science presupposes. Hume's scepticism did not abolish science, nor was it intended to.

purely metaphysical inquiry, in *Philosophie première*,[1] and of an ethical one in *Traité des vertus*.[2]

In his *Philosophie première* he distinguishes three philosophies, which may be enumerated in reverse order, since they proceed from the accountable world to its unaccountable origin, and from the quidditive scientific perspective of applied reason to the quodditive one of radical contingency and irrationality. The third is concerned with the 'relatively' contingent world of natural events, observed, accounted for and incorporated into a body of synthetic truths, of knowledge: a storehouse of experience for the benefit and facilitation of subsequent experience. The second deals with the rational world of analytic truths, in which the criterion is that of consistency: the world of rationality. The first reverts from necessity to gratuity. Its domain is as 'positive' as that of the third, indeed even more irrationally 'posited', in that it points to the contingency not only of what is, but of the whole system of relationships connecting its parts. What the first philosophy seeks is not the other order of reason, but the 'Tout-autre ordre' (the utterly different order) which is both meta-empirical and meta-logical, or truly metaphysical. If, however, the first philosophy were devoted merely to drawing attention to the utterly unjustified givenness of the universe, it would merely reiterate a commonplace, and could consist of only one proposition, since having pointed out the contingency of all things taken as a whole, it would indeed be obliged to follow Wittgenstein's precept, and thenceforth be silent, since there would be nothing more to add. It is not, however, quite as simple as that. Radical contingency does not merely stand at the beginning of things as an act of cosmic creation, it runs through them and fills the interstices of reality and the instants of time. It is true that this comes near to assimilating it to the 'relative' contingency of events described by synthetic propositions. But not quite, I think, because the contingency of the fact, for example, that the sun will rise tomorrow, is one which in practice has no influence on our decisions and behaviour. It is a bit of Humean virtuosity which

---

[1] P.U.F., 1953.
[2] Bordas, 1949.

can be put on as a conjuring trick for our intellectual delectation, but which, as contingent, is almost irrelevant to the serious business of living.[1] Radical contingency, or *quoddity*, on the other hand, is liable to show up in a crisis, in connection with some happening which we are desperately anxious to account for, or justify, and which we find, to our consternation, grief, or other disagreeable emotion, unaccountable. It is therefore particularly relevant to moral philosophy, and perhaps refers, using a fancy name, to no more than the subjective, unguaranteed status of value-judgements.

The *Quod* does, however, elaborate considerably upon the bare position of the empiricist, because it relates, phenomenologically, to the affective attitude which the empiricist is anxious to exclude. It may belong to pure metaphysics, but it has nothing to do with meta-ethics. Furthermore its realm extends beyond that of verdicts, normative or evaluative or in any sense moral, back to the fundamental attitude from which verdicts spring. I have said that quoddity is not merely the mystery of the ultimate origin of things or of their eschatological winding-up, it is that of creation or absolute discontinuity in all its aspects, and not least in those which touch our everyday lives. Death is one of the meeting-places of the empirical and the metaphysical. The death of another is, despite its solemnity and any sympathy we may feel, biologically accountable and what happens to us all. My own death, however, has for me an absolutely unique significance, but I shall not be there to feel its impact. The death of a near one perhaps alone combines the objective naturalness of 'the death of another' with the inconceivability of one's own.[2] The attitude, as we have seen, which befits the peculiarly intense force of life unrationalized is 'seriousness'.

We may say that the first manifestation of metaphysical *seriousness* was the acceptance of the entirely-different-order and the

[1] Not *quite* irrelevant, however, since any truth which changes our way of looking at things is always waiting for its chance to slip across the no-man's land which philosophers have laid down in the name of the 'naturalistic fallacy', to colour our conduct.

[2] *Phil. prem.* p. 4.

refusal to reduce to differences of degree – diminutions or augmentations – the absolute difference of kind, the fundamental heterogeneity of this order and 'the other'.[1]

All discontinuity opens up beneath our feet a yawning chasm of irrationality, all suspension of being implies an interval of nothing, beyond which the resumption is as miraculous as the first beginning.[2] Now this sounds pretty familiar. Descartes postulated a process of continuous creation by which God intervenes at every instant with a renewed creative act. Only thus could he account for the fact that the inertia of the universe is overcome. Hume restated this in untheological terms when he discredited the notion of cause as a dynamic agent. But these are statements of a universal truth. Put into the context of experience as understood phenomenologically, it is not a universal truth, or rather not interesting as such. In the human context there are events which are explainable, in the sense that they form part of a familiar sequence, and at the same time not explainable, because our feelings about them (which are not regarded as intrusive agents of distortion) present them to us as unique. And there are events which, though *in principle* accountable, are in practice not so, or which, when retrospectively accounted for, are over and done with, and part of our facticity, so that the explanation is otiose. We may strive, in the manner of scientific man, to conceptualize and ironize our past, and to make our future increasingly predictable, so that we live in a world of schemata rather than of situations, but this, by existentialist standards, is not living, or rather is not existing. It is, on the contrary, trying to ignore and override the irreducible nature of reality (that is, human reality), and moreover it is foredoomed to failure. For we cannot live outside the world, we must live in it. The instants of time are not to be fused into comfortable intervals, or ideally into one interval, spanning what should be the adventure between birth and death, they are potentially creative and should be made actually so, by a perpetual reassessment which is the denial of what has been: 'only that soul which at one stroke opens itself wide to the new order,

[1] *Phil. prem.* p. 2.   [2] ibid. p. 58.

by saying No! to the previous one, shall experience the actual transfiguration of its being'.[1]

The discussion in *Philosophie première* revolves round a number of related topics: the danger that the elusive first philosophy will degenerate into the second, the 'nature' of Quoddity as act and its irreducibility to essence, the curiously ambiguous nature of the instant. Let us begin with the objects of the three philosophies. The third deals with things, the second with relations and the first with the act, in the singular, that is, with initiative and origination. The task of philosophy is most often that of rescuing the act from its own conceptualization and essentialization; would-be first philosophy tends to drift into second philosophy, in other words, and needs to be constantly on its guard. This drift is evident in some of the greatest thinkers. In Plato, for example, the demiurgic productivity of the *Timaeus* is an arrangement rather than a creation, the *poiētēs* being primarily an orderer, copying a pre-existing model in the shape of the Idea.[2] Plato's attachment to models[3] shows that he was a half-hearted metaphysician who entered upon the infinite regress of originating entities but tired at the second stage. I think that Jankélévitch might very well say that there is no metaphysical second philosophy, or at least that the field which it usurps belongs legitimately to mathematics, logic and the formal studies generally. What metaphysics is properly concerned with is the 'anhypothetical', thetic positivity[4] which he regularly calls the *Quod*, or quoddity. What is examined here on a highly abstract plane is no more than the immediacy of experience, which is a theme round which contemporary philosophy weaves many variations, not only within the frontiers of phenomenological thinking, but across philosophical and national frontiers too. Professor Gilbert Ryle's refutation of 'the ghost in the machine' could conceivably be equated with Jankélévitch's discrediting of the pre-existence of our acts in the form of transcendent models. Similarly

---

[1] ibid. p. 59. Cf Merleau-Ponty, *Phenomenology of Perception*, Routledge, p. 30. 'The miracle of consciousness consists in its bringing to light, through attention, phenomena which re-establish the unity of the object in a new dimension at the very moment when they destroy it.'
[2] ibid. p. 194.   [3] ibid. p. 219.   [4] ibid. p. 103. Cf also p. 82.

the pseudo-problem of knowing how we know how we do things has its Gordian knot cut in Rylean style: we 'become blacksmiths by shoeing horses and zitherists by playing the zither; what would have to be foreknown in order to be done is learnt by being actually done'.[1]

The Other-Order is, then, no order at all. There is no first 'order' because the utterly other is nothing *existing*, he says. Order is the privilege of the meta-empirical world of tautologies, necessary truths, halfway between the disorder of the empirical world and something other (*un je-ne-sais-quoi-d'autre*) which is neither order nor disorder, and which must be recognized as the fount of order, *fons ordinis*.[2] Now this source is both divine and human, divine in that everything flows from it, but human too in that man's intention issues from it, and is as originating as the divine creative act. We are, of course, in a world which could go on without, or independently of, each of us (although to allow it to do the latter would be to act inauthentically, as Sartre would say) but our choices and decisions are nevertheless supplementary 'creative' acts analogous to God's. 'Is it not possible that the inexistent which confers existence (*l'inexistent donneur d'existence*) may be of the nature of decision?' he asks.[3] Now this seems a peculiar speculation, because it appears to make decision into an 'acte gratuit', without antecedent acts, assessments or evaluations. But I think that here, as elsewhere, philosophy leaves everything as it was, and only a man as naïve as Gide would, on the strength of this, suppose that someone might commit an outrageous act for the purpose of demonstrating that he could dispense with motive. What is meant, I think, is that an act, which may be purely mental, that is, not publicly committed in the observable world, and which moreover may be regarded as a decision on the strength of data or similarly the solution of a problem, is not *preceded by* an appraisal of the data, but is simultaneous with the apprehension of the whole situation, which presents itself meaningfully – that is to say, articulated in terms of its own requiredness. There are acts which follow an analysis of a situation as a kind of extra datum, but these are of the nature of

[1] op. cit. p. 184.   [2] ibid. p. 88.   [3] ibid. p. 98.

repetitions, or lend themselves to repetition and belong to the interval. Quidditive acts and repetitions bear the same relation to authentic acts that blueprints or maps bear to machines or landscape paintings. 'Genius (and is not the Act elementary genius?) itself invents the problem; it raises and solves it at one stroke.'[1]

At this stage it is necessary to examine the notion of the instant, which has been associated with quoddity. It is first presented rather metaphorically as an infinitesimal fraction of time,[2] which intuition mysteriously apprehends. Eventually, however, we find that the instant is not at all some mathematical irrational, but is unexpectedly and fully in the world. It, or its content, is the immediately apprehended form or meaning which unites the parts of any object or situation perceived or appreciated, and the justification for equating it with the instant is that it partakes of the same non-temporal nature. Non-temporal in the sense that no lapse of time covers the supposed process of receiving a set of sensations and putting an interpretation on them: the whole is a simultaneous unity.[3] 'Simplicity would probably be a better word than unity to give to this atomic focus (*ce foyer ponctuel*) . . . in which parts, at first merely juxtaposed in space, interpenetrate and coincide.'[4] This is a phenomenological view of experience and it has much in common with Gestalt psychology, which conceives perception as the apprehension of shapes and groupings as wholes, not the piecemeal and chronologically measurable elaboration of reality from atoms of sensation.

[1] Cf Merleau-Ponty, op. cit. p. 36. 'It would follow from this that the mind runs over isolated impressions and gradually discovers the meaning of the whole, as the scientist discovers the unknown factors in virtue of the data of the problem. Now here the data of the problem are not prior to its solution, and perception is just that act which creates at a stroke, along with the cluster of data, the meaning which unites them – indeed which not only discovers the meaning *which they have*, but moreover *causes them to have a meaning*.'

[2] Cf *Phil. prem.* pp. 113 and 119.

[3] 'The idea of time which leads us to think of sensation as anterior to knowledge is a construction of the mind.' Lagneau, *Célèbres Leçons*, quoted by Merleau-Ponty, op. cit. p. 37, note 2. Cf also ibid. p. 38, 'Perception is nowhere, for if it were situated in a place, it could not cause other things *to exist for itself.*'

[4] *Phil. prem.* p. 161.

The 'atomic focus' may, then, be 'spread' in time and space. It may take time, or more accurately Bergsonian 'duration', to constitute itself, as in music; but most characteristically the *meaning* of the situation is instantaneously grasped, hence the non-temporal character attributed to it. But, instantaneous as its apprehension may be, it is a form, ensemble or grouping, and, in the case of visual perception, occupies a field of space, though again this may not be determinate, and may contain 'gaps' of irrelevant material, and shade off towards vague limits. In other words, however much these forms (which are in effect valuations) overlap, and however imprecise be their boundaries, they are, *for me*, units of experience, and bear no relation to the instants of chronological time or any clear-cut divisions of space. These units are felt to have some sort of connection with each other, but this is, from a rational point of view, highly arbitrary, and, like all units, they are discontinuous, therefore contingent. The fact remains, however, that once the portions of experience have been allowed to coalesce and occupy the whole of consciousness, there is no end to the process, with the result that the at first apparently clear distinction between the *Quid* and the *Quod* becomes blurred. 'One may ask whether continuation, in so far as it involves us in alteration, modulation and becoming, is not itself a *continuous creation*,[1] and whether the interval is not after all an infinite proliferation of instants.'[2] The individual's life itself is perhaps a 'great instant' in its production of a pattern which is unique and non-recurrent, in 'the unfathomable quoddity of selfhood', which, 'bounded by birth and death, appears to itself in the form of a thetic act'.[3] Yet the instants of which the 'great instant' is made up are not all, or even for the most part, value-producing. They are 'rather promotive than creative, rather propulsive than thetic'.[4] It is no use our being perfectionists in this matter. It is God who is totally and unremittingly creative; on the human plane the instants, though all potentially creative, are in fact only intermittently so,[5] with the result that the *Quod* becomes quiddified, and the *fiat* takes to pottering along in a cosy routine.[6]

---

[1] Italics mine.   [2] ibid. p. 200.   [3] ibid. p. 246.
[4] ibid. p. 209.   [5] ibid. p. 186.   [6] 'l'embourgeoisement du *fiat*', p. 243.

JANKÉLÉVITCH'S MORAL PHILOSOPHY

When we come to ask what is the significance of all this, and what relevance it has to ethics, which is a constant preoccupation of Jankélévitch, I think we shall do well to bear in mind the affinity for him, not to say the virtual identity, of awareness of a situation and evaluation. This relationship is implied rather than stated, but it is none the less the bridge between the 'is' and the 'ought'; or perhaps one should say that it is the dissolvent of the 'is'. Our situation is always changing and our authenticity consists in our keeping alive a corresponding elasticity and renewal of initiative. There is therefore a hierarchy of virtues. Those of origination are preferred to those of continuation. Courage, love, charity and humility are better than fidelity, friendship, justice and modesty.

It is clear that the quodditive impulse *par excellence* is the categorical imperative. It has no content, or bears no necessary relation to any content, and is, in Jankélévitch's conception of it, equatable with Bergson's 'totality of obligation', which weighs everywhere upon men, but by imposing almost limitlessly variable duties upon them. It is the moral version of radical contingency:[1] '... *the almost-nothing of Duty*, in which the will feels that it must do, without knowing what, is the only form in which man experiences the *nothingness of the Good*'.[2] Now there is a certain amount of Jankélévitchian sleight of hand here, because although any sector of the totality of obligation is indeterminate, it is never empty; for every call to duty there is an appropriate act. We are never frustrated by feelings of dutifulness which can find no outlet, as we might conceivably be by feelings of irritability when there is no enemy to hand on whom they may be vented. Nevertheless, within the context of contemporary continental philosophy, Jankélévitch is here saying something. For here there *is* an 'almost-nothing of Duty' and a 'nothingness of the Good', and this is what makes existentialist ethics so self-stultifying. It is one thing for a meta-ethical philosopher to maintain that goodness is irreducible to any natural quality, and quite another for a moralist (however much he hides his hand and evades the appellation,

[1] 'There is no proof that it is necessary to do.' ibid. p. 109.
[2] *Phil. prem.* p. 244.

which, incidentally, is not the case here) to tell his fellow-men that in order to be good (i.e. authentic) they must be for ever active, adding, however, that if he prescribes forms of worth-while activity he will be inviting them to become inauthentic through habitually pursuing them. I think, in spite of this, that it is possible to state their position fairly sympathetically, and this I shall in due course try to do.

Let us meanwhile return to the quoddity of the categorical imperative. This lies in the fact that it is not related to calculable results, and the difference between the array of antithetical virtues presented to us in *Traité des vertus* is that some, the second-class or second-order virtues, the virtues of the interval, are calculating, whereas the real ones are not. 'Fidelity is the virtue of continuous time as courage is the virtue of going into action.'[1] Modesty is related to irony, bearing ultimately less relation to one's neighbour than to oneself, '. . . a detached attitude of the self towards itself'.[2] In this it seems to me commendable and not manifestly imperfect; it is admitted to have 'no mercenary pretensions';[3] and it does not, in its genuine form, seek so to manipulate the world within its reach as to win some compensation for its show of selflessness. But this is not quite good enough for our Kierkegaardian philosopher, who deplores that, unlike humiliation, it does not plumb the depths of despair and strike 'the springboard of a fruitful nothingness'. Jankélévitch understands the incomprehension of modern man in face of the evangelical abdication of will, but he does not appear to share it.[4] In a section entitled 'Blessed are the poor in spirit' he recognizes that the scandal, in reality, is not that such a one should be first, but that in general there should be the first and the last. Justice, with its symbol of the scales, is almost too obviously quidditive to require any discussion, but Jankélévitch elaborates interestingly on any topic, new or well-worn, and draws on an inexhaustible source of metaphor to give life and even a look of familiarity to the most rarefied and bloodless categories. Respect has almost always been wrongly bestowed, but love which is sincere is never mistaken. This is

[1] *T. des v.* p. 214.   [2] ibid. p. 318.   [3] ibid. p. 329.
[4] ibid. pp. 349–56.

important because once more the content, or object, of an attitude is seen to be secondary in comparison with the attitude itself. Justice and love are compared;[1] both are πρόσ ἕτερον, relative to the other, but in ways different in kind, one directed towards the rights of the other, the other towards his personal being; one recognizes only his works, the other loves the person because he is that person, regardless of his merits. Justice is dispensed on the basis of abstract and administrative generalities, love is bestowed in concrete situations. It is possible, of course, to be a philanthropist, loving the whole human race, but then mankind assumes the figure of 'one's neighbour', 'le toi d'un moi', and ceases to be an abstraction. If, on the other hand, the neighbour remains a remote figure, humanity is never more than an impersonal and cosmic entity: the neighbour is 'the other'. Justice is blind, and fittingly so, for it represents not man, but the logos.[2] To which one may point out in reply that not for nothing is charity described as cold, and that confidence is better placed in an unbending justice which at least shows its hand than in a beaming, Tartuffian charity well versed in the self-seeking manœuvrings of the interval. Jankélévitch would agree,[3] perhaps adding, however, that his treatise is not a set of precepts for smoothing out life's way, and that if we want to play for safety we had better go back either to John Stuart Mill, who will make us good citizens, or else first to La Fontaine, who will make us worldly, and then to La Rochefoucauld, who will give us a clear conscience about being so.

The *Traité des vertus* does not merely establish a distinction between the quodditive and the quidditive virtues, it attempts a further hierarchy of the former, and this is superimposed on something analogous to Kierkegaard's 'stages on life's way'.[4] Firstly there is the 'hither' innocence, which is that of childhood

[1] ibid. p. 425.

[2] ibid. p. 17. 'This arbitrating third party is the logos.'

[3] Countering with 'The precariousness of every acquisition is expressed in the virtue of *humility*. Is it not a strange irony that the refusal of all virtuous respectability (*embourgeoisement vertueux*) should itself be a virtue?' ibid. p. 145.

[4] See ibid. p. 757.

before temptation, then mediocre semi-consciousness, which sees possibilities, but is too attached to the self to go beyond caring for its honour, the virtue of the mediocre. Thirdly comes the extreme consciousness of wisdom which strikes a balance between myself and others. It is self-love 'sobered by the impartial logos'. Socrates is the supreme model of this ideal, which is essentially ironical. Finally ulterior innocence is thoroughgoing altruism, beyond all intermediarity. Courage is the initial virtue here,[1] concerned not with exhibitionism, not with theatrical attitudes in front of mirrors, not with the initiative displayed at War Office Selection Boards to impress the resident psychiatrist, but with the genuine initiative which has no second thoughts to distract it from sacrifice-for-the-other. Sincerity is inherent in the attitude required, hence modesty, which has its quidditive admixture and leads on, or should lead on, by the criteria of existentialist salvation, to humility. This is the negative quality to which charity corresponds, and this is the ultimate virtue.

It is good will, and good will is evident in no predetermined set of actions, nor is it attainable by following any set of rules: it is tact which is the rule.[2] 'Everything is in the manner. Strictly speaking evil does not exist. . . . Evil is not *this or that*, in the sense, for example, that it is to be sought in instinct, or pleasure, or the senses, or the bodily nature. It is neither something nor somewhere. There is no evil, but there are wicked people and perverse dispositions of the will.'[3] Conversely goodness, or rather good will, has an almost infinite variety of actions at its disposal, and these will take their moral colouring from the intention behind them, not from their own specific nature. *The* fault is absence of love.[4]

Virtue resides in disposition, and this once again carries a certain ambivalence into the notion of contingency which the quodditive impulse implies. It might seem that the virtuous desire must be unmotivated and precarious, because the idea of motive is almost necessarily linked with that of selfish motive. This, however, is the sort of sophistry which underlies La Rochefoucauld's

---

[1] *T. des. v.* p. 764.   [2] *Du Mensonge*, p. 98.   [3] *T. des v.* p. 593.
[4] ibid. p. 572.

view of motive, because when he says that all my actions are selfish, he means that all my actions are mine, which is a tautology.[1] If we say that a generous motive is a selfish one, we misuse words and contradict ourselves. Taking this hint, however, we might give the word 'selfish' a new meaning and say that all my motives are certainly selfish in that they are an expression of myself. It is myself who am good or bad, and my 'selfish' actions will be judged on the strength of their allowing a good or bad self to be intuited behind them. Now this lands us once more with a substance, not a flash-in-the-pan event. If we say now that the quality (good or bad) of this substance is to be considered quodditive and contingent, we are back in the theologian's conception of grace, and grace is a term from which these French writers do not flinch. A writer of Christian sympathies, such as Jankélévitch, may be expected to find room for it, but it occurs equally in the atheistic wing.[2]

Sartre's word 'facticity' partly covers the notion in its non-religious version, and it is significant that the idea of facticity is stressed by Sartre in relation to the for-itself.[3] There are certain conditions within which our freedom can work, so that it is conditioned without being determined, and this in practice leaves considerable latitude in one's choice of self. 'To become what one is' is a precept put forward in the *Traité des vertus*.[4] Bearing in mind that being is existentially conceived as becoming, this appears to be a tautology. But this would not be conceded, because 'to be' means here to be what one has it in one to be, and to forgo that is 'to be' in the sense in which objects are: in themselves, without potentiality. The human being has an entelechy or form which has a certain kind of being, but which nevertheless has to be realized. 'Thus all begins with totality.'[5] The illusion of the pure present is resolved on analysis into social, intellectual and motive elements which spill over the punctuality of the Nunc. Now duration is not a succession of atomic instants . . . disjoined by a continuum of

---

[1] Cf Nowell-Smith, *Ethics* (Pelican), p. 142.
[2] Cf Simone de Beauvoir, *Pour une morale de l'ambiguïté*, p. 59.
[3] e.g. *L'Être et le néant*, pp. 121-7.   [4] *T. des v.* pp. 267 ff.
[5] See *Bergson*, passim.

oblivion; it is a fidelity.'[1] So, in the moral sphere too, we find that the distinction between the *Quod* and the *Quid* is not clear-cut and that we live and work in a continuity which is neither a field for calculation and evasion, nor for drift, nor yet for repetition and vicarious living on the values of others, but for originality. By this we are not to understand the constant production of novelty, or expression of caprice, or chameleon-like changefulness, but a certain spontaneity of action which is evidence of sincerity, and which comes by no means easily for being a free expression of the self.[2]

I feel, despite the emphasis constantly placed on charity, that it is perhaps sincerity which is the basic virtue, if not the highest, in Jankélévitch's hierarchy, and I am sure that this is true of existentialist philosophers as a whole. Courage serves sincerity, and without sincerity love is impossible. The problem of sincerity and misrepresentation runs fitfully through his whole work, from the discussion of irony and oblique expression which is meant to be understood, but not believed, through *Le Mensonge* where sincerity is shown as inseparable from good will and selflessness, to the *Traité des vertus*, where, 'if the last word is left to purism, it is to the purism of charity and not to the inhuman purism of veracity . . .'[3] Again in a still later work, *Le Je-ne-sais-quoi et le presque-rien*,[4] there is discussion of misrepresentation in which the empirically unverifiable intention may alone distinguish the act from mime. Only spontaneity and creation leave no room for the duplicity of repetition or the repeatable.

It is difficult in a short space to give an adequate account of the philosophy of Jankélévitch which, beneath a superficial air of highly sophisticated slapstick, is profoundly serious, and involves a degree of genuine commitment to a moral position not evident in some more strident champions of 'engagement'. What I have tried to make clear, however, is that in his insistence on the importance of quoddity and creativeness he is in the tradition under consideration, namely that which condemns action which is conceived as a hoarding of resources, action to end action by accumu-

[1] *T. des v.* p. 11.   [2] Cf *L'Austérité et la vie morale*, 1956, p. 180.
[3] *T. des v.* p. 294.   [4] 1957.

lating goods on which it is vainly hoped to live in spiritual retirement. He is for values in preference to norms, for the open in preference to the closed morality.

13

Detail and atmosphere. René Le Senne

Two of Jankélévitch's themes are dealt with by René Le Senne. One, that of the 'organ-obstacle', whereby value is conceived as brought into being through overcoming, or at least meeting, the resistance of reality, and 'transcending' the 'contradiction', is already familiar, and receives in *Le Devoir*[1] a more than usually Hegelian treatment, although acknowledgement goes to Maine de Biran.[2] In an earlier work, *Obstacle et valeur*,[3] this theme is discussed, but in relation to the notion of value as atmospheric rather than determinate. Le Senne uses the term *extraversion* to refer to the move from 'atmosphere' to 'detail', and *introversion* for the reverse procedure.[4] In so far as the self apprehends detail, it is the perceptive and expressive self, the public self, which is in question, whereas atmosphere is related to the intimacy of the private self. We are warned against confusing introversion, a term borrowed from Jung, with introspection, a hybrid operation involving self-consciousness and discrimination. Introversion consists in opening oneself to atmosphere, giving preference, over the detached scrutiny of a picture, to the undivided feeling of its totality.[5] Value is atmospheric, because it is not made up of parts.[6] Norms can therefore be expected to be analysable into details which are in opposition to atmosphere and destructive of it, as the social is to the intimate.[7] Le Senne's dislike of 'determination',

---

[1] P.U.F., 1949.

[2] V. op. cit. p. 203. Cf also pp. 20, 25, 55, 57, 87, 203, 228, 235, 250 and *Obstacle et va eur*, p. 148.

[3] Aubier, 1934.   [4] *Obstacle et valeur*, p. 197.   [5] ibid. pp. 198–9.
[6] ibid. p. 176.   [7] ibid. p. 215.

'detail' and objective being as components of the world of value is exceptionally strong, and he is led to suppose experience in general as an 'act', in Lavelle's sense, which is basically undifferentiated, with the result that it does not ideally lend itself even to the formation of values, but only to that of Value.[1] The encounter of this spiritual flow, or upsurge (*essor*), with the obstacles presented by reality, gives rise to acts of will and produces 'determinations'. The upsurge is to be distinguished from the will. In the former, the power of the self is not specified by any definite intention; it aims at value.

> Some obstacle has to break the continuity of the upsurge before the self, concentrating upon it the energy which it receives from the body, begins to will. Identical with existence at its beginning, this will coincides with a determination at its end: from being will at the outset, it becomes volition. It is an atmospheric rushing into localization.[2]

This may say no more than that as long as we are alive our energy is either held in reserve, or expended in specific situations, devoted to meeting specific challenges. In fact it is difficult to see how it can mean any more than this, because the spiritual undercurrent which in fact, though presumably not necessarily, throws up acts and determinations, is completely indeterminate, as far as one can see. Therefore it is much too volatilized to be what we are at this stage looking for, namely something corresponding to Sartre's 'original choice', and which must be some rather generalized form (*Gestalt*) of consciousness, one still associated with the individual, and one which will allow his overt acts to be pronounced consistent or inconsistent with it, that is to say, authentic.

---

[1] Cf ibid. p. 179, 'Value is absolute or it is not value.'
[2] ibid. pp. 209–10. This opposition is later expressed in theological terms as the *double cogito* and the *theandric relation*; see pp. 224 ff. 'God, from whom the self experiences alternately the divine will in the obstacle and the divine grace in value, and the *self* which limits the experience of value through the determinations proper to its nature . . .'

PART FOUR

TOWARDS A DEFINITION
OF AUTHENTICITY

14

The instant

We have seen that an evaluation appears as contingent and gratuitous. In a way this is natural, yet in another it seems to demand some explanation. Phenomenology sees significant reality as human reality, a world for me, in which the intentional structure of my experience is constituted instantaneously, not built up piecemeal. We can analyse experience as we would dismantle a machine, but experiencing is not analogous to assembling component parts.[1] We immediately apprehend reality, or any object in it, in terms of a horizon of other objects, including experiences, memories and feelings, which sustain the object and are sustained by it. There is no strictly meaningless reality such as would correspond to a chaos of perceptions or a completely isolated sensation.

Yet there is much talk of the instant, which, in the context of Gestalt psychology or phenomenology, ought to be excluded from the start, just as the notion of a pure sensation is unceremoniously brushed aside.[2] The main reason why it comes in for a good deal of discussion is to be sought, perhaps, in the stress placed on contingency, which goes back to the writings of Kierkegaard. Now contingency is more naturally associated with units than with continuities. It is possible, in accordance with V. Jankélévitch's 'first' philosophy, to think of the whole of reality as contingent, and necessarily so, since it is unique. But this is of very limited interest. The contingency of time, conceived as a succession of separate instants with related contents, struck

---

[1] Cf Jankélévitch, *Bergson*, p. 30. 'Fabriquer consiste bien plus à défaire qu'à faire.' Also p. 32 where he says that when I reconstruct a melody note by note, I succeed because I know the melody immanent in each note, otherwise I could arrive at it only by a series of lucky shots.

[2] Cf the first pages of Merleau-Ponty's *Phenomenology of Perception*.

Descartes, and the idea of the contingency of events[1] is familiar enough. But the contingency of choices, personalities, and attitudes, seems to present problems, since these are presumably related to assessments of reality, indeed in existentialist thinking they *are* such assessments. One might maintain that, this being the case, there remains absolutely nothing to be said. But by revealing self-commitment they acquire a moral force, and have a certain emotional intensity and consistency which leads to effort being made, perhaps quite unnecessarily, to confer upon them a respectability denied to mere expressions of caprice.

The existentialist tendency seems to be to begin with Descartes's problem: how can there be any passage from one instant to another, when instants, though separated by nothing, are yet without intercommunication?[2] The instant is, in fact, conjured away by Sartre in favour of continuity. It is no length of time, and in isolation is therefore timeless; so temporality is less real multiplicity than quasi-multiplicity: an adumbration of dissociation in the heart of unity, a unity which multiplies *itself*.[3] Time thus loses its own substance and becomes the mere mode of being of a being which is itself outside itself; the for-itself 'temporalizes itself' by existing.[4] It is constantly outrunning itself in the direction of self-realization, and cannot exist in the limits of the instant. There is no instant when the for-itself is, and time hurries on as a refusal of the instant.[5]

15

Choice

This refusal is not undertaken in the interest of a mere succession of instants, which is really no more meaningful or imaginable. What is required is something transcending the instant, and of a

[1] Conceived, roughly speaking, as units of history, or process of any kind.
[2] *E.N.* p. 176 (*B.N.* p. 131).   [3] *E.N.* p. 179 (*B.N.* p. 136).
[4] *E.N.* p. 180 (*B.N.* p. 136).   [5] *E.N.* p. 196 (*B.N.* p. 149).

different kind from it; and this I propose to call the form, in the sense of the *Gestalt*. This is radically different from any content that the instant could conceivably have, and it is also more homogeneous and self-subsistent, on the other hand, than pure duration could be. In fact Bergsonian duration presupposes a sort of variable density corresponding to the forms which our duration projects.[1] Duration is heterogeneous, but not amenable to fragmentation into any arbitrary discontinuity (*ne tolère pas une discontinuité quelconque*).[2] Now what underlies much contemporary French philosophy is the question how these 'structures' come to be projected, how they are maintained through time, how they persist in spite of resistance offered to them, and according to what principles they change. In a sense they are, of course, contingent, and ultimately have to be taken for granted, but they are not contingent in the sense in which the succession of instants is, in other words, in the sense in which the fact that things just happen is contingent. The 'original choice' which orientates, or tends to orientate a life, and colour a personality, just happens, in a way, and yet continental philosophers are not prepared to leave it at that. They would say that such a dismissal of the problem indicates that what is essentially for-itself is being objectively and exclusively viewed as in-itself.

To choose is seen as presenting the peculiar difficulty that I choose by virtue of what is there and by virtue of myself,[3] and yet that choice does not leave either things or me as they and I were.[4] It is, of course, obvious that choice is self-expression in relation to what is, and that something must come of it. But I think it is rather a question of exceptional, 'costing' choices such as affect one's choice of oneself. That there is some original choice of outlook on life, or what amounts to it, is convincingly argued by Sartre in *Being and Nothingness*, where he is urging his own type of psycho-analysis in preference to the Freudian, and where he devastatingly exposes the fatuity of Bourget's would-be deterministic

[1] Jankélévitch, *Bergson*, p. 50.   [2] ibid. p. 51.

[3] 'I know that I shall choose in terms of what I now am.' ibid. p. 91.

[4] Cf J. Wahl, *Etudes kierkegaardiennes*, p. 75. 'What is chosen must be there . . . and yet it must be posited by choice.'

account of Flaubert's career. Sartre emphasizes the facticity of this choice, yet though he regards the past as in one sense inviolable, he does concede that we can change its significance by present action, since it is an ex-present which had a future.[1] This affects such drastic decisions as conversion, either to or from religious belief, where the apparent stability of the earlier attitude may have been illusory, and merely masked the accumulating energy of the impending change.[2] William James's study of the varieties of religious experience, with its wealth of illustration from actual cases of decision in this sphere, is as good a practical treatise as one could find to give ballast to the volatile theoretical considerations paraded here.

In *Le Choix*[3] Jean Grenier recommends that we act in such a way that the choice is dictated by our own nature. We must tend towards indifference by way of a nature which we have chosen.[4] The man who seems to have chosen on his own account and by 'his own free will' is merely ratifying a choice which appears to him to have been made by something which transcends him. Thus the revolutionary believes that it is possible to help, and that he is in fact helping, an inevitable historical tendency. Moreover, in religious belief, those who are most firmly convinced of divine omnipotence and predestination have often been precisely those who have most firmly insisted on the need for individual effort towards salvation. What conclusion can be drawn other than that choice is ambivalent, and that 'it means nothing if it is not the expression of a necessity' not external to the agent?[5] On the quodditive aspect of action Grenier points out that though man is not 'a first beginning' he is nevertheless an initiator. As one might expect, Jankélévitch has something explicit to say about this. In his excellent book on Bergson he discusses 'the immanentist conception of liberty' and holds that acceptance of it does not deprive decision of its value as a *beginning*. Bergson has no need, he says, to bring home to us the solemnity of the *fiat* by exaggerating,

---

[1] *E.N.* p. 160.   [2] See William James, *Varieties of Religious Experience*.
[3] 1941.   [4] *Le Choix*, p. 120.
[5] ibid. pp. 120-1. Cf J. Wahl, *Etudes kierkegaardiennes*, p. 74. 'Choisir suivant sa valeur éternelle. L'homme devient lui-même.'

as Renouvier does, the discontinuity of free acts.[1] For Bergson, and in this he is representative of many contemporary continental philosophers, the free act is pre-existent in the traditions which prepare for it, and yet it is a 'true beginning', for at every moment in one's inner life there is a Rubicon to cross, a perilous leap to be undertaken: ' "to take place" is not an empty formality'.[2]

To render the ambivalence of free choice Jean Grenier compares the free agent to an actor who has a part to play, and yet who, if he is a good actor, contrives to invent and 'play' the part as he recites it. The tendency to see man as an actor, usually in a tragic part, is not uncommon in modern writers,[3] who conceive the human condition as one in which each of us is here to act his part, but creatively and with conviction, quodditively and not repetitively, as a man and not as a puppet.[4] This is seriousness, in the Jankélévitchian sense, or authenticity in Sartre's, as demonstrated by Orestes in *Les Mouches*. It must be admitted that the actor-ideal put forward in Camus's *Le Mythe de Sisyphe* is not authentic, because he is in search of discontinuity, repetition, exhaustion of possibility, and the reason for this is that he has no faith in any purpose which would seem to require, and be implied by, consistency. For here it is not a question of acting one part, which would impose some unity on life's 'performance', but of acting many parts, in fact as many as possible, with the object of keeping oneself occupied, at least aesthetically.[5]

Now the idea put forward by Camus of going through many parts and living vicariously and uselessly does in fact correspond to Kierkegaard's aesthetic stage, which is that of the non-recurring; the ethical one on the other hand is that of the ever-recurrent. 'Life is affirmation and reaffirmation, and particularly the life of the spirit; the spirit alone can repeat itself, that is, renew itself in its permanence.'[6] The ethical domain is, furthermore, that of reaffirmation, duty and fidelity to the self, the domain of choice and self-committal.[7] The existentially ethical stage, then, is less that

---

[1] op. cit. p. 99.   [2] ibid. p. 101.   [3] Cf Nietzsche, Camus, Anouilh.
[4] Cf *Le Choix*, p. 124.
[5] Cf Camus's Don Juan and Simone de Beauvoir's 'adventurer'; *Pour une morale de l'ambiguïté*, pp. 86 ff.
[6] J. Wahl, *Et. kierk.*, p. 76.   [7] ibid. p. 72.

of what is universally required than of what is personally required, in terms of 'one's eternal value', in virtue of which 'man becomes himself', aspiring to the marriage of freedom and necessity.[1] Existence is a task,[2] an enterprise of self-discovery by becoming, which involves outstripping oneself towards what one is.[3] My free actions are, therefore, of all those of which I am the author, the most essentially mine; so freedom is a kind of superior necessity: the determination of the self by the self.[4] The freedom of an act is to be judged by the extent to which it is more or less expressive of the person, issuing from an organic necessity, and in form meaningful.[5] What appears to me to be in question here is rather spontaneity than freedom, since Jankélévitch goes on to describe freedom in terms of a demand made upon us, and as 'the duty to remain as far as possible *contemporary with our own actions*, and to seek refuge neither in the past of efficient causes nor in the future of retrospective justifications. . . . And its name is *sincerity*.'[6]

I think this is revealing and important. We are told that freedom is a demand made upon us, and that the acts most essentially ours are subject to a superior necessity. Sartre says that we are condemned to be free, and Simone de Beauvoir is perhaps the most explicit in her *Pour une morale de l'ambiguïté*.

> The drama of the original choice is that it operates instant by instant throughout the whole of life, that it operates without reason, before all reason, that freedom is present in it only in the guise of contingency; this contingency is not unlike the arbitrary incidence of the grace distributed by God to men according to the doctrine of Calvin; here too there is a sort of predestination originating not in external tyranny, but in the acts of the subject himself. We think, however, that the recourse of man to himself is always possible; there is no choice so unhappy that it cannot be redeemed. (*Pour une morale de l'ambiguïté*, p. 59)

---

[1] J. Wahl, *Et. kierk.*, p. 74.   [2] ibid. p. 266.
[3] *E.N.* p. 196 (*B.N.* p. 149).   [4] Jankélévitch, *Bergson*, p. 102.
[5] ibid. p. 103.
[6] Cf A. N. Whitehead, *Religion in the Making*, Cambridge, 1930, p. 5.

To the objection that this kind of freedom is no kind of freedom at all, and that if we are necessarily free we cannot opt out of freedom, Simone de Beauvoir has her answer.[1] Freedom is not a thing or an attribute of a thing, otherwise we would indeed possess it or not possess it. But it is 'fused with the very movement of that ambiguous reality called existence', and is given only to him who conquers it. But this does not seem convincing. To be free is certainly an attribute which may or may not be present, and existentialists themselves recognize that a man can refuse it, in which case his rejection of freedom is still a free choice. All this is unnecessarily confusing, and, as I have indicated earlier, I think the notion of freedom in existentialist philosophy is entirely otiose. The word 'free' in existentialist parlance should be replaced by 'spontaneous', or 'sincere', which would adequately convey the 'ambiguous' quality of the free (i.e. unconstrained) act in relation to the personality which it expresses and the novelty which it brings about. The duty to remain contemporary with our own actions, though perhaps too colourfully expressed for some tastes, then begins to mean something. It expresses phenomenologically the obligation which *can* be either incurred or rejected, to remain attentive to the forms which experience directly assumes, not to allow them to become dulled by familiarity, schematized through intellectual or moral laziness, or standardized through desire for conformity, or through habit. It is a matter of common experience that the impact of a perceived reality can be blunted by repetition, and when we consider that, phenomenologically speaking, perception is never 'pure', that its 'horizon' is as much temporal as spatial,[2] and that therefore my memories are constitutive elements of it, it becomes clear that the intentional structure of the world for me is in some measure dependent on myself, on my alertness and readiness to see its meaning. This is why Jankélévitch says that a free act is a significant act.

If it were not rooted in my past it would not be significant, but would merely be the idiotic 'acte gratuit' of Gide. But this is not all; it would not even be possible, because I should, unweighted by any facticity which is indispensable to the for-itself, be in the

[1] op. cit. p. 36.   [2] Merleau-Ponty, *Phenomenology of Perception*, pp. 68–9.

position of Buridan's ass in the face of a choice: immobilized by indecision. We do not decide without reason; Buridan's dilemma arises from the supposition of a for-itself bereft of its own facticity; we try to 'manufacture the spiritual *ex nihilo*, and condemn free will to die of hunger'. The organic, which is ordered in time, is a factor in reality; I always find in the plenitude of my past the wherewithal to make a decision where I am un-decided.[1] Mathematics deals in reversibles, but life and art have direction and meaning.[2]

This meaning, however, is discoverable only in the face of the situation, and moreover directly in action. Action, we must re-member, may be mental action, and does not necessarily imply the production of physical change. This action I have described as dependent upon (and perhaps it is even identical with) alertness and a kind of intuitive understanding. It is the revelation or 'un-veiling' (*dévoilement*) of the human reality, and it implies a 'per-petual tension' to keep being at a distance, to tear oneself away from the world and assert oneself as 'freedom'.[3] Keeping being at a distance is seeing the implications or requiredness of a situation, in other words, seeing a situation in terms of another situation to which it points. Failing to keep being at a distance is avoiding the tension (or 'anguish') of choice by fleeing into the object itself and becoming absorbed into it: 'in the servitude of seriousness,[4] original spontaneity tries to deny itself'.[5] Inauthenticity of this kind may take the form of trying, from the subjective side, to build something into the already organically total structure of experience in the form of some sort of duplication or phantom operation. Inauthentic consciousness may create a ghost in the machine to keep itself spiritual company in the loneliness of the human condition. This makes possible the bad faith of maintain-ing that we *could* have done more than we did and are better than our history. What one's actions express is oneself, not pre-existing, disembodied actions. From the objective side, becoming

---

[1] *Bergson*, p. 273.   [2] ibid. p. 235.   [3] *Pour une morale*, p. 34.
[4] For Simone de Beauvoir 'seriousness' is playing for safety, seeking a routine, being 'right-thinking' – the antithesis of Jankélévitch's 'sérieux'.
[5] *Pour une morale*, p. 38.

absorbed into the object may involve seeing our evaluations and interpretations as inherent in things themselves, and overlooking the fact that intellection discovers the true sense by supposing it. Reasoning is always subject to the pre-existence of a datum, but action creates itself in its entirety, for it exists only as complete and total. It is by speaking that we learn to speak.[1]

Such conclusions are suggested in large measure by the syncretic character of phenomenological thinking, in which all mental operations, including the most rational, partake, by virtue of being for oneself, of the nature of evaluation. Experience is immediate, and ought to be immediate, any attempt to stuff mediatory material or processes into it being vain *and* immoral. This stress on immediacy seems to be characteristic of modern philosophy as a whole, but the attempt to make a value of it is peculiar to phenomenology and existentialism.   René Le Senne emphasizes the positivity of action in *Le Devoir*. We do not know what we want to do until the moment when we complete our action. The work becomes the extension of the intention, but adds to it and adds itself to it.[2] Obligation arises out of the impotence of a necessity to realize what it would realize, if on the one hand another necessity did not oppose it, and if on the other the self were not indispensable to the invention of every augmentation of reality.[3] Le Senne goes so far as to adopt, in the matter of judgement, a voluntaristic position similar to Renouvier's. He holds that, by instructing us to suspend judgement until the will is determined from the outside by data supplied to the understanding, Descartes in effect condemns us to leave every problem unsolved. Descartes, of course, saw the will as a factor in error, in so far as it wrongly anticipates clear and compelling evidence. Le Senne insists that sufficient conditions cannot *be provided* for judgement. The will to judge finds reasons for judging. He concedes that as soon as we commit ourselves (presumably willingly) to certain postulates, our choice cannot fall on simply any conclusion. But I must give my assent to the conclusion which I reach: in short, I am not bound by necessity, but by obligation, and judging is a free act.[4]

[1] *Bergson*, p. 99.   [2] op. cit. p. 220.   [3] ibid. p. 263.   [4] ibid. p. 251.

16

The authentic and the everyday. Camus

It is rather doubtful if judging is quite as free as Le Senne holds. There seems to be, in this attitude, that lack of cosmic piety with which Bertrand Russell taxes American pragmatists. What we choose, in the language of phenomenology, is surely whether or not we place ourselves in the scientific perspective; but once in it we are in the perspective which has the peculiarity of being nobody's perspective, and in which we have the overwhelming impression of undergoing truth rather than inventing it, despite the mental effort involved in reaching it. If we set aside, however, as an open question whether or not truth is a value in the sense just discussed, we are on ground common to empiricists and phenomenologists in regarding the justification for any 'original choice' as being dependent on the person in question. There is no absolute value in anything, and 'the passion consented to by man finds no external justification. . . . But that does not mean that it cannot . . . give itself reasons for being which it does not possess.'[1] Simone de Beauvoir goes on to add that Sartre says man makes himself into a lack, *in order that* there may be being. She is on surer ground when she shows that there is really nothing arbitrary in natural choice and that where the lack is not the expression of a real need, we tend to be suspicious of it and to regard it as a pseudo-project. Authenticity may have no universal content, but it is not empty. The 'parlour Socialist' and 'bourgeois intellectual' are often looked on as not quite genuine participants in the working-class struggle.[2]

Authentic man and his opposite are discussed concisely but with insight by Simone de Beauvoir in *Pour une morale de l'ambiguïté*.[3] Inauthentic man cannot avoid being present in the world, but his mode of being there is at the level of bare facticity, of in-itself. The impression created by many self-centred people

---

[1] *Pour une morale*, p. 18.   [2] ibid. p. 28.   [3] pp. 58 ff.

is one of lacking sufficient energy and sympathy to interest themselves positively in anything outside the narrow limits of their own world. Such persons are not actively evil, but suffer from a kind of defect of being. This is the existentialist conception of immorality. The subman is the one who restrains his natural and spontaneous self (*ce mouvement originel*). He aspires to the peace of the grave, but within life; he vegetates and takes refuge in the ready-made values (Polin's norms) of the 'serious' world. But he is capable of inauthentic activity too, and is in these circumstances at his most dangerous. 'In lynchings, pogroms, all the bloody and riskless enterprises organized by the fanaticism of right-thinking respectability and moral indignation, it is among the submen that the labour force is recruited.'[1] A bitter, but justified indictment.

Who is the villain of Anouilh's *Antigone*? Neither Antigone nor Creon, who are both authentic in their conflicting ways. Antigone's 'project' is to withstand the pressure of legality, which Creon has undertaken to maintain. She is committed to non-commitment, socially speaking, whereas he has assumed responsibility for the community. The scenes in which they are face to face constitute philosophical dialogues on the meaning of existentialist commitment. The incarnation of evil is neither of these but a collectivity, sufficiently small to appear on the stage, yet anonymous: the guards, with their spokesman and guard commander, the apotheosis of the Sartrian 'salaud'. His projects are extra allowances and not carrying the can. The guards are the unaffected survivors at the end of the play, busy with their game of cards, serene, ready to accept any leader's values and to place themselves at his disposal: themselves spiritually sterile, the tools of power.

The citizens of Argos, in Sartre's *Les Mouches*, are inauthentic, remorse-ridden and bogged down in the shabby misdeeds of their own past. But it is the citizens of Oran, in Camus's *The Plague*, who are, of all, the most elaborately conceived symbol of the self-induced anchylosis of consciousness.

The abstract data here are: the ineradicable illusion of progress,

---

[1] ibid. p. 64.

the indestructibility of evil, the difficulty of making man conscious of the absurd, and having once done so, the greater difficulty of ensuring that he continues to behave as if salvation were possible and 'the walls of absurdity' surmountable. Continuance of life and action while remaining fully conscious of the human situation are therefore the achievements of man worthy of his humanity. One may therefore say that *The Plague* is 'about' making people who are creatures of comfortable habit conscious of the power of contingency to invade and shatter their world. Chance is no man's servant: 'Ils pariaient en somme sur le hasard et le hasard n'est à personne.' Those whom Camus ironically labels 'our fellow-citizens', the people of Oran, hope their luck will hold because they lead an unquestioningly optimistic and materially undisturbed life. They are the type of the modern 'everyday man' whose basic belief is in the permanence of 'normalcy'. Camus pillories complacency and habit unremittingly from the first paragraph. No man can escape from the absurd, but to be unaware of it is to be a prey to reality in a sense in which Rieux and the physically doomed Tarrou are not. The citizens are shown living in a false sense of security, which causes life to be lived in the form of habit – 'since our city favours habit, it may be said that everything is for the best'. Camus even uses the language of the doctrine of pre-established harmony. Habit is a defence against modest novelty; against catastrophe it struggles in vain to survive, but its struggle is not readily abandoned, even among those professionally responsible for meeting the challenge of the unexpected, perhaps least of all among them.

The doctors of Oran are unwilling collectively to recognize and deal effectively with the plague: no panic at any price, they say. 'Our citizens were no more guilty than others, but they forgot to be modest; how could they be expected to think of the plague, which eliminates the future . . .' The normal is not compatible with the idea of a medieval disease. 'On the other side of the window-pane the bell of a tram rang suddenly, and in an instant cruelty and pain were refuted.' The people are 'plunged in stupid human confidence', and to them disaster is an alien idea. The word 'étranger' is significant and variable in Camus. In the novel of that name Meursault is 'outside' the habits and conventions of his environment. In *The Plague*, Tarrou is similarly apart, by reason of his awareness, from the sluggish and habit-ridden citizens. They, for their part, and conversely, are 'strangers' to the intransigence of the absurd, and are symbolized by the Parisian Rambert who is caught in Oran by the collective quarantine restrictions and refuses to 'belong' – 'I am a stranger in this town', 'I don't belong here', express an attitude which dies hard in him.

The collective effort, then, is to maintain contented inertia intact against the force of contingency in its most acute form, 'to put out of reach of the plague that part of themselves which they were defending against any incursion'. Here a word about the symbolism of plague is appropriate. An artistic symbol never coincides exactly with the idea or set of ideas for which it stands; it has a life and a discursiveness of its own which overlap or fall short of the discursive arguments which might conceivably re-place it (and which in *Le Mythe de Sisyphe* do). Bubonic plague is chosen and well handled by Camus as a symbol of contingency and evil. Its pandemic ravages in Europe and the west declined from the time of the Black Death to the beginning of the eigh-teenth century. By the mid-nineteenth it had withdrawn to its endemic centres in Asia, but at the end of the nineteenth century it showed some tendency to spread again, in a very limited way, but disturbingly, in South America and also in British com-munities. In 1900 over thirty cases occurred in Glasgow, causing fifteen deaths, and in the same year Sydney had over a hundred cases of whom about a third died. Isolated cases occurred in Suffolk and Liverpool before and after the First World War, these being of the invariably fatal pneumonic variety. This recrudes-cence of a disease normally associated with uncivilized conditions of overcrowding, verminous filth and malnutrition offers an appropriate symbol for the moral and material setbacks which our apparently well-established and prosperous civilization has suffered in recent years. The plague clearly stands often for Camus's recol-lection of war and occupation – he actually uses the term 'new order' once. The cheapness of life, mass burials, the loss of human dignity in life and death are constantly brought into relief, so that the novel becomes a slightly disguised material history of our time, and an entirely undisguised moral one. The plague stands for all the primitive evil which is immanent in reality and which 'progressive' man has learnt to know only abstractly. His revolt is provoked only when he is forced to know evil concretely in his own life and through his own senses. For as long as possible he cultivates the security of habit, and the more sophisticated escape of a pseudo-rational, or what one may call bureaucratic, complacency. The face of a scientific society is saved by the speed and efficiency with which it buries its dead and, unlike earlier ages, keeps accurate mortality records; organization is good and the prefect well pleased. All of which forces Rieux to remark: 'Yes! it's the same burial; but we keep card indexes. Progress is undeniable.' The citizens live in a world of rubber stamps 'which regulate our lives and deaths . . . we are destined to die ignominiously, but duly card-indexed'. Tarrou remarks that all that is left is accountancy, and Dr Richard derives satisfaction from his excellent graph of the course of the plague. Camus enjoys sending his bacteria against all the tidy people who, in one way or another, have the plague explained. Father Paneloux, who sees it as an act of divine judgement, and poor M. Othon who is no more than a judge of ordinary misdeeds and who behaves creditably throughout the book, are all carried off for their judicial presumptuousness. The crime of the priest and the judge in Camus's eyes is to *accept* the idea of condemnation: every human being is condemned to death, but his duty is revolt and not acquiescence. To judge, docket, or condemn is to make a thing of a person, to side with fate against man, to betray our fellows, to bring more determinism into human life than even a hostile reality ordains. It is always an act, not of equity, but of hatred; let us leave inhumanity to the plague.

Paneloux's sermon had the effect of 'bringing home to certain people the idea, hitherto vague, that they were condemned for an unknown crime to an unimaginable imprisonment'. The bitterest words against Paneloux are those of Rieux: the priest speaks in the name of truth because he has not seen enough people die; he's an academic priest; a parish priest would be too busy relieving suffering to try to demonstrate its excellence. As for legal judgement, we are told that the plague was particularly severe in the communal life of prison, and that the governor, warders and prisoners were all equally under sentence, so that for the first time justice really reigned. Othon on the other hand is perhaps no more than a figure of grim fun. 'How can one help a judge?' asks Tarrou, and finds that in life or death, or both, 'he had had no luck'. Tarrou's father was a lawyer who 'innocently' drove his son from home by professionally obtaining the death sentence for a criminal.

The question of inter-human evil, evil of human provenance, 'le scandale', man's inhumanity to man, whereby through his free will he widens the rift which is the pre-condition of 'absurdity' is one which receives searching treatment and calls for an extension of the symbol of disease. Society is infected with a kind of moral sleeping sickness, again a version of habit, which renders it insensitive to the significance of its acts. It complacently accepts evil as an ally and an element of social stability. This is a failure to answer the call to awareness, and to meet the challenge of the instant which demands a new, and above all a *felt*, an 'authentic' response. The conventional value is the symptom of moral plague, and Tarrou conceives immunity as man's duty. 'I didn't want to be infected with the plague, that's all. I thought the society in which I lived rested on the death penalty, and that by fighting it, I was fighting murder.' He rejects the argument that the infliction of death is the means of banishing from the world the killing of one's fellow-man, that murder does away with murder. (This is the theme of *Les Justes*.) Or, more precisely, he recognizes its partial and occasional truth, but confesses himself 'incapable of remaining in this order of truths'. To refuse evil as an auxiliary, as part of man, is to choose the hard way and ultimately to *pretend* that evil is entirely set over against man and outside him. To maintain human freedom against hostile fate is to over-simplify, but this is a nobler error than sleepily to believe in the condemnation of man by man, in whatever form, as a 'necessary evil'. The only necessary evil is the extra-human 'walls of absurdity', and ultimately death, which is the reduction to thinghood against which life struggles; but 'the slumber of men is more sacred than life to the plague-ridden'. To sink into the restful torpor of resignation and anaesthetized conscience is easy, to remain healthy is difficult: 'Yes, Rieux, it is tiring to be a victim of the plague. But it is even more tiring not to want to be.' Put into abstract and non-symbolical terms the struggle is between the acceptance of conventional value, which in its sophisticated form involves applying laws (scientific and social) to individual cases which they always cover but never fit, and on the other hand recognizing the uniqueness of the individual and the fact that his death is never merely a case of Death: there is no death, there are only dead people. Tarrou generalizes: 'I have realized that all human unhappiness derives from the fact that people do not use clear language.' Nothing strictly relevant is ever said in general terms, or when man acts in an official capacity. Meursault's trial in *The Outsider* is not about his murder, but about his failure to weep at his mother's funeral. Public money is spent on fitting him into what Tarrou here calls 'the convenient category of the accused'.

The social importance of convenient categories and euphemistic designations is brought into ironical prominence in the account of the meeting of the doctors of Oran to decide on emergency measures. It is a chapter on verbal taboos and the vain attempt to evade reality by refusing to name it. The novel purports to teach us that cases are never entirely covered by the words, forms or attitudes which are evolved to receive them. The 'good citizen' always has something ready, but it is seldom adequate. The attempt to rationalize evil away is a version of the 'leap' from absurdity into eternity and salvation which Camus condemns. There is a place for human ingenuity and reason, but it is in ever-renewed action, not in graphs or card-indexes. These things do not dispose of evil, at best they merely represent it in schematized form, and seek a sort of spurious escape through representation. The distinctively human reason thus parodies itself by its creation of pseudo-entities and substances. Its proper function is to introduce not rigidity, but flexibility into the mind which only thus is fitted to deal with the recurrent challenge of contingent reality.[1]

[1] Camus, with his excess of satirical zeal, generally speaking misrepresents

Man in revolt is a pluralist who sees in every case a new beginning and who lives quantitatively by performing tasks as they occur. He is 'everyday man', but transformed and elevated by his awareness of how he stands and how temporary as well as temporal is everything he does: 'Your victories are always provisional', says the sagacious Tarrou, and Rieux replies that this is no reason for giving up the fight. The struggle is not a blind one in which the motive is hope, but the lucid and active acceptance of an 'interminable defeat'. Paneloux is brought to this in a more Christian version, which he defines as active fatalism.

It might be said that the 'divorce' presented in The Myth of Sisyphus is an oversimplification on the part of Camus, by his own standards. This is made evident in the novels, where in concrete terms Camus shows that as bacteria, particles of malignant, non-human reality, invade the body and thrive there, so fragments of 'material' evil reside and breed in the soul. They partake of the nature of matter in that they resist disintegration, they endure, and by flourishing at the expense of the host they impoverish his living variability. They live on his life and their simplicity persists to the detriment of his complexity.

Thus the modern writer questions the wisdom of the ages, and its values. Does evil reside in change or changelessness? The traditional hierarchy of values has favoured that which endures. But the philosophies of life show the desire of eternity as the desire of death. Simplicity and rigidity are principles of death, whether in the world of micro-organisms, good citizens or good organizers. What then is goodness? A principle for which action is undertaken and man held in constant readiness, but one which Camus does not name; he accepts it as a thing intuitively but not discursively known. It is manifested in the principle of revolt, it shows itself in the outrage felt at the death of a child. It is also the blind principle of sacrifice in a world where values cannot be rationally upheld. 'Nothing in the world justifies one in turning aside from what one loves. And yet I too turn aside without knowing why.'

---

reason, which he consistently shows as mere mental habit, a parody of 'constituted' reason. He seems to overlook constituting reason altogether.

The Outsider is more complicated as far as symbolism is concerned. Meursault is an ambiguous character, who begins by being an 'everyday' drifter, glad to see the end of each interruption of his routine, and taking the line of least resistance, whether this involves evasion or assent. He drifts into murder, but then having, as Sartre's Orestes does, incurred guilt and ratified his act, he moves progressively towards authenticity, while conversely society comes to stand for the betrayal of the genuinely human. Sartre has described the novel as Humean. It is Humean in presenting, principally in Meursault's character as initially portrayed, the absence of that necessity which has been discussed. He is aimless and atomic, and he believes as little in his own substantial soul as does the prosecuting counsel.

But here an interesting point arises. Camus is less concerned with discontinuity than with artificial continuity. He is worried about the sort of 'Gestalt' which is nobody's project, but which society somehow strings together with bits of Christian doctrine, Old Testament vindictiveness and the law as a great many people's living. The trial brings to light the psychological and sociological fictions of character, motive and cause, in which everybody believes implicitly, except Camus and Meursault. To the latter the whole proceeding is a curious ritual irrelevant to his life and acts, for when, asked what caused him to commit the crime, he mentions the only circumstance closely related in his own mind with the deed, namely the sun's light and heat, everyone laughs. He cannot identify himself with the social values which are other people's, nor can he place himself in the 'category of the accused' to which society assigns him. What he represents is not so much the discontinuity of spineless drift as a man initially and half-consciously in search of values, and who refuses social norms. The inauthentic is the universal, and its condemnation here 'reveals the existential vanity of pure determination',[1] of what is embodied in the legal and social structure of a community, accepted by all because it is too much trouble to reject it, yet which is, strictly speaking, irrelevant to every instance, concrete situation and particular case for which it is invoked. The incompatibility of

[1] R. Le Senne, *Obstacle et valeur*.

inhuman necessity – even when, in the form of law, it is of human provenance – and human requirement is seen throughout Camus's work.[1] In real life it is seen outside any prison in which a murderer is being executed, and where is measured the distance between justice as an abstract provision and as the concrete enactment; to take place is indeed no mere formality.

17

Universality and particularity

The open and closed moralities are commonly distinguished in large measure by their insistence respectively on particularity or universality of requiredness. The distinction is variously made by different writers in France,[2] but it is a widespread preoccupation there, and has excited some interest recently among English philosophers.[3] The latter generally consider that a moral position is possible only on the basis of some universalizable maxim whereas continentals tend to hold that universalizable morality is closed morality, and inferior to what is uniquely required for me in my situation.

The tendency of recent French philosophy to see morality as simply one part of value-creating mental activity which, being inventive, is concerned with what essential novelty shall be brought into being, as distinct from what will by its own nature come about, is seen in René Le Senne's *Le Devoir*. 'Science is the knowledge of what is, and, in what is, of what cannot not be;

[1] Cf *Les Justes*, concerned with the conflict between revolutionary zeal for the millennium, accessible through a single act here and now, and reluctance to sacrifice the innocent.

[2] Cf Le Senne's 'moralité' and 'morale'. See *Le Devoir*, p. 83.

[3] See *Proceedings of the Aristotelian Society*, 1954–5, papers by E. A. Gellner, 'Ethics and Logic', and R. M. Hare, 'Universalisability'. Also Alasdair MacIntyre, 'What Morality is not', in *Philosophy* (Vol. XXXII, No. 123), October 1957, and W. F. Frankena, 'MacIntyre on defining Morality' in *Philosophy*, April 1958.

morality is concerned with what must be, or with what cannot be, since there would be no occasion to order it, if the objective course of events were destined to produce it necessarily as an effect. . . . To order is to propose to oneself, or to others, in the light of some conflict, an object to be made. Science is about the realized, morality about the realizable.'[1] By virtue of this, of course, the putting forward of universal maxims would be regarded as a kind of manufacture of morality in terms of the realized (analogous to the retrospective discovery of determinism in decisions), and thus fall outside morality altogether and into determinism. The existentialist criticism here would be the familiar one that man was imitating the operations of inanimate nature, and trying to find a morality in the in-itself instead of in the for-itself. Morality, then, adds to reality, and enriches being, which means that it is quodditive and not merely repetitive. Real morality cannot be looked up in books or codes, but only intuited here and now.

What does this amount to? In his *Traité de morale générale* Le Senne seems very close to Bergson's conception of open morality, in requiring that, once 'moral anonymity', or the reduction of morality to mass customs, has been set aside, we can approach 'the description of the noblest ways of living which have been proposed to mankind'.[2] But a model is, surely, no less universal than a maxim, for a maxim can be highly complex and detailed. The reply would no doubt be that the quality of moral insight, which provides ethical inspiration of an indeterminate but none the less lofty kind, works on us by its 'atmosphere', and that we attend to detail at our peril. The fact remains that one feels more inclined to identify the real way of the open morality as the Sartrian one, where no objectifications of any sort, past or present, are offered. The for-itself finds its own way restlessly and intangibly forward. There are difficulties here too, but difficulties less fatal to the whole outlook.

It is, however, only in the *Traité de morale générale* that Le Senne seems disposed to vest moral excellence in 'the minority of heroes and sages'. Elsewhere, and pre-eminently in *Le Devoir*, he is concerned with the 'contradiction', or conflict of obligations, as the

[1] op. cit. pp. 83–4.   [2] *T.M.G.* p. 107.

real source of moral choice and creativeness. Obligation is generally, among French philosophers, seen as one 'intentional structure' among many, and indeed, the requiredness of every unique situation being unique, there is little tendency to classify it as even moral, and less to relate it to any particular maxim or precept. However, Le Senne keeps universalism in sight, for he says that what is required of each one of us is not that he should do everybody's duty, but *his* duty,[1] and this changes with situation, temperament, personal past, and so on.

> At the same time as it is the same for everybody, in the sense that no concrete duty can be a duty without applying the imperative universally, it is true, because of the inexhaustible fecundity of duty, that this duty, which imposes itself upon me, at such and such an instant, is a historical duty, that no other person is called upon to face, and which is incumbent upon me only by reason of what I am and what I want. So it is more appropriate to stress the personality of duty than its universality; or rather to show that abstract universality . . . is only a pointer to concrete universality. (*Le Devoir*, pp. 270-1)

How does this 'personalism of duty' work out? In fact, in vigilant and vigorous resistance to unquestioning social conformity, in 'the reaction of individual intelligence against social truth'.[2] Now it would be generally agreed that the ability to see immorality in existing social customs and institutions, and willingness to raise one's voice against it, are what constitute a social conscience; but the moral novelty advocated is necessarily universalizable, whether it be the right of slaves to be free, of all men to life, liberty and the pursuit of happiness, or all people to treatment in sickness, regardless of their ability to pay a doctor. Morever, reformist zeal may be qualified, and insert provisos and details into its laws. In fact, as R. M. Hare says,[3] one can load any amount of detail into a maxim without destroying its universality, yet make it in practice personal, and particular in its

[1] See below concerning MacIntyre's points, and *Philosophy*, XXXII, No. 123, p. 328.
[2] op. cit. p. 278.   [3] loc. cit.

P

relevance. But all this logical argument is beside the point. The problem is surely a psychological one.

It is not a question as to whether the moral implications of a unique situation are or are not theoretically universalizable. It is a question of my state of mind in the face of moral choice, or of a situation calling for a moral judgement. If I think that everyone shares my indignation at some scandal, and *a fortiori* if there is some law under which action can be taken in the matter, my anger will tend to subside and I shall probably leave the matter to other people, feeling reasonably assured that something will be done. At the other extreme is the case where I am the only person to feel outraged, and then exceptional courage may be needed to speak out and act. The comparatively common intermediate case is where I am one of a substantial minority which feels strongly about something, and then I shall probably consider associating myself with some concerted effort to right the wrong, which, by existentialist standards, would be a kind of semi-moral action. By these standards there is no moral issue where everybody is agreed and where the law is clear. Legislation which is good does not so much embody morality as kill it by depriving its advocates of the role of men in revolt or of martyrs.

> Shall we eliminate sacrifice from morality? This is the declared or tacit aim of every morality. It has found expression in objectivity; and one must recognize that the aim of all moral research is to formulate rules which, when applied, exempt others, and the moralist too, from having to invent them. (*Le Devoir*, p. 193)

Le Senne adds, with an almost audible sigh of relief, that in trying to substitute intellectual for affective or practical morality, we do not thereby evade morality. There is no goodness to end all goodness, and the belief that there is, he might have added, is simply Sartrian 'bad faith'.

There will always be room for moral pioneering, which is the only sort of moral activity recognized by the kind of writers I am concerned with. What characterizes the state of mind of the moral pioneer is the feeling of conscious and active committal to a position which usually encounters some 'everyday' resistance, based on habit, traditional values, calculation of interest, communal or sectional, and so on. Bergson has relevant things to say in the early part of his *Two Sources*, when discussing the feeling of obligation as ordinarily experienced, and where no conflict of duties is involved. Obligation as a single, untrammelled duty is almost always fulfilled automatically, he says, and usually doing one's duty is reducible to a kind of self-abandonment and relaxation of tension.[1] It is in society's interest that it should be habitual and involve little strain or need to brace oneself for the task, and that, in short, it should be well within reach, not to say the normal form of behaviour, of 'everyday man'. In a sense doing one's duty in this way is unconscious; it is a manifestation of a closed morality. Some degree of paradox is involved, since this unconsciousness is the condition of a comprehensive objective consciousness. It is, says Merleau-Ponty,[2] 'by giving up part of his spontaneity, by becoming involved in the world through stable organs and pre-established circuits that man can acquire the mental and practical space which will theoretically free him from his environment and allow him to *see* it'. What we see, by thus sacrificing spontaneity, is common property reality, and this is by no means a negligible acquisition. But this objective perspective must occasionally be disrupted in the interest of reality-for-me. This involves a moral conflict, a conflict between my moral insight and objectified value, and here my act becomes conscious and authentic. The consciousness takes the form of 'anguish', perhaps genuine fear,[3] accompanied perhaps by some hesitation; indeed, says Bergson,[4] this hesitation *is* consciousness, the habitual act passing almost unnoticed. We see why Bergson stresses suspension of judgement as a distinctively human phenomenon. It represents resistance to the forces of habit, or instinct, or inertia. To say No! particularly in a social context, can be as authentic an act as any,[5] the important thing being that we should be

---

[1] *Les Deux Sources*, p. 13.   [2] *Phenomenology of Perception*, p. 87.
[3] Cf *E.N.* p. 66.   [4] op. cit. p. 13.
[5] Cf for example Kaliayeff's refusal to throw the bomb, in Camus's play *Les Justes*.

contemporary and compresent with our acts, whether we give or withhold participation.

To be conscious and in a way resistant, then, is the prime characteristic of the authentic act. Its antithesis is the act which is in conformity with either our own habitual behaviour or the received social pattern. What is existentially required is something over and above this.[1] Alasdair MacIntyre, discussing the matter at the logical level, instances what theologians call 'works of supererogation' as examples of moral acts which are 'by definition not numbered among the normal duties of life',[2] and are therefore non-universalizable.[3] It does not make sense, he maintains, to say that Captain Oates did what he ought to have done. Yet it is possible for a man to set himself the task of performing a work of supererogation, and feel guilty if he does not carry it out, without finding such failure in others blameworthy. Now it is true that a work of supererogation would be an excellent example of an existentially moral act. But what one needs to remember is that what makes it a work of supererogation is not what it involves (because it may, given the appropriate change in moral climate, cease to be one and become universally required) but the contingent fact that no one at present expects it to be performed. Authenticity, then, is a state of mind, in relation to an action, which is independent of the content of the action.

Any valuation is of course logically independent of the thing valued, but the precepts of closed morality can generally be justified in terms of social utility, whereas authenticity is not concerned with this. It sets out to be 'pure' morality, and it is for this reason that some moral heroes of existentialist literature appear so perverse. The writer's object being to present a character committed to his own acts, these are thrown into the clearest relief when they are such that they could not possibly be confused with the demands of routine morality. I do not think there is any intention, with such characters as Orestes, Meursault and Jean Genet, of

[1] The expressions 'par surcroît' and 'par-dessus le marché' are typical of what is frequently found in French.

[2] loc. cit.

[3] There is here a first person, but not a third person, use of moral valuation.

confusing the issue, but of showing clearly 'what morality is not'.

Existential morality is notorious for its lack of content. But it does not cease for that reason to be morality. Everything is in the manner, as its sponsors would, and do, say.[1] What is important is not what we believe in, but that we should really believe in it. There is a conservative tendency, not entirely discreditable, to try, in Carlyle's language, to wear old clothes when they no longer fit. But, says Le Senne,[2] any institution or precept must be believed in, and be an object for which sacrifice is possible, if it is to endure. From the fact that some do not endure, we must conclude that 'their collapse reveals the existential vanity of pure determination'. Simone de Beauvoir, in her *Pour une morale de l'ambiguïté*, shows determination as the snare of morality. The objectified values of 'seriousness' are the refuge of the subman.[3] This is a thoroughly familiar theme, and for the most part she follows the Sartrian line, discussing the content of a moral position only in so far as it is existentially fruitful, and not in terms of its possible universality.

There is, however, one important respect in which she departs from Sartre's position, and bridges the abyss that yawns between the curious, half-deterministic, half-tautological kind of morality just discussed, which seems to say that we must do what some inner necessity requires, and the other which seems to demand, perhaps illogically but none the less imperiously, that at least as much recognition be accorded to the claims of other people's interests as to those of our own. Sartre's attitude to others, on the philosophical plane at least, as revealed in *Being and Nothingness* and *In Camera* (where it is summed up in the celebrated statement: Hell is other people), seems to be basically one of fear and hostility, arising out of the feeling that, with the appearance of the other, his world is stolen from him,[4] that his being ebbs away from him beneath the other's gaze,[5] and that the mere existence of the other brings about his apprehension of himself as a bit of nature.[6] The fact that Sartre's political opinions seem to belie this

---

[1] 'Sensibility is nothing but attentive presence in the world and to oneself.' S. de Beauvoir, *Pour une morale*, p. 60.

[2] *Obstacle et valeur*, p. 187. [3] *Pour une morale*, pp. 63 ff. Also p. 38.

[4] *E.N.* p. 313. [5] *E.N.* p. 319. [6] *E.N.* p. 321.

basic conviction, and that by all accounts his personal affability is at variance with it, suggests that he is in the grip of some everyday morality in all but his creative moments. Be that as it may, he appears to take, in an extreme form, the view that one needs to work out one's own values in absolute independence, and undertake one's own acts (which Garcin fails to do). He speaks of being in a state of servitude when ready-made values are imposed on him, and in danger to the extent that he is the instrument of possibilities which are not his own possibilities, which 'deny his transcendence'. This danger is furthermore no fortuitous and temporary predicament, but the permanent structure of being-for-others.[1]

Now Simone de Beauvoir does not accept this view of other people in her *Pour une morale de l'ambiguïté*. A morality of ambiguity, she says,[2] is one which refuses to deny *a priori* that separate beings can be associated, or that 'their separate liberties can forge laws valid for all'. This seems an important advance on the positions earlier examined, and a move towards universality. No man can save himself alone, she says,[3] and she is aware that any human work needs to be sustained not only by the conviction of its author, but also by the recognition, if not of posterity (for which many will sacrifice their present), then at least of a handful of faithful devotees. Complete moral isolation is enough to shake most men's confidence in their beliefs and acts, and nothing rings more true in the Gospel narratives than the ultimate faltering of Jesus when in such a situation.

There is, then, a reciprocity of consciousness, and it is not the case that 'each consciousness seeks the death of the other', as Hegel is quoted as saying.[4] Simone de Beauvoir has little time for this excessively virile and aggressive brand of self-realization. She makes no direct attack on Sartre, but quotes with disapproval the preface of Georges Bataille's *L'Expérience intérieure*, where each individual is said to seek, imperialistically, to dominate and absorb everything (*chaque individu veut être Tout*). She retorts that such hatred is naïve and self-destructive, for if I were indeed every-

---

[1] *E.N.* p. 326.   [2] op. cit. p. 26.   [3] ibid. pp. 88–9.
[4] ibid. p. 99. Cf supra, p. 54.

thing, there would be nothing outside me, and I should be not so much a void as non-existent, having nothing to possess, or against which to measure myself and confirm my separate individuality. I soon learn that others, by robbing me of my world, also give it to me, since a thing is given to me only in the act whereby it is taken away. To desire that there should be being is to desire that others should be there to endow the world with human meanings. A project becomes determinate only through its relation to those of others, and our being is realized only through communication with others. Every human being, as she claims to have shown in her *Pyrrhus et Cinéas*, needs the freedom of others, and without it is fixed in the absurdity of facticity.[1] She maintains that by thus pointing the way to altruism she is giving a content to existentialist morality, and refuting those who complain that it has none, by 'indicating to each one concrete actions to be performed'.

One sign of a renascent universalism, and the restoration of the norm to its rightful dignity, is a recent book by M. Jean Pucelle, *La Source des valeurs*.[2] All established philosophical tendencies have their stereotyped fringe of repetitive, imitative and dull writing; the philosophies of existence no less than others. This book brings a breath of fresh air into the stifling atmosphere of anguish and vertiginous liberty. Pucelle states unequivocally that personal relations can promote values only by repeated acts. We are caught between the demand for purity and that for 'duration or expansion'.[3] There is a balance to be struck between the 'precariousness' of a value and its 'consistency'. The first is not mere arbitrariness and the second does not promise absolute security and sink into the morality of the hypocritical formalist. What is stressed is that it is of the essence of value that it be shared, made authentic by *consensus*, and consolidated by objectification in an organized society provided with norms.[4] A salutary distinction is observed between 'values of unity', such as love or friendship, and universalizable values, which we have generally seen neglected and discredited. Pucelle, while recognizing the sincerity, prophetic vigour and conviction of existentialist writers such as Kierkegaard,

---

[1] *Pour une morale*, pp. 100–1.   [2] Vitte, 1957.
[3] op. cit. p. 76.   [4] ibid. pp. 78–9.

Buber and Berdiaeff, nevertheless feels that their denunciations of objectivity are carried too far, and that some sense of proportion needs to be restored. He remarks, perceptively, that Germanic and Slavonic thought (to which recent French philosophy owes not a little) have always, for different reasons, shown aversion to the Latin juridical spirit, but that there is no reason why we should follow them all the way in this direction.[1]

A certain proportion of the book is profitably devoted to the examination of writings on jurisprudence, and to considerations arising out of these. Will is dissociated, for all practical purposes, from legality.[2] Law arises out of 'bonds of consensus'; no creative activity can be an expression of it, because it is a 'principle of limitation'.[3] But it is a condition of creation, for 'if a promise excludes capricious liberty, it exalts and deepens creative liberty'.[4]

Ethical values oscillate between the two poles of charity and justice, the personal and the impersonal, the spiritual and the juridical, gratuitousness and obligation.[5] If our relations with others, it is wisely pointed out, involve direct valuation, we are in the realm of love and friendship; but if they are regulated by pre-existing norms, then we are in the realm of justice.

18

Saint-Exupéry

Before a final summing-up is attempted, it is worth while to devote a few pages to a writer whose reputation rests on the literary, rather than the philosophical, value of his work. Yet in so far as a novelist, who is entitled to pose problems without solving them, can be considered a philosopher, at least by the standards of this study, Saint-Exupéry's claims are not negligible. His temperament and outlook show a dualism which illustrates

---

[1] op. cit. p. 92 footnote.   [2] ibid. pp. 100–1.   [3] ibid. p. 110.
[4] ibid. p. 121.   [5] ibid. pp. 153–4.

what has been said in the foregoing pages about the two poles of a settled and, where it is wisely used, fruitful past (in-itself), and a restlessly progressive present-becoming-future (for-itself). There is enough strictly phenomenological interest in his writings to make some of his descriptions relevant to Merleau-Ponty's *Phenomenology of Perception*.[1] And if the 'circle of selfhood' is anywhere manifest it is in these novels and autobiographical writings.

The dualism referred to above is variously displayed at different times, and the relative importance of the elements constituting it also varies greatly. Basically and simply one may say that these elements are, on the one hand a desire for tranquillity and security, and on the other the quest of action and change. Or, more precisely, there is the *desire* for tranquillity while action and acceptance of change are seen by him as the fulfilment of an *obligation* to himself and others. The life of the child is spent in the sheltered haven, and initiation into manhood means the voyage into the unknown, and only through this undertaking does the boy grow up (or 'build himself', as Saint-Exupéry is fond of saying), and, thereby ceasing to be self-sufficient, assume responsibility for others and integrate himself into his community.

In every one of his works there is, somewhere or other, prominently or incidentally, the nostalgia for a past which represents irresponsibility (protection by others) and stability (freedom from threat and change, particularly the threat of death). It is significant that this clinging to a secure past is most evident in situations of danger and exposure, for example, in the fourth section of 'L'Avion et la planète' (*Terre des hommes*), where, forced down in the desert, he lies and meditates on his predicament, 'naked between sand and stars, separated from the poles of my life by too much silence'. He thinks of the house where he lived as a child, and of its park with dark fir trees and limes. 'It mattered little whether it was far or near, or that, being now no more than a dream, it could neither warm my flesh nor shelter me: its mere existence was enough to fill my night with its presence.' This thought of security in insecurity underlines the relationship

[1] See op. cit. pp. 84, 456.

between them, and even the dependence of one on the other. He thinks of his old nurse Paula, for whom thoughts of a hard and alien life were simply barbarous. His dreams of adventure as a child made no impression on this simple, homeloving woman, and he pitied her. But that night, in those circumstances, he tells us, he saw things with her eyes. In other words, by action and the embracing of the contrary ideal, he has won the right to value hers. The challenge and uncertainty of modern life is a challenge to be met; the man who evasively tries to conserve his possession of innocent happiness is failing in his duty and also deluding himself (for his attempt is doomed to failure); but the man who tears himself away from his attachments wins two worlds: that of self-realization through action and concrete achievement, and, in consciously apprehended and idealized retrospect, that of his 'amies d'enfance ennuyeuses mais chères, toutes ses petites infirmités d'homme' (*Vol de nuit*, Chap. IV).

A further instance of the retrospective vision won by the distance he has travelled from it, or of a kind of redemption through suffering, is to be found in *Pilote de guerre* (Chap. XIX). He is on a reconnaissance flight, and exposed to attack by German fighters. It is now, he says, that childhood becomes sweet, and not only childhood, but all past life. The memory of Paula is an obsession throughout the flight; the first paragraph of the following chapter is significant. He returns to childhood as to a kind of charm which shall preserve him from his present danger: 'Paula, your shade was my shield . . .' There is of course here the straightforward desire for the impossible: a protection in manhood as adequate as that provided by those who look after us as children. But there is also the feeling that the value of life is fully apprehended only after it has been offered as a sacrifice. The experience of fighting one's way through to the peace of contemplation is communicated in the very last paragraphs of both Malraux's *L'Espoir* and *Les Noyers de l'Altenburg*. Might not the same truth be expressed symbolically in Chapter XVI of *Vol de nuit*, where Fabien emerges, above the storm, over the moonlit clouds?[1]

In the two early works *Courrier Sud* and *Vol de nuit* what one

[1] Cf also *Terre des hommes*, 'Coll. pourpre', Gallimard p. 45.

may, in the light of Saint-Exupéry's characterization and symbolism, call the woman's world of conservation and non-purposive
relationships occupies an important place. In the first, which is a
kind of preparation of *Vol de nuit*, the pilot Jacques Bernis and
Geneviève respectively incarnate these hostile yet mutually complementary worlds. Geneviève is associated with Bernis's old
home, and this is one of Saint-Exupéry's most striking symbols
of the 'affective refusal of time'. The house represents the cult of
conservation, the fear of change and decay, and ultimately of
death (Chapter III). Whatever could these great beams be defending the house against? Against time, the great enemy in our home.
We protected ourselves against it by tradition and the cult of the
past. The object of this poetic chapter is to show the vanity of
such a cult. The struggle to keep the home and its inmates
staunch against the flow of time is a losing one. We alone, says
Saint-Exupéry, knew that the house was launched like a ship, and
in its holds we alone knew where it had sprung a leak. They, the
children, exploring the loft, knew the hole in the roof which time
had bored and through which shone the star which was a portent.
They would then turn back; it was the star which brought sickness
and death.

The summing up of the eternal affinity and incompatibility of
the two worlds is admirably performed in the short Chapter V
(Part III) of *Courrier Sud*. We are left somewhat suspended between the two, as again we are, despite a certain Nietzscheanism
of tone, in *Vol de nuit*. For Rivière too has his doubts, and wonders
whether there is adequate justification for tearing men away from
their individual happiness in the name of a project which is little
more than a gamble. Is not the first necessity to preserve individual
happiness? Here the conclusive misgiving asserts itself: 'And yet
one day, inevitably, the golden sanctuaries vanish like mirages.
Age and death, more pitiless than he, destroy them.' Ultimately
this is the impulse which compels action and the acceptance of
time, so that men, in losing themselves, are saved.

The idea that happiness and security are fragile and menaced,
and that a kind of miserly concern with their preservation leads
only to disappointment and disillusionment, causes the alternative

of action and self-expenditure or self-exchange (*s'échanger*) to be sought. But there is no question ultimately of turning from one to the other. They are not really alternatives; they are mutually dependent, and the word which perhaps best expresses their relationship is bipolarity. It is an illusion to believe that life can be satisfactorily lived by remaining, or trying to remain, at one pole, that of secure happiness and the golden age of childhood. This is best seen from the opposite pole of manhood and its responsibilities. Happiness is most nearly achieved by a kind of circular route via realization and creation. In *Lettre à un otage* he is dealing with this question, and writes: 'The essential thing is that there should remain somewhere that on which we have lived. Customs, the family occasion, the house of memories. The essential thing is to live for the return' (Chap. II). A little later he recalls the experience in the desert recounted in *Terre des hommes*: 'Almost unreal poles magnetize the desert from afar; a childhood home which remains alive in memory . . .' *Pilote de guerre* deals with the fragmentation of his country and his experience. Here he is concerned with the fate of the detached fragment which seeks return and re-integration. War is in these works the agency of detachment, and since Saint-Exupéry regards war as an evil (a disease, like typhus) one might think that in a more civilized world the initial fragmentation would be avoidable. But this is not so. War is the symbol of what other writers have called 'absurdity', but it is not the whole of it, and men will always find that the paradise of their own experience must be jeopardized and broken before it can be reconstituted. The detachment of the human fragment is voluntarily undertaken for *the sake of the return*, and the essentially paradoxical and contradictory nature of human experience is thus brought to light.

Never did I feel a greater love for my home than in the Sahara. Never were men nearer to their betrothed than the Breton mariners of the sixteenth century, when they rounded Cape Horn and grew older in the teeth of adverse winds. From the moment of departure they were already beginning to return. It was their return that they were preparing with their heavy hands as they hoisted the sails. The shortest route from the Breton port to the house of the betrothed ran via Cape Horn. (*Lettre à un otage*, Chap. I)

The emigrants are the real travellers, for their return may perhaps never be.

The man's destiny then is that of the traveller, *homo viator*, and Fabien's wife visiting the company's office after the death of her husband comes as an intruder into a world whose values are not hers. She is a living but ineffective reproach: 'What was the good of the lamp, the dinner served, the flowers. . . . She guessed with a feeling of embarrassment that here she expressed a hostile truth. . . .' Hostile as it is, Saint-Exupéry understands and respects it, for it is the other pole of his life, and one which draws him almost irresistibly. He says on the first page of *Pilote de guerre* that usually a schoolboy does not fear the future, but that he is rather an odd schoolboy, one 'who knows his happiness, and is in no hurry to face life'.

Now what of the other pole? For Saint-Exupéry this is the truly positive pole. It appears at first somewhat Nietzschean, with its insistence on self-discipline, and at least the risk of self-sacrifice. It is true that there is always the altruistic element, but the building of the self is at least as important as the building of an external and visible structure. *Vol de nuit* is the first full and almost unrepentant expression of this ideal. Rivière is the leader who is represented as caring for those whom he leads, but in such a way as to ensure their self-expenditure rather than their self-preservation. We have seen that preserving one's happiness by turning in upon it and nursing it jealously depends upon a delusion. Through the roof of the stable childhood home peeps the star of death: there is no eternity in the past. But there is at least a relative eternity, or durability, in the future for those who take the trouble to build it. 'It is a matter of making them eternal . . .' The leader sympathizes with suffering, but even more he pities death, and imposes on his people the task of building a structure capable of outlasting it (Chap. XIV). This is not an absolute eternity, but it is the best that can be had.

Rivière is an anticipation of the 'chief' in *Citadelle*, and assumes responsibility for the organization which he represents, and for those who serve it. He integrates the self-fulfilment of each individual pilot into the external and tangible structure which is his own creation. He stands, vicariously and also in his own right, for the will to power and the increasing domination over external reality and over the resistance which it offers to the human will. He brings more predictability into life, and by a transference of his own will brings the aircraft out of the night to their destination. The pilots are encouraged to challenge not only predictable hazards, but also what might legitimately be regarded as insuperable obstacles. The margin allowed for hesitation and prudence is reduced to nothing. A value is therefore attached to the fulfilment of purpose which ignores the ordinary claims of justice and fairness. Fairness is regarded as having its context at the ordinary bourgeois level of equitable and negotiated living, but Rivière's world transcends this, and values must be created 'beyond good and evil' which will ensure a commensurate achievement. The will to win makes its own laws and conventions: 'what is living jostles everything to survive, and creates, in order to live, its own laws' (Chap. XI). There are no sacrosanct values which must take precedence over those dictated by experience and the demands of concrete achievement. In the world of action the concrete realization, the event is all-important, what is met or brought into being, not what is merely found. Rivière says, 'it is events which I serve' (Chap. XI).

Now this acceptance of time and action as the field of man's effort differs significantly from that of some contemporary writers. Camus and Sartre are concerned with the concrete situation, and it would appear that Rieux's provisional victories over disease which is never abolished, but which always lurks as an element of evil and irrationality in man's path, correspond to Rivière's ever-renewed burden of a fresh mail to see through. 'It would always be so. Always . . . an effort without respite and without hope' (Chap. II). 'There is no peace. There is perhaps no victory. There is no final arrival of all mails.' But this is not the whole story. There is no suspicion of the nihilist about Saint-Exupéry. To him an atomistic view of reality is quite unsatisfying. And he is aware that 'participation' or committal may promote such a view since reality is never as tidy as we should wish it to be. In the peace of contemplative leisure we can find the links and relationships which give meaning to our past. But the present hurries by and the future rushes towards us, so that we are always liable to be caught at a disadvantage and fail to see significance in the present. It is against this that we must fight. The enemy is fragmentation: bits of the self divided against the remainder of our nature, or ourselves against our context and heritage. Action is not undertaken merely for its own sake or for 'living dangerously', which Saint-Exupéry regards as foolish, nor even for the fiction of an ultimate, 'eternal' purpose which transcends all mundane purposes (see *Vol de nuit*, end of Chapter XIV), but for the sake of bringing into reality a significance which, so long as it remains unrealized, is not even potentially clear. So life becomes a version of artistic creation which makes sense of disjointed and indiscriminate reality.[1]

The works pre-eminently representative of this view are *Pilote de guerre*, *Lettre à un otage*, and *Citadelle*, and even *Le Petit Prince*. Making links (*créer des liens*) is a key-phrase of Saint-Exupéry, and humanly speaking, the creation of links is equivalent to the assumption of responsibility. It is the relation of the airman to his family, so that he must save himself for their sake; it is the relation of the wartime pilot to his country, and of the little prince to his rose. The idea of responsibility and human bonds is fairly straightforward; what is less so is the more general idea of integration treated in *Pilote de guerre*. The general symbol of the work is the French defeat of 1940, which stands very adequately for the 'décalage' of all experience. There is, we are told, one impression which dominates all others at this end of a campaign: that of the absurd. Everything is collapsing round about us (Chap. I).

Saint-Exupéry shows the ambiguous nature of token resistance.

[1] Cf *Citadelle*, Chap. III. 'I have discovered a great truth, to wit, that men have a habitation, and that the meaning of things varies for them with the meaning of home. And that the path, the field of barley and the slope of the hill are different for man, according as they do or do not make up a domain. For all at once this disparate matter is drawn together . . .'

It is futile and in a sense criminal in involving useless sacrifice, yet by maintaining the fiction that 'there's a war on' (when it is virtually over) there is the gesture of resistance not only to the enemy without, but to the enemy within: disintegration. The narrator perceives both the nonsense and the sense of his situation and that of the country: in the general collapse, he says, we are ourselves broken into pieces, 'et les morceaux n'émeuvent pas'. Bits have no value. The preparation for a reconnaissance flight for the collection of unutilizable information appears like the preparation for an empty ritual in the service of some dead god. This emptiness and fragmentation is further represented by the evacuation of the civilian population, who pile their possessions on to carts in an effort to preserve their home, but the pathetic will to conservation is immediately seen to be vain. For once out of their spiritual context, the *form* which gave them significance, these chattels are merely unrelated objects: 'objets de bazar, qui montrent leur usure' (Chapter XVI). Everywhere is disintegration: 'everything is divided against itself. . . . France in collapse is now nothing but a flood of fragments not one of which has a face to show. . . . The troops, fed up and weary, disintegrate into absurdity' (Chap. XVII).

Defeat is the division of man from man, and from himself. A defeated army is no longer an army at all, for victory alone binds men together. This seems highly questionable, but it is also what Stendhal has to say in his famous description of the Battle of Waterloo. So, even though resistance may be folly, it is also wisdom, for the fiction of possible victory redeems the defeated and enables them to re-integrate their lives: 'orders build the world up again' (Chap. I). They behave *as if* their reconnaissance were able to turn the tide of retreat and chaos, and serve some purpose: 'we are struggling desperately against the self-evident. . . . In spite of the fact that nothing can serve any purpose, we blow up bridges just the same, to play the game' (Chap. XIII). The idea of a redemptive pretence, which is not hypocrisy, but the salvaging of something at least intangible from defeat, is constantly emphasized: 'You are on duty to play the part.' The reinforcements who are trying to fight their way through the fleeing civilians to meet the foe have only one reply to their clear-sighted and less romantic fellow-citizens: 'On fait la guerre.'

The purpose of the pretence is as much personal as patriotic, as we see at the beginning of Chapter XXIII. The commanding officer maintains the pretence and, like Rivière, who is not always quite sure that the game is worth the candle, keeps his men from personal disintegration by enforcing loyalty to a cause which is lost. 'We clung, you above all, to the letter of a duty whose spirit was dimmed. You instinctively drove us, no longer to conquer, which was impossible, but to become.'

Reintegration, then, is very largely effected through action, here a kind of gratuitous action. But Saint-Exupéry has not forgotten his other pole. There is an entirely inner peace and reconstitution of things accessible to the contemplative spirit, and which is favoured by night. At night we are delivered of the exigencies of action and can think of the links that bind us to our world and give us a motive for continuing the struggle. Significantly and typically, we notice that the idea of substance takes precedence under these circumstances over that of process. Events give way to forms and continuities. 'Reason sleeps . . . things are . . . they resume their form . . . and survive the destruction of daylight analyses.'

We are back in the quest of tranquillity. After imposing a form and order on chaos by purposive action, comes the discovery of form in what is undergone. The death of others is seen in this light (end of Chapter II, but the same discussion occurs elsewhere, notably in *Vol de nuit*, concerning Fabien's death). Death is apprehended by two faculties, the spirit and the intelligence. It is first understood by the intelligence, which on the day of the funeral is busy going through the forms and practical concerns connected with burial. These are disjointed bits ('the dead person is still in pieces'); he acquires 'étendue' and significance by the action of the spirit, which comes to realize loss through the times and situations when the dead one is felt as not there. 'The person will not really die until tomorrow, in the silence.'[1] Our own being and substance is impoverished by his absence, which acquires a positive quality.

[1] Cf Merleau-Ponty, *Phenomenology of Perception*, pp. 80-1.

Q

Here again is the antithesis of the idea of reality as inherent in isolated occasions; the reality asserts itself through 'duration', through a period which has significance; in this case the significance is felt as a lack. Similarly defeat is felt not as the individual manifestations of chaos, but more keenly later, as a continuity of experience which can be apprehended only as a whole, as a state (see Chap. XVIII).

The genuinely authentic is thus not the event, but the shape of a series of events or apprehensions, or the content of duration or (to use Saint-Exupéry's word) *étendue* (extension). This content, moreover, must be on a human scale. Thus in Chapters X and XI he shows how flying in the stratosphere, even in the presence of mortal danger, is not an adventure compared with the entirely human situation of having to tear oneself away from one's bed in an unheated billet in order to light a fire! The authenticity of an experience depends on whether its domain is that of intelligence or spirit. Intelligence is the power of perceiving abstract relationships and remains fairly constant. Spirit (*Esprit*) depends on favourable circumstances for its activity, on a certain tranquillity and retrospect, permitting an apprehension of the sense (*sens*), direction and meaning of experience (Chap. II). The life of the spirit is intermittent, whereas that of intelligence is constant, or almost so. The analytical powers can always be brought into play, as a tool is put to use. But Spirit is not concerned with limited points or areas of application, but with the significance which whole situations display: 'it considers the meaning which interlinks them'. The links which constitute this meaning may be absent or lost, so that Spirit passes from complete vision to absolute blindness; one's native land may become a mere collection of disconnected objects; a piece of music may lose all the meaning it once had; one's wife may become a focus of worries. It is possible to become blind to Being.

In France's defeat, more is involved than a military and political capitulation. There is a loss of everything continuous and spiritual, and a division of reality into its constituent parts. The commanding officer cannot see his men otherwise than as 'objects in the general incoherence'. We are fragments, says Saint-Exupéry, of a great construction, which we shall need more time, more silence and more perspective to discover. Intelligence is capable of manipulating a situation, but not of evaluating it. It is related to the parts of which reality is built up, and can deal with those parts, but it cannot apprehend significance: 'The important thing is to pursue an end which is not manifest in the instant. This end is not for the intelligence, but for the spirit.' The Spirit forges the links between people and things, in time and space, and this forging of links Saint-Exupéry regards as the sole worth-while activity. Here the basic identity of the ideas of spirit and form, continuity and significance is seen in the use of the word *étendue*. 'True extension is not for the eye, but is accorded only to the spirit.'

The idea of unified substance emerges from Saint-Exupéry's writings. Man is not a collection of acts, but the meaningful sum of them. France, he suggests, has succumbed because she has been unmindful of this. 'We nearly perished in France through intelligence without substance. The substance, or essence, is constituted by a continuity, a linking of act to act, of instant to instant, in a certain direction and with a certain meaning: a system of links which is the means of becoming.' The book ends with a non-allegorical exposition of his idea of the essential substance of French civilization. The journey of Saint-Exupéry is back towards his starting point. We cherish secure happiness, the happiness of childhood, but discover that we must leave childhood whether we want to do so or not. We are therefore launched into Valéry's 'ère successive', where salvation is to be found in action. But not in disjointed action. Form is imposed on the atomic content of experience. Life is art, and if our first, childlike structure of a durable reality proves a failure, perhaps the second, built from the resistant stuff of the external world, may be a worthier thing.

Saint-Exupéry is interesting because, in spite of strong suggestions throughout his writings of an illiberal political outlook, and a tendency to say things of incredible inanity,[1] he is, nevertheless, what could be described as having an existentially

---

[1] e.g. 'We are all agreed that man is greater when he is mystical than when he is egoistical.' *Carnets*, p. 94.

integrated outlook. This has fundamentally much in common with Lavelle's, and he sees his world as one in which participation holds a fruitful place for the past as well as for the future. There is, in his writings, none of that feeling, conveyed by Sartre's purely philosophical works at least, that one's past and other people are objects from which to flee. Saint-Exupéry's sense of community and of its basis as shown in *Citadelle* is strong and, in its nature as there revealed, somewhat disquieting. But on the purely personal plane, one has the impression of a man with a feeling of integrated living to communicate, and this feeling is one which existentialism values in a world which it sees as generally hostile to it.

That the notions of living coherence and meaningfulness were more than merely literary preoccupations is seen in the posthumously published notebooks.[1] Saint-Exupéry shows his hand on the second page, where he criticizes democracy for 'moving in the direction of statistical probabilities, increase of entropy, fragmentation of authority', liberation of the individual in the name of the liberation of 'man',[2] man being presumably a euphemism for the nation. This lucubration ends with the consoling thought that sometimes there arises a man who sets his face against 'the increase in entropy' and statistics and, espousing life, initiates a programme of moral rearmament.[3] However, the unfortunately not unfamiliar spectacle of an incarnation of energism thus becoming a propagandist for 'un homme à poigne', though it may appear rather depressing, need not deter us. What it is important to see is that there is in Saint-Exupéry a constant search for coherence, of which his quasi-totalitarian political views are merely one aspect. The interesting part of the *Carnets* is the second section, devoted to the concept, which is seen as the linguistic ratification of a vision, or some act of rational insight.

What discourages me in advance of creative effort is that *I do not know what I am going to say*,[4] or rather I do not know how to

---

[1] *Carnets*, Gallimard, 1953.   [2] op. cit. p. 16.

[3] 'réarme l'homme et rétablit les potentiels'.

[4] This suggests a search like Valéry's, for a pre-existing rational pattern for the use of creators.

build my bridge between the unformulated world and consciousness. I must invent a language for myself.

Now this taste for coherence is so keen that man, sooner or
later, accepts the language which provides him with it. And
there he is: Christian, Cartesian, Newtonian, Marxist according
to the latest synthesis.[1]

When, he says, I create a grouping or totality from hitherto
disjointed elements, I bring a face to view,[2] and what is even more
important, I put the new totality into circulation. A concept is the
individualization of a totality or structure, and it gains currency
as an invariable.[3] He seems to be putting forward a coherence
theory when he says that knowledge is not possession of truth,
but a coherent language. Hence, he goes on to add enthusiastically,
beatitude is the possession of the sovereign concept, bringing a
point of view of the universe as a whole. This provides no greater
knowledge of the universe in itself, but destroys the barrier[4]
between the universe and me.[5] Saint-Exupéry seems to be striving
for some system of universal concepts which shall not preclude
those personal 'values of unity', as M. Pucelle has called them, the
existence of which make reality into human reality.

[1] *Carnets*, pp. 92, 95.   [2] ibid. p. 101.   [3] ibid. p. 103.
[4] 'litige ou... contradiction irréductible'.   [5] ibid. p. 113.

CONCLUSION

My aim in this study has been to show, in the writings of a number of authors, philosophical and literary, a varied but, I think, basically homogeneous body of ideas. From the starting point of a familiar mood of questioning, I have traced the growth, by way of a feeling of the strangeness of reality, of the notions of absurdity and facticity. From these beginnings in emotional attitudes, which involve feelings of tragic isolation, spring for the most part dynamic doctrines. Being is conceived as active rather than passive and static, though 'the act' need not involve physical and visible action. Being, in the human sense of being for onself, or existence, is fundamentally a process of valuation, which means that present, possibly past, experience is always pointing to its future. Our facticity is never self-subsistent and self-sufficient.

Depending on whether we conceive our life as escape from a past and present self into a future one, or as a process of building the whole of life into an integrated work, the act will be seen as pure transcendence or as participation, which latter accords some value to the in-itself. I have indicated, in speaking of Alquié, Bachelard and Morot-Sir, and to some extent Valéry, a rationalist movement running parallel to this quasi-moral existentialist one. Bachelard conceives an 'open' rationalism analogous to Bergson's open morality. What is curious is that most French existentialists give the impression of being unaware of the rationalistic philosophy of negation represented by some of their own compatriots. I say this because the assault on 'everyday' thinking (*quotidienneté*) generally slides into an indictment of rationalism as the cult of habit. This distortion, which could be expressed by saying that all reason is assimilated to 'constituted' reason, is used to pillory science in *The Plague*. Outside the ranks of philosophers of science, properly speaking, only Alquié appears to present reason itself as always directed towards reality, which it renews and modifies as much as any other process, while itself being a source of activity, not some kind of model which is copied.

Existentialists' hostility to reason, and their blindness to its being an activity 'for itself' as much as any other, is peculiar, since objectivity is regarded by phenomenologists not as *the* perspective, but as one among a number, and so one might think that it ought to stand on an equal footing with the rest. But it is spurned undoubtedly because it is the perspective accessible only to the person who is prepared and able to set aside his own personal one; it therefore easily comes to be looked upon as inauthentic. This view, however, does no credit to existentialism and is unnecessary to it. Anti-rationalism is perhaps also exacerbated by the tendency of recent French rationalism (represented by Meyerson and Lalande) to stress the idea of assimilation, which, to the artistic mind, suggests 'uniformity', 'bureaucracy' and generally the stifling of originality. I think I have shown, in discussing Lalande's philosophy, that this is a misinterpretation; but the terms involution, dissolution (Lalande's original term which he abandoned) and assimilation may well suggest boredom to sensitive souls and heroic energists.

A would-be evolutionary ethic is put forward by Bergson. I have tried to show the confusion to which this leads, while stressing the great importance of the distinction which Bergson makes between open and closed morality. It leads directly to the parallel distinction between values and norms, which is at the core of existentialist ethics, and round which the questions of personalism and objectivity, particularity and universality, turn.

Having established the position of existentialism as personalist and particularist, it was necessary to inquire to what such a morality could be regarded as anchored. Choice and decision, in this context, appeared as in a sense contingent and in another sense as necessitated, otherwise liable to become inseparable from caprice. This ambiguous basis of ethics seems to point to some 'original choice' to which subsequent choices throughout life are subordinated. Fidelity to the original choice is authenticity, the existentialist virtue. Betrayal of it, and acquiescence to habitual morality, imposed from outside, is refusal of human reality and the assimilation of the self to an object, an in-itself. Setting aside the continental jargon, this differs little from first-hand virtue as presented by Professor P. H. Nowell-Smith, and his distinction between virtue and conscientiousness corresponds to the existentialist one between authenticity and its opposite. I have said that sincerity and self-committal to an attitude, in other words a state of mind, are what constitute authenticity. Nowell-Smith writes:

> Aristotle held that a man was not really good unless he enjoyed doing what is good, and I am inclined to agree. The sense of duty is a useful device for helping men to do what a really good man would do without a sense of duty; and since none of us belongs to the class of "really good men" in this sense, it is a motive that should be fostered in all of us. But it plays little part in the lives of the best men and could play none at all in the lives of the saints. They act on good moral principles, not from the sense of duty. . . .[1]

I think that this is as sober and straightforward a summary of what the closed and open moralities amount to as one could desire. But existentialists carry to the limit the demonstration that the object of our pro-attitude, or the content of the 'good moral principle', is gratuitous and arbitrary. So for them, instead of the good man's enjoying doing what is good, goodness consists primarily in 'enjoying' doing. It is obvious that this can cover anything from saintliness to war-crimes, and the existentialist recognizes this. His aim is to inculcate above all, and even at the expense of all else, sincerity, and more particularly 'good faith' with oneself, in the conviction that given the basic virtue, the remaining traditionally recognized virtues will follow, but that in any case without it, any attitude is poisoned at the source.

This reduction of morality, if not to the absurd, at least to the impracticable, not to say illegal, forces us to take account of conscientiousness, the substitute virtue, *alias* 'everyday' morality or inauthenticity, which is, after all, the distinctive modern ethic.

[1] *Ethics*, Pelican Books, 1954, p. 259.

As Mr Bernard Mayo points out,[1] ancient philosophy emphasized virtue and character instead of rules and principles, and existentialism has tended to revive this tendency. It is since Kant, Mayo says, that the ideal of universal law has dominated ethical thought. Mill and the Utilitarians stressed legislation as the means to the good life for all. In modern societies, achievement is held to be more important than character, so education becomes increasingly functional, and the quality of the person is ignored.

In noticing the extent to which the philosophy of the English-speaking world differs from that of continental Europe, partisans on each side are prone to claim that a revolution in philosophy has brought about the millennium, empiricist or phenomenological, in which they alone now bask. British empiricists see their movement as the return to philosophical sanity after Hegelian and metaphysical aberrations. Continentals, for their part, consider that only since their liberation from positivism has philosophy become respectable. But these differences of tone and preoccupation are not recent developments, and if we are inclined to think that they are, we have only to look at Hobbes's objections to Descartes's *Meditations*, and Descartes's replies. It is true that both the French and the British in the eighteenth century were predominantly empiricist, but after a promising start on linguistic analysis by the ideologists,[2] an abrupt change occurred with Maine de Biran, and the two nations thenceforth went their separate philosophical ways, never again to be reunited, the British straight forward towards utilitarianism, the French forking off towards voluntarism and the tendencies I have examined. Positivism was not in the main stream of French philosophy, despite its one-time vogue which has generally been taken as signifying more genuine positivistic conviction than in fact existed in writers such as Comte, Taine and Renan.[3] French philosophers have been on the whole idealistic, and have emphasized the contribution of the

---

[1] *Ethics and the Moral Life*, 1958.

[2] Chiefly Destutt de Tracy, who wrote in the immediate post-revolutionary period.

[3] For a detailed argument of this contention see D. G. Charlton, *Positivist Thought in France during the Second Empire*, Clarendon Press, 1958.

mind in ordering reality into a meaningful whole. English philosophy has been more object-centred. However, reality has to be ordered; this order cannot, moreover, be arbitrary; we may have a purpose to fulfil – phenomenologists say that we *must* bring an intention to the situation – therefore the order will be arbitrarily selective. So the French tend to pit an autonomous self against a resistant objective world, and to dramatize this into 'Man versus Cosmos'. From this emerges the idea of a divorce between rational man and the irrationality and evil of things. The word 'human' occurs with extraordinary frequency in French writing, in opposition, stated or implied, to the scientific and objective. Science generalizes, phenomenology concerns itself not only with the particular case, but with the particular case coloured by its attendant emotions. This is the heart of the matter. From the Cartesian idea that the will gives assent under the persuasive influence of clear ideas, comes the idea that will shapes reality as best it can. French rationalism is thus, like Bottom, translated. It has given way to a new primitivism, a revulsion from the scientific view of things and situations as utensils and means, to a physiognomic view of them as endowed with a sort of face, expression or personality, friendly or hostile.

When this way of envisaging things is generalized it produces a feeling that the universe is either friendly, or indifferent, as Vigny and Camus have seen it. So, it is felt, we have to adopt some attitude to the world in order to live, and this is really a religious quest. The fact that Nietzsche, Camus, Sartre and others are professedly irreligious in the ordinary sense, does not make them any the less concerned with finding an attitude to life, a way to live, and therefore something in the nature of salvation, however indignantly they would repudiate the term.[1] People who think that organized religion has outlived its usefulness are quick to intuit in much modern French philosophy the application, in fact however little in intention, of the thin end of a vaguely Christian wedge. The call to men to develop and rely on their own inner resources is taken as an invitation prematurely to neglect the

---

[1] They do not always repudiate it. Simone de Beauvoir actually uses it. Cf *Pour une morale*, p. 43.

organization of their environment. Not that the two concerns are necessarily mutually exclusive, but in practice they have tended to crowd each other out. It is feared that discomfort and suffering may be looked upon as legitimate bits of the voluntaristic obstacle race. In short, that 'absurd' man may sooner or later tire of his 'gratuitous' restlessness and decide to take the logical step of getting right with a resuscitated God.

I think that the existentialist challenge, as it has been called, has been a healthy corrective, or at least criticism, directed at the encroachments of universality, legality and scientific organization on human life. But this can go too far, and one can sympathize with the impatience of some English philosophers with existentialism. English empiricists tend to be universalistic and legalistic, and ethically negative. They think of morality as designed to secure the minimum of unhappiness for the maximum number of people. And this is best achieved by political legislation. Those moral problems which cannot be solved by legislation are not moral problems at all, but personal problems. Almost all positive happiness is a personal concern. Salvation is a personal problem, and as soon as it is universalized and organized by religion, concern with it tends to take the place of what is legitimately the business of organization, namely the lessening of widespread poverty, discomfort and suffering. I think that Nietzsche said somewhere that pigs and Englishmen seek happiness. English moral philosophy has tended to be concerned, indirectly perhaps, but at least by implication, with minimum standards of contented living, with avoidance of unhappiness, rather than with models to imitate. For this reason the English philosopher is as good an example as any of man as a political animal.

We, political differences apart, want in the most general sense a bigger and better welfare state, and we shall console ourselves for cosmic hostility when we have swept away removable evils and injustices. We want to put our house in order first and animadvert on divine shortcomings afterwards. Bearing in mind that we are reputed to be a puritanical people, it is strange that we should have been so severely criticized by other Europeans, in the recent past, for our highly discreditable pursuit of happiness.

Mr G. J. Warnock, in a recent book,[1] 'hazards the idea' that metaphysical speculation has often been no more than theology in disguise, and that in a period of rapidly decaying religious belief it is undesirable 'to *pretend* to suffer from cosmic anxieties'. He seems to take it for granted that any religious or quasi-religious quest is likely, at the present time, to be 'synthetic or simulated'. Continental philosophy seems the only possible target for such criticism; it seems unfair to impute insincerity to its exponents, though in many cases, it is true, its expression seems irritatingly melodramatic. This study has tried, however, to show something more than a 'metaphysical revolt', which was largely literary and quickly spent. My concern, as stated at the outset, has been with a certain philosophical dilemma, or rather dualism, which indeed probably has its roots in an emotional attitude. To be 'nauseated' by everyday physical reality suggests psychological derangement, but Grenier's 'we are not in the world' is the sort of quasi-emotional response to reality from which philosophizing can legitimately arise. The manifest fact that in a physical sense we *are* in the world may well prompt us to ask how the feeling and evidence of detachment come into existence.

It is a question with which probably only Merleau-Ponty comes effectively to grips. His analysis of the perceptual object and, from this, of the concept and the norm, shows effectively what phenomenologists mean when they speak of the ambiguity of consciousness. Consciousness exists by virtue of the perceptual or conceptual unities, or experiences in the plural, which constitute experience as a continuity. These acquired *meanings*, which is what they are, are at the service of consciousness in its further explorations, and they subsist or are disrupted in answer to the needs of its perpetual and essential meaning-giving activity. The status of error here is important. It is not a diminishing area of imperfection eaten into by the incursions of absolute truth, but immanent in experience and, in a sense, its motive power. We are always learning more about ourselves-in-the-world, but we have never finally learnt everything, or rather we have never completed our transactions with reality. Our foothold in the world takes the

[1] *English Philosophy since 1900*, Oxford, 1958, p. 145.

form of the 'cultural objects' (in which ideas are included) which we create, but as stepping stones, not as resting places. The phenomenological criticism of objective thinking is that it tends to be too attached to its objects. Where, however, this criticism is persistent and strident, the notion of 'objectivity' attacked is usually outdated. There is, in any case, as I have tried to show, a phenomenology of rationality which accords a place to both constituted and constituting reason, and shows them as mutually complementary.

Consciousness makes what it can of a reality at once resistant and compliant, and, in the process, projects provisional unities in the significant forms of the percept, the concept and the norm. One might, of course, in criticizing the 'constituting' activity postulated, object that there is little resistance offered to the meaning-giving activity of perception in the vast majority of the objects which surround us. There is no room, it might appear, for personal evaluation in the perception of, for example, chairs and tables. They are obviously, unambiguously and universally what they are, and we ought to be discussing, if anything, whether the relevant sense-data correspond to anything objectively existing in the place where we think we see them. But Merleau-Ponty is content to take it for granted that they do so correspond, and to use the analysis of perception as a stage towards the description of lived experience. The difficulty of seeing the intentional core of perception is the difficulty of seeing the wood for the trees when we are dealing with familiar, 'cultural' objects. We are almost entirely surrounded by such objects. Chairs and tables are man-made for a specific purpose, and they have their intention *built into* them, so that the tension of intentionality is entirely removed, and, in Merleau-Ponty's sense of perceiving, we do not really perceive them at all, because we do not have to make sense of them. The sort of example by which he and Sartre illustrate their arguments is that of the mountaineering situation, where a certain rock face may present itself as instrumental in its very obstructiveness. It will appear to different people as a 'way through' or simply as part of a view.

It is in the realm of brute, inhuman materiality that 'initiating' perception has full play and is brought to light, just as it is at the boundaries of knowledge that creative rationalism operates, and in the 'situation-limite' that the act of supererogation is performed. The crux of the matter is that the habitual situation is not in the realm of full consciousness, but only of semi-consciousness. The philosophers here dealt with are not primarily interested in the repeated response to a familiar situation to which norms are applicable, but in creative thinking and acting. The emphasis placed, in one way or another, on the value, which is able to impose a requirement necessarily relevant but not universalizable, places the mentality behind this kind of philosophy in a category which is artistic rather than intellectual or moral. But then the retort from its sponsors would be that traditional categories have no place here, and that this is as much a revolution in philosophy as any neo-positivism.

BIBLIOGRAPHY

(English titles published in London, French in Paris, unless otherwise stated)

Introductions to contemporary philosophy

COPLESTON, F. C. *Contemporary Philosophy*, Studies in Logical Positivism and Existentialism. Burns & Oates, 1956.

CRUICKSHANK, JOHN (Editor). *The Novelist as Philosopher*, Studies in French fiction, 1935-60. Oxford University Press, 1962.

FARBER, MARVIN (Editor). *L'Activité philosophique contemporaine en France et aux Etats-Unis*, Vol. II, P.U.F., 1950.
(English version) *Philosophic Thought in France and the United States*, New York, Univ. of Buffalo, 1950.

KLIBANSKY, RAYMOND (Editor). *Philosophy in the Mid-century: a Survey*, 4 vols, Florence, La Nuova Italia, 1958-9.

LAVELLE, LOUIS. *La Philosophie française entre les deux guerres*, Aubier, 1942.

MOUNIER, EMMANUEL. *Introduction aux existentialismes*, Denoël, 1947.
Eng. trans. Eric Blow, *Existentialist Philosophies*, Rockliff, 1948.

PASSMORE, JOHN. *A Hundred Years of Philosophy*, G. Duckworth & Co., 1957.

SPIEGELBERG. *The Phenomenological Movement: a historical introduction*, 2 vols, The Hague, Nijhoff, 1960.

WAHL, JEAN. *Les Philosophies de l'existence*, Armand Colin, 1945.
Tableau de la philosophie française, Fontaine, 1946.
Petite histoire de l'existentialisme, Ed. Club Maintenant, 1947.

Philosophical works

ALQUIÉ, FERDINAND. *Le Désir d'éternité*, P.U.F., 1943 (in series 'Initiation philosophique', 1960).
La Nostalgie de l'être, P.U.F., 1950.
La Découverte métaphysique de l'homme chez Descartes, P.U.F., 1950.
Philosophie du surréalisme, Flammarion, 1955.
Descartes, l'homme et l'œuvre, Hatier-Boivin, 1956.
L'Expérience, P.U.F., 1957.

ARON, RAYMOND. *Introduction à la philosophie de l'histoire*, Gallimard, 1938.

BACHELARD, GASTON. *L'Intuition de l'instant*, Stock, 1932.

Les Intuitions atomistiques, Boivin, 1933.

Le Nouvel Esprit scientifique, P.U.F., 1934.

La Formation de l'esprit scientifique, Vrin, 1938.

La Philosophie du non, Alcan, 1940.

Le Rationalisme appliqué, P.U.F., 1949.

Le Matérialisme rationnel, P.U.F., 1953.

BACHELARD, SUZANNE. *La Conscience de rationalité*, P.U.F., 1958.

BASTIDE, GEORGES. *Méditations pour une éthique de la personne*, P.U.F., 1953.

Traité de l'action morale (Coll. 'Logos'), P.U.F., 1961.

DE BEAUVOIR, SIMONE. *Pour une morale de l'ambiguïté*, Gallimard, 1946.

BERGSON, HENRI. *Essai sur les données immédiates de la conscience*, Alcan, 1889. Eng. trans. entitled *Time and Free Will*, by P. L. Pogson, Sonnenschein, 1910.

Matière et mémoire, Alcan, 1896. Eng. trans. W. S. Palmer and N. M. Paul, Sonnenschein, 1911.

Le Rire, Alcan, 1900. Eng. trans. C. Brereton and F. Rothwell, Macmillan, 1911.

L'Evolution créatrice, Alcan, 1907. Eng. trans. A. Mitchell, Macmillan, 1911.

L'Energie spirituelle, Alcan, 1919. Eng. trans. entitled *Mind-Energy*, by H. Wildon Carr, Macmillan, 1920.

Durée et simultanéité, Alcan, 1922.

Les Deux Sources de la morale et de la religion, Alcan, 1932. Eng. trans. C. Brereton and R. A. Audra, Macmillan, 1935.

La Pensée et le mouvant, Alcan, 1932. Eng. trans. entitled *The Creative Mind*, by Mabelle L. Andison, New York, The Philosophical Library, 1946.

BOUTROUX, EMILE. *De la contingence des lois de la nature*, 1875, P.U.F., 1895.

BRUNSCHVICG, LÉON. *La Modalité du jugement*, Félix Alcan, 1897.

Nature et liberté, Flammarion, 1921.

L'Expérience humaine et la causalité physique, Alcan, P.U.F., 1922.

Le Progrès de la conscience dans la philosophie occidentale, P.U.F., 1927.

La Connaissance de soi, Alcan, 1931.

Les Ages de l'intelligence, P.U.F., 1934.

La Raison et la religion, P.U.F., 1939.

La Philosophie de l'esprit, P.U.F., 1949.

CAMUS, ALBERT. *Le Mythe de Sisyphe*, Gallimard, 1942.

L'Homme révolté, Gallimard, 1951.

CUVILLIER, ARMAND. *Anthologie des philosophes français contemporains*, P.U.F., 1962.

DUFRENNE, MIKEL. *La Notion d' 'a priori'*, P.U.F., 1959.

GILSON, ETIENNE. *L'Essence et l'existence*, Vrin, 1948.

GRENIER, JEAN. *Le Choix*, P.U.F., 1941 (Coll. 'Initiation philosophique', revised and re-entitled *Absolu et choix*, 1961).

GUSDORF, GEORGES. *Traité de l'existence morale*, Armand Colin, 1949.

JANKÉLÉVITCH, VLADIMIR. *L'Odyssée de la conscience dans la dernière philosophie de Schelling*, Alcan, 1932.
La Mauvaise Conscience, Alcan, 1933.
L'Ironie, Alcan, 1935.
L'Alternative, Alcan, 1938.
Du Mensonge, Arthaud, 1947.
Traité des vertus, Bordas, 1949.
Philosophie première, P.U.F., 1954.
L'Austérité et la vie morale, Flammarion, 1956.
Le Je-ne-sais-quoi, P.U.F., 1957.
Le Pur et l'impur, Flammarion, 1960.

JEANSON, FRANCIS. *Sartre et le problème moral*, Le Myrte, 1946.

JOLIVET, RÉGIS. *Les Doctrines existentialistes*, Fontenelle, 1948.
Aux sources de l'existentialisme chrétien, Kierkegaard, Arthème Fayard, 1958.

LALANDE, ANDRÉ. *Les Illusions évolutionnistes*, Alcan, 1930 (revised edition of doctoral thesis: *La Dissolution opposée à l'évolution dans les sciences physiques et morales*, Alcan, 1899).
Vocabulaire technique et critique de la philosophie, Alcan, 1926. 8th edition, P.U.F., 1960.
Les Théories de l'induction et de l'expérimentation, Boivin, 1929.
La Raison et les normes, Hachette, 1948.

LAVELLE, LOUIS. *La conscience de soi*, 1933.
Le Moi et son destin, Aubier, 1936.
L'Erreur de Narcisse, Grasset, 1939.
Traité des valeurs, P.U.F., 1951.
La Dialectique de l'éternel présent:
   I. De l'être, 1928.
   II. De l'acte, 1937.
   III. Du temps et de l'éternité, 1945.
   IV. De l'âme humaine, 1951.

LE SENNE, RENÉ. *Introduction à la philosophie* (Coll. 'Logos'), P.U.F., 1925.
Le Devoir, P.U.F., 1930.
Obstacle et valeur, Aubier, 1934.

Traité de morale générale (Coll. 'Logos'), P.U.F., 1942.

Traité de caractérologie (Coll. 'Logos'), P.U.F., 1949.

MADINIER, GABRIEL. *La Conscience morale*, 'Initiation philosophique', P.U.F., 1954.

MARCEL, GABRIEL. *Etre et avoir*, Aubier, 1935.

Homo Viator, Aubier, 1944. Eng. trans. Emma Craufurd, Gollancz, 1951.

MERLEAU-PONTY, MAURICE. *La Structure du comportement*, P.U.F., 1942.

Phénoménologie de la perception, Gallimard, 1945. Eng. trans. Colin Smith, *Phenomenology of Perception* in 'International Library of Philosophy and Scientific Method' ed. A. J. Ayer, Routledge & Kegan Paul, 1962.

Humanisme et terreur, essai sur le problème du communisme (Coll. 'Les Essais'), N.R.F., 1947.

Sens et non-sens, Nagel, 1948.

Aventures de la dialectique, Gallimard, 1955.

Signes, Gallimard, 1960.

MEYERSON, EMILE. *De l'explication dans les sciences*, Payot, 1921.

La Déduction relativiste, Payot, 1925.

Le Cheminement de la pensée, Alcan-P.U.F., 1931.

Réel et déterminisme dans la physique quantique, Herman, 1933.

MOROT-SIR, EDOUARD. *La Pensée négative*, Aubier, 1948.

Philosophie et mystique, Aubier, 1948.

MOUNIER, EMMANUEL. *Révolution personnaliste et communautaire*, 2nd edition, Temps présent, 1947.

Qu'est-ce que le personnalisme? Editions du Seuil, 1946.

Le personnalisme, 'Que sais-je?' series, P.U.F., 1950.

NABERT, JEAN. *Eléments pour une éthique*, P.U.F., 1943.

Essai sur le mal, P.U.F., 1955.

PARAIN, BRICE. *Recherches sur la nature et les fonctions du langage.*

L'Embarras du choix, Gallimard, 1946.

PATRI, AIMÉ. 'Sur les notions d'essence et d'existence', Cahiers du Collège philosophique, 1948.

POLIN, RAYMOND. *La Création des valeurs*, P.U.F., 1944.

La Compréhension des valeurs, P.U.F., 1945.

Du laid, du mal, du faux, P.U.F., 1948.

PUCELLE, JEAN. *La Source des valeurs*, Vitte, 1957.

Le Règne des fins (Pref. by J. Nabert), Vitte, 1959.

RICŒUR, PAUL. *Philosophie de la volonté*. I. Le volontaire et l'involontaire, Aubier, 1950.

RUYER, RAYMOND. *Le Monde des valeurs*, Aubier, 1948.

Philosophie de la valeur, Armand Colin, 1952.

SARTRE, JEAN-PAUL. *L'Imagination*, P.U.F., 1936.
Esquisse d'une théorie des émotions, Hermann, 1939. Eng. trans. *Outline of a Theory of the Emotions*, B. Frechtman, Philosophical Library, New York, 1948; also *Sketch for a Theory of the Emotions*, trans. Philip Mairet, Methuen, 1962.
L'Imaginaire: psychologie phénoménologique de l'imagination, Gallimard, 1940. Eng. trans. *The Psychology of Imagination*, trans. Frechtman; Rider, 1949.
L'Etre et le néant: essai d'ontologie phénoménologique, Gallimard, 1943. Eng. trans. Hazel Barnes, entitled *Being and Nothingness*, New York, Philosophical Library, 1956; London, Methuen, 1957.
L'Existentialisme est un humanisme, Nagel, 1946. Eng. trans. Bernard Frechtman, *Existentialism*, New York, Philosophical Library, 1947; Philip Mairet, *Existentialism and Humanism*, Methuen, 1948.
Baudelaire, Gallimard, 1947. Eng. trans. Martin Turnell, London, Horizon, 1949; New York, New Directions, 1950.
Situations I, Gallimard, 1947. Cf Annette Michelson, *Literary and Philosophical Essays*, Rider, 1955.
Situations II, Gallimard, 1948. Contains celebrated *Qu'est-ce que la littérature?* Eng. trans. B. Frechtman, *What is Literature?* New York, Philosophical Library, 1949; London, Methuen, 1951.
Situations III, Gallimard, 1949.
Saint Genet, comédien et martyr, Gallimard, 1952.
Critique de la raison dialectique, Vol. I, preceded by *Question de méthode*, Gallimard, 1960.
WAHL, JEAN. *Etudes kierkegaardiennes*, Aubier, 1938.
Existence humaine et transcendence, Neuchâtel, La Baconnière, 1944.

Studies on individual writers

BERGSON

ALEXANDER, IAN W. *Bergson*, 'Studies in Modern European Literature and Thought', Cambridge, Bowes & Bowes, 1957.
ARBOUR, ROMEO. *Henri Bergson et les lettres françaises*, Corti, 1955.
CHEVALIER, J. *Bergson*, Plon, 1926. Eng. trans. Lilian A. Clare, Rider, 1928.
JANKÉLÉVITCH, VLADIMIR. *Bergson*, Alcan, 1931 (revised edition, P.U.F., 1959).
LINDSAY, A. D. *The Philosophy of Bergson*, Dent, 1911.
THIBAUDET, ALBERT. *Le Bergsonisme*, Gallimard, 1923.

CAMUS

BRÉE, GERMAINE. *Camus*, New Brunswick, New Jersey, Rutgers U.P., 1959.

CRUICKSHANK, JOHN. *Albert Camus and the Literature of Revolt*, Oxford University Press, 1959.

MOUNIER, EMMANUEL. *Carnets de route*. 3. *L'espoir des désespérés*. Editions du Seuil, 1953.

THODY, PHILIP. *Albert Camus. A Study of his Work*, Hamish Hamilton, 1957.

SARTRE

ALBERES, R. E. *Sartre*, Editions universitaires, 1954.

CAMPBELL, ROBERT. *J.-P. Sartre ou une littérature philosophique*, Ardent, 1944.

CRANSTON, MAURICE. *Sartre*, 'Writers and Critics', Oliver & Boyd, 1962.

DESAN, WILFRID. *The Tragic Finale: an Essay on the Philosophy of Jean-Paul Sartre*, Harvard University Press, Cambridge, Mass., 1954.

GREENE, NORMAN N. *Jean-Paul Sartre: The Existentialist Ethic*, University of Michigan Press, Ann Arbor, 1960.

THODY, PHILIP. *Jean-Paul Sartre: A Literary and Political Study*, London, Hamish Hamilton, 1960; New York, Macmillan, 1961.

VALERY

SCARFE, FRANCIS. *The Art of Paul Valéry: a study in dramatic monologue*, Univ. of Glasgow Publications, 1954.

SEWELL, ELIZABETH. *Paul Valéry*, 'Studies in Modern European Literature and Thought', Cambridge, Bowes & Bowes, 1952.

SUTCLIFFE, F. E. *La Pensée de Valéry*, Nizet, 1955.

THIBAUDET, ALBERT. *Paul Valéry*, Grasset, 1923.

SAINT-EXUPERY

CHEVRIER, PIERRE. *Antoine de Saint-Exupéry*, Gallimard, 1949.

IBERT, JEAN-CLAUDE. *Saint-Exupéry*, Editions universitaires No. 10, 1953.

INDEX